The Grammar You Need

G M Spankie

MACMILLAN
PUBLISHERS

©copyright text G M Spankie 1987
©copyright illustrations Macmillan Publishers Ltd 1987

First published 1987

Published by *Macmillan Publishers Ltd*
London and Basingstoke
Associated companies and representatives in Accra, Auckland, Delhi,
Dublin, Gaborone, Hamburg, Harare, Hong Kong, Kuala Lumpur, Lagos,
Manzini, Melbourne, Mexico City, Nairobi, New York, Singapore, Tokyo

Design and artwork by Jordan and Jordan

Typeset by Kempshott Phototypesetting Services, Basingstoke

Printed in Hong Kong

British Library Cataloguing in Publication Data
Spankie, Greig M.
   The grammar you need.
1. English language — Text-books for foreign speakers
I. Title
428.2'4   PE1128
ISBN 0-333-41261-3

Contents

Preface

All over the world, people are learning English as a foreign language by various methods and systems. At a fairly early stage, whatever the general teaching methods may be, learners find it necessary to cope with English that is not merely comprehensible but grammatically acceptable too, at formal and informal levels. That is to say, they need grammar in order to give full meaning to what they say, hear, read and write. Grammar is essential to meaning. Were this not so, a grammar would be of little value to learners of English.

No previous formal instruction in grammar is required by anyone who uses *The Grammar You Need*. In writing this grammar I have used only simple, well-known grammatical terms which are explained as and where they occur throughout the pages of the book. Explanatory text is in straightforward, clear language, examples are uncomplicated, meaningful and within the compass of general experience. The method is the one that has seemed most apt for each point that arises on each occasion, eg descriptive, inductive, ostensive, paradigmatic, pictorial.

The work in *The Grammar You Need* has been set out under thirty-four main headings which deal progressively with the parts of sentences, the parts of speech in their functions and the relationships among them. There are examples on the left-hand side of the page, with commentary and explanation immediately opposite, on the right-hand side. There is a good, clear index in which most items are mentioned at least twice.

The Grammar You Need is for learners at all stages who have already passed through beginners' classes. The book can be used as a grammar course from cover to cover, though teachers might easily re-arrange the order of items, without loss of coherence, to suit their own pupils' needs at any time. *The Grammar You Need* can also be used for remedial teaching and as a reference book throughout normal English courses. Explanatory text and examples of all points in this book will be very helpful to teachers in the preparation of exercises and tests involving the use of relevant grammar.

While *The Grammar You Need* has been written in British English, I have been careful to mention American English whenever it has seemed helpful to do so. There are very few absolute differences in grammar between these two main forms of English but there are some differences in the meanings of words, eg 'pavement' (Br)='sidewalk' (Am).

In preparing *The Grammar You Need* I have been able to draw copiously from long, first-hand experience as a teacher of English as a foreign language in Britain and abroad and have also derived considerable insights from the works of previous writers in this field to whom I now express my thanks. *The Grammar You Need* is my latest contribution towards easing the ways to teaching and learning English as a foreign language.

G M Spankie   1987

Symbols

We use these phonetic symbols in The Grammar You Need in order to indicate the sound of grammatical items, only when it is helpful to do so.

A stress mark (ˈ) shows that the next syllable bears stress eg adˈventure = adventure.

Ⅹ...Ⅹ This sign marks an example of incorrect English.

▶ This symbol denotes a cross reference to another chapter or section.

Br = British English, which is compared with Am = American English eg **lift** (Br) = **elevator** (Am).

consonants		vowels	
p	shi**p**	iː	sheep
b	**b**ook	ɪ	ship
t	ho**t**el	e	hotel
d	chil**d**	æ	apple
k	**c**rooked	ɑː	half
g	**g**o	ɒ	hop
tʃ	**ch**ild	ɔː	saw
dʒ	**j**am	ʊ	put
f	**f**ish	uː	too
v	**v**erb	ʌ	up
θ	**th**in	ɜː	bird
ð	**th**en	ə	driver
s	**s**ize	eɪ	day
z	si**z**e	əʊ	go
ʃ	**sh**ip	aɪ	life
ʒ	mea**s**ure	aʊ	house
h	**h**ot	ɔɪ	boy
m	**m**an	ɪə	here
n	**n**o	eə	there
ŋ	lo**ng**	ʊə	poor
l	**l**eg		
r	**r**ed		
j	**y**es		
w	**w**icked		

1 Basic sentences: *the parts*

A Subjects

Subjects can be people, animals, tools, machines or any other things that name the doer of an action.

a **She** works hard.

b **Mary** works hard.

c **The tall girl** works hard.

d **The tall girl with red hair** works hard.

a A subject can be a personal pronoun.

b A subject can be a noun or a name.

c A subject can be a phrase with a noun.

d A prepositional phrase after a noun, eg **with red hair,** can describe it and is part of the whole subject. A phrase is two or more words that go together and make sense.

B Verbs

Verbs in basic sentences can be words that name the subjects' actions.

1 **a** The dog **barked.**

  b Someone **was coming.**

  c We **had been waiting.**

  d They **might have been sleeping.**

We have one-word verbs (**a**) and (in **b, c, d**) verb phrases with one or more auxiliary verbs, eg **was, had been, might have been.** The verbs in **a-d** do not take objects; they are intransitive verbs.

2 **a** I **was writing a letter.**

  b She **posted the letter** yesterday.

  c The man in London **can't have received it.**

These verbs have objects. Verbs with objects are transitive verbs.

C Objects

Objects follow the verbs. The object in a basic sentence can be a noun, a noun phrase or a personal pronoun.

a Peter has bought **a new house.**

b I shall make **fresh biscuits** today.

c The children always eat **them.**

The action of a subject and verb can produce an object (**b**) or do something to the object (**a** and **c**). Personal pronouns have object forms (**c**) but nouns do not.

D Complements of state verbs

State verbs do not name actions. They mention feelings, impressions and states: **appear, be, become, feel, seem; appear (to be), seem (to be),** are the more usual ones.

1	The man	is	tired.
	Robert	seems	ill.
	Everyone	became	happy.
	Nobody	felt	angry.
	The baby	looked	excited.
	My sister	sounds	well.

The complement of a state verb can be an adjective. The adjective says something about the subject of the state verb.

2	The men	were	doctors.
	You all	seemed to be	officers.
	A few women	appeared to be	engineers.
	They	became	professors.

3 They became **very good young officers of the Navy.**

The complement of a state verb can be a noun. Nouns in the complements repeat the subjects but with other words.

Noun complements can be as long as noun subjects and objects. They are complement phrases.

E Complements of prepositions

We say that prepositions govern their complements. *Preposition + noun or pronoun complement = prepositional phrase.*

1		*Preposition + complement*	
a	Father works	**in**	**an office.**
b	I like tea	**with**	**sugar.**
c	Mary ran	**towards**	**me.**
d	We can meet	**after**	**the lesson.**

Most prepositional phrases can follow a noun or a pronoun and say something about it — **tea with sugar** (b). They can mention a place — **in an office** (a); a direction — **towards me** (c); or a time — **after the lesson** (d) as adverbs do, after the verb.

2 a Father works **in an office/on the top floor.**
  b I'll be free **after the English lesson/on Monday.**
  c He'll take Mary **to the party in a taxi.**
  d A man **with a moustache** called a girl **in a white coat.**
  e The girl listened **to him** and looked **at us.**

We can have more than one prepositional phrase. They come after verbs without objects (a, b), after the objects of verbs that have them (c) and after the nouns they describe (d). Pronoun complements of prepositions are in the object form (e).

F Adverbs as complements

  a Your sister plays the piano **beautifully.**
  b Please put your suitcase **here.**
  c I didn't see him **yesterday.**
  d He wasn't **here at the usual time.**

Adverbs do not come between verb and object. Adverbs follow objects in basic sentences. When there is no object, adverbs follow the verb (**here** in **d**). A prepositional phrase can be adverbial and take its place in the sentence as an adverb (**at the usual time** in **d** and ▶ **E 1 a-d**).

2 Basic sentences: *word order*

A basic sentence need not have a subject when the verb is imperative (▶ **A**). When the verb in a basic sentence is not imperative, we must have a subject (▶ **B**).

In the affirmative forms, basic sentences can be made up in various ways.

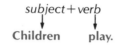

subject + verb
Children   **play.**

subject + verb + *object*
Children   play   **games.**

Subject + verb + object + *adverb*
Children   play   games   **happily.**

subject + verb + object + adverb + *prepositional phrase*
Children   play   games   happily   **in the garden.**

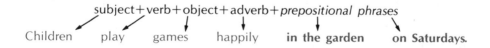

subject + verb + object + adverb + *prepositional phrases*
Children   play   games   happily   **in the garden**   **on Saturdays.**

NOTES

1   Many verbs do not have or cannot have objects, eg **go, come.** Basic sentences for them are the same as the sentences in the diagram but without an object.

2   We can have more than one adverb in a sentence. Prepositional phrases often mention place and time, like adverbs, and we can have more than one of them in a basic sentence. They can take other positions in the sentence and we shall see them later in this book. Do not put prepositional phrases and adverbs between the verb and its object.

3   There are some differences in word order of subject and verb in the negative and in the interrogative forms; you can see them in **C, D** and **E.**

4   The verb is sometimes more than one word, eg **is playing, will arrive, must be waiting.**

3

A Imperative

a **Go! Wait!**

b Go **there.** Wait **there.**

c Go **to the market.**
Wait **at the market.**

d Buy **fruit** at the market.
Sell **fruit** at the market.

e Buy fruit **carefully** at the market.
Sell fruit **quickly** at the market.

f **Do not go** to the market today.
Do not buy fruit at the market.

g **Do** sit down, please.
Do keep quiet.

a An imperative verb can stand without other words and be a sentence.

b An adverb can follow an imperative verb.

c A preposition with its noun (or pronoun) can follow an imperative verb.

d When there is an object, it follows the imperative verb immediately.

e An adverb does not come between a verb and an object; adverbs usually follow objects.

f **Do not** (or **Don't**) comes before the imperative verb. Someone requests or orders us **not to go, not to buy** etc.

g **Do** sometimes comes before a polite request or a firm command when the verb is imperative.

B Verbs with subjects: affirmative

1 a **I** am waiting here for Tom.
b **Father** was working in the garden.

2 a **Mary** served **coffee quickly.**
b **You** can see **the manager in the office.**

Except in the imperative, verbs have subjects. A subject comes immediately before its verb. The verb can be a one-word verb or a phrase (**am waiting, can see** etc).

Objects follow their verbs. Adverbs and prepositional phrases follow the objects.

C Negative verbs in statements

1 a I **am not** waiting here for Tom.
b Father **was not** working in the garden.

2 a The car **has not** been running well.
b I **will not** be using the car today.
c You **must not** park here.
d People **should not** have told lies.

3 a We **do not** watch television often.
b Mary **does not** like TV programmes.

4 a I **did not** meet Carlos yesterday.
b We **did not** go out last Saturday.

Not comes between the only auxiliary verb and the **-ing** verb in present and past progressive tenses.

When we have more than one auxiliary verb, **not** follows the first.

The simple present tense takes **do not** between subject and verb; the third person singular takes **does not** between subject and verb.

The simple past tense takes **did not** between subject and verb, for all persons, singular and plural, in the negative.

1 After **do** and **does** in the simple present and after **did** in the simple past tense, we use the *base verb* only, for all persons. The base verb is the form we find in dictionaries; we can also call it the *bare infinitive* or the *infinitive without 'to'.*

2 Except after **I am** or **I'm,** speakers often shorten **not** to **n't,** eg You must**n't** speak. Do**n't** go away. He did**n't** understand. She is**n't** my sister. **Shan't** = shall not; **won't** = will not; **can't** = cannot.

D Interrogative verbs

1 a **Am I** driving too fast?
  b **Are you sitting** comfortably?
  c **Was John playing** the piano?
  d **Were the children going** to school?

The speaker asks an open question. The answer can be affirmative or negative. *Present progressive* and *past progressive:* the usual parts of **be** — **am, are, is** and **was, were** — come before the subject. The **-ing** participle does not change.

2 a **Do you know** my brother?
  b **Does he meet** you at work?
  c **Did everyone go** to the party?

Simple present: we place **does** before the third person singular (**he, she, it, the man** etc) and **do** before all other subjects. *Simple past:* **did** comes before all subjects. The verb is in the base form (▶ **Note 1**).

3 a **Will you telephone** tomorrow?
  b **Shall I make** some coffee?
  c **Would Peter sell** his house?

Will/shall and **would/should** come before the subject + base verb.

4 a **Can you see** that little boat?
  b **May I come** in?
  c **Must we stay** here all day?
  d **Need you make** so much noise?
  e **Ought you to smoke** so much?
  f **Used she to live** in London?

Other auxiliaries — **can, could, may, might, must, need** — can stand before the subject + base verb. **Ought** and **used** stand before the subject and full infinitive (▶ **Chapter 21, B**).

5 a **Have you met** Charles Grey?
  b **Has the doctor arrived?**
  c **Had John gone** to bed?

Present perfect: **has** comes before third person singular and **have** comes before all other subjects. *Past perfect:* **had** comes before all subjects. The verbs do not change form. They are past participles.

6 a **Have you been waiting** long?
  b **Should I have taken** an umbrella?
  c **Will you be working** there tomorrow?
  d **Must you be asking** so many questions?
  e **Could Charles have been playing** cards?

An affirmative sentence can have more than one auxiliary verb with its main verb (▶ **C2a** and **b** above). In questions, the first auxiliary comes before the subject.

E Negative-interrogative verbs

1 a **Aren't you** taking the car today?
  b **Wasn't John** feeling well?
  c **Don't you** like dogs?
  d **Doesn't Mary** know John?
  e **Won't she** go there tomorrow?
  f **Wouldn't Peter** help us?
  g **Can't you** see that little boat?
  h **Couldn't we** leave early?
  i **Hasn't my brother** arrived?
  j **Hadn't you** paid the workers?

Speakers ask these questions when they think that the answers will be negative, eg **No, I'm not. (1a)**, **No, he wasn't. (1b)**. After auxiliaries, **not** becomes **-n't** in conversational English (▶ **C Note 2** above). *Auxiliary verb* + **n't** comes before the subject in negative-interrogative sentences. Speakers expect negative answers, eg **No, he wouldn't help.** but the answers can also be affirmative — **Yes, he would help. (1f).**

2 a Is **John not** feeling well?
  b Will **he not** be using the car?
  c Have **you not** been studying?
  d Should **we not** have gone there?
  e Could **they not** have been visiting friends?

We place an *auxiliary verb* + **n't** before the subject in conversational styles of English. When we write or speak more formally, **not** comes between the subject and main verb; **not** follows the subject and comes before other auxiliaries, when there are any.

F Basic sentences and emphasis

1 a Why didn't you wash your hands?
  b I '**did** wash them.
2 a Money doesn't matter to him
  b Money '**does** matter to her.
3 a They haven't done their homework.
  b They '**have** done it, I'm sure.
4 a Why are your hands so dirty?
  b My hands '**aren't** dirty.

When someone asks a question or makes a remark and another person protests or disagrees or makes a contrast in reply, we have an auxiliary with the main verb. When we speak, we stress this auxiliary verb. We do not shorten it.

3 Nouns: *plural forms*

A Regular plurals

Nouns are words that can be subjects of verbs, objects of verbs, complements of verbs and prepositions (▶ **Chapter 1, A-F**).

1

boots, bricks, cats, clocks, coats, cuffs, drinks, hats, lips, photographs, puffs, roofs, stamps, steps, tents, myths, fifths, tenths

The singular form of the noun ends with one of the sounds /f/, /k/, /p/, /t/, /θ/. Add **-s** to make it plural. The sound is /s/ as in **say, sister, saw, sock, sun.** ▶ also **A7** below.

2

clubs, beds, buds, baths, caves, doves, heads, hands, maids, paths, rogues, sounds, waves

The singular ends with one of the sounds /b/, /g/, /d/, /v/, /ð/, /z/. Add **-s** to make the plural. The sound is /z/ as in **zoo.**

3

balls, buns, dolls, doors, floors, horns, lambs, lungs, mothers, pairs, pills, stairs, things, thumbs, tongues, vans

The singular ends with one of the sounds /l/, /m/, /n/, /ŋ/ /r/. The sound is /z/ as in **A2** above.

4

boys, cows, crews, days, keys, laws, nephews, paws, views

The singular noun ends in a vowel sound. Add **-s** for the plural. The sound is /z/ as in **A2** and **A3** above.

5

buffalos, dynamos, Eskimos, sopranos
heroes, Negroes, potatoes, tomatoes, torpedoes, vetoes
kilos, photos, taxis, minis, maxis

The singular noun ends in **-o**. To some of them we add **-s** for the plural, others take **-es**. The sound of **-s** and of **-es** is /z/.

Short forms of longer words can end in a vowel; the plural form is **-s** pronounced /z/.

6

baby/**babies**; body/**bodies;** cry/**cries**; dummy/**dummies;** fly/**flies;** lady/**ladies;** ruby/**rubies**; spy/**spies**

The singular noun ends in a *consonant* + **-y**. For the plural, change **-y** to **-i** and add **-es**; the sound of **-es** is /z/.

days, donkeys, keys, monkeys, plays, toys, trays, ways

When we have a vowel before **-y**, we form the plural with **-s** as in **4** above.

7

calf, elf, half, knife, leaf, life, loaf, shelf, thief, wife, wolf

The **-f** or **-fe** at the ends of these singular nouns become **-ves** in the plural: **calves, elves, halves, knives, leaves** etc. Some singular nouns in **-f** add **-s** for the plural as in **1** above.

8

| boxes, branches, bridges, brushes, classes, fences, foxes, garages, horses, kisses, masses, matches, oranges, pages, races | The singular ends with a sibilant sound: /s/, /ʃ/, /tʃ/, /dʒ/, /z/. When the spelling of the singular ends with **-e**, add an **-s** for the plural. When the singular does not end in **-e**, add **-es** for the plural. The sound of **-es** is /ɪz/. |

B Plural in compound nouns

1

| seaman, schoolbag, schoolgirl, playmate
gas-meter, oil-filter, drawing-board
bus driver, egg beater, steam engine | We join two or more words and form a compound noun, eg **gentle + man** makes **gentleman; hand + full** makes **handful.**

We write some compound nouns as one whole word, some have a hyphen between the parts and most are two words without a hyphen. |

2

| seamen, schoolbags, schoolgirls, playmates
gas-meters, oil-filters, drawing-boards
bus drivers, egg beaters, steam engines
handfuls, spoonfuls, cupfuls, mouthfuls
second lieutenants, deputy-sheriffs, vice-presidents | The first part of these compound nouns describes the second part. Only the second part becomes plural in form. Measures ending in **-ful** also add the plural **-s** to the end. |

3

| commanders-in-chief, courts-martial, notaries public, men-of-war (battleships), attorneys-at-law, brothers-in-law, mothers-in-law | The second part of these compound nouns describes the first part. Only the first part becomes plural. All **-in-law** relationships take the plural in the first part. |

4

| menservants, women-servants, women teachers, gentlemen farmers, men teachers, women doctors but policewomen, workmen, craftsmen, chairwomen, chairmen | The first noun in a compound can be **man, woman,** or **gentleman.** Both parts of the compound become plural. Exceptions are **man-eaters, man-haters, woman-haters.** |

5

| bystanders, onlookers, overseers, incomes, outgoings, undertakers, underwriters, overtakers, outlaws | The first part of a compound noun can be a prepositional or adverbial particle. Only the last part takes the plural form. |

6

goings-on, hangers-on, lookers-on, passers-by, runners-up, tellings off

A compound noun can end with a prepositional or adverbial particle. Generally, the first part takes the plural.

blackouts, blow-outs, breakdowns, breakthroughs, close-ups, forget-me-nots, hold-ups, knock-outs, lay-bys, leftovers, setbacks, takeovers

When the first word has the same sound and spelling as the verb it comes from, the plural comes at the end of the whole compound noun.

7

goalkeepers, centre-forwards, half-backs, javelin throwers, obstacle racers

Compound nouns for sportsmen take the plural ending on the final part.

C Irregular plurals

1

child/**children**; foot/**feet**; goose/**geese**; louse/**lice**; man/**men**; mouse/**mice**; tooth/**teeth**; woman/**women**

We make the plural of some common nouns by changing the vowels.

2

aircraft — **craft** = boat(s) or ship(s), deer, dice, fish, series, sheep, species

Singular forms of some nouns also serve for the plural. The names of most kinds of fish usually have one form for both singular and plural. Some kinds can also have the **-s** plural, eg **sardines.**

3

Burmese, Chinese, Japanese, Portuguese, Sudanese; Swiss

We have one form for singular and plural nouns of nationality in **-ese**. They mention one or more persons by race or nation. **Swiss** also has one form only.

4 a Beef cattle do well on rich summer grass.
  b Country folk lead quieter lives than **city folk** do.
  c Vermin damage crops and infect **people.**

cattle = cows and other oxen
folk = people
people = a number of persons
vermin = rats, mice and other pests
  These nouns do not end in **-s** but are plural and as subjects they take a plural verb.

D Pair plurals

1 a I shall wear my dark blue **trousers** today.
  b She never puts on **jeans** to go to the office.
  c You can't wear **shorts** with no belt on them.

Some of our clothes have two legs or have a place for the left leg and a place for the right leg. These articles of clothing are always plural in English.
eg **jeans, knickers, pants, pyjamas, shorts, tights, trousers, trunks, underpants**

2 **a** You can draw a circle with **compasses.**
   b Don't use my **scissors** for cutting paper.
   c John isn't wearing **sunglasses** today.

Some tools and instruments have two legs or sides that work together as a pair.

eg **bellows, binoculars, compasses, clippers, pincers, pliers, scales, scissors, shears, tweezers**
Also, **glasses = spectacles.**

3 **a** I need **a pair of** sharp **scissors.**
   b There is **a pair of scales** on that shelf.
   c There are **three pairs of jeans** in the wash.
   d **Four pairs of tights** have holes in them.

We can say **a pair of trousers, one pair of shorts** and so on and when we mention more than one **pair** we say **pairs:** two/three/several/many **pairs of trousers** etc.

4 **a** Mary needs **some** reading glasses.
   b I'll buy **some** pyjamas today.
   c The boys need **some** swimming trunks.
   d You'll find **some** pliers in the tool-box.

Some can be either singular or plural in meaning, before pair nouns. Pair nouns cannot have **a** or **an** immediately before them, because these nouns are plural in form and grammar.

E Count nouns

1

one boy, **two** cats, **three** girls, **twenty** horses, **fifty** kilos

A count noun is a noun that can have an arithmetical number with it and make good sense. Nouns with **the** in **A** and **B** above, and with **pair** in **C** above are all count nouns.

2

a few bricks, **some** stamps, **a lot of** mice, **many** knives, **a few pairs** of shorts

We can have indefinite plural number with count nouns, eg **a few = a small number; many = a large number.** Only count nouns become plural; other nouns are always singular (▶ **F** below).

F Nouns without plural

1 **a** Winter **clothing is** essential in Finland.
   b The **news** on TV **wasn't** very good.
   c **Housework keeps** me busy all morning.
   d Our **mail comes** about midday.
   e My doctor gave me **some** good **advice.**
   f We usually have **some homework** for school.
   g Our agent has sent **some information.**

In English, some nouns are always singular. When they are subjects, the verbs are singular.

eg **advice, baggage = luggage, clothing, furniture, homework, housework, information, knowledge, luggage, mail, money *work.**
   *▶note after **G** below for **work.**
These nouns are singular but **a, an** and **one** do not go with them: we can have **some** in place of **a** or **an.** They are not count nouns, in English.

2
a Two **pieces of news/information.**
b Several **articles of clothing/luggage.**
c Five large **sums of money.**
d Many **items of furniture/knowledge.**
e Some **pieces of work/news/advice.**
f A few **articles of clothing/furniture.**
g **A lot of** homework/housework.

a piece of advice; an article of clothing; a sum of money. **Piece, article** and **sum** are count nouns, as in **E** above, so they can be plural.
Some with plural nouns has its usual meaning: an indefinite number of pieces of luggage, information etc.
NOTE
the works of Shakespeare
three works by Chopin
a work of art (etc.)
in which **work** is a count noun.

G Nouns ending in -s

1
a **Arms are** not normally carried by British policemen.
b **The customs** often **search** travellers' luggage.
c **The contents** of the bottle **were** green in colour.
d Our business **premises have become** too small for us.
e **The troops live** in barracks or in camps.

Some nouns have particular meanings in the plural with **-s.**

eg **arms** = weapons
customs (at an airport or frontier)
contents (of a box, bottle or other container)
premises (a shop, office etc.)
troops = a body of soldiers, an army

2
a My winter **clothes are** in that large wardrobe.
b Our home is on the **outskirts** of the city.
c Its **surroundings are** very pleasant in summer.
d **Oats are** given to horses as extra food.
e Please do not leave **valuables** in the cloakroom.

Some nouns are always plural,
eg **arrears, clothes, earnings, goods, oats, odds, outskirts, soapsuds, surroundings, thanks, valuables**

3
a A new car is **beyond my means** at present.
My best **means of transport** is a number 12 bus.
b Mary's **savings** from her salary pay for her holidays.
A saving of a few minutes is important to busy men and women.
c I'm glad I wasn't born in **the Middle Ages.**
Parents of **middle age** often have adult children.
d **The tropics** have the hottest climates on earth.
The equator lies between **the Tropic of Cancer** and **the Tropic of Capricorn.**

A few nouns are usually plural but can be singular, sometimes with a change of meaning.
eg **means** = money or other income;
a means of transport
the tropics = that part of our planet;
the Tropic of Capricorn/Cancer
the Middle Ages = a historical period;
middle age = part of a person's lifetime
my savings = money I have saved;
the **saving** of life, energy, electricity.

4 a Politics is the art of government.
The government's **politics were** always changing.

b Mathematics is an essential part of most sciences.
My **mathematics were** incorrect so I made no profit.

c Ceramics is one of the oldest art forms on earth.
One ceramic in the exhibition **was** 3,000 years old.

d Classics is basically the study of Latin and Greek.
Tolstoy's 'War and Peace' **is a** Russian **classic.**

e Statistics is a branch of mathematics.
A statistic that shows my salary above the cost of living can't be right.

The name of a science, subject of study or a form of art or craft can end in **-s.** Such words are singular, but not count nouns, in this sense.
eg **athletics, *ceramics, *classics, graphics, linguistics, mathematics, physics, politics, phonetics, *statistics**
They can also be plural with a plural verb, as when we mention several examples of political, mathematical or statistical operations.
*These can also be count nouns without **-s** in the singular.

5 a Skittles is a game rather like ninepins.

b Billiards demands a good eye and steady hands.

c Darts is a favourite game in English pubs.

d So is dominoes, especially in the country.

The names of some games end in **-s** but these usually take singular verbs when they are subjects.
eg **billiards, darts, dominoes,*draughts, fives, skittles, ninepins**
*draughts (Br) = checkers (Am)

NOTE
specific sums of money, as subjects, usually take a singular verb.

H Collective nouns

1 a A large audience was waiting for the speaker.

b The whole family lives in one large house.

c The Metropolitan Police is a fine organisation.

d That gang of crooks has reason to know this.

e A swarm of flies was buzzing round my head.

f A pack of wild dogs has attacked our flock.

These collective nouns name a group or class of people as a singular unit. A singular collection takes a singular verb.

Some collective nouns are:
audience, class, club, committee, crowd, family, faculty, gang, government, nation, (political) party, race, staff, team, workforce, army, navy, police

We can mention other living things collectively in the same way.
eg **flock** (of birds, sheep)
herd (of cattle, elephants, goats)
pack (of dogs, wolves)
shoal (of fish)
swarm (of insects)

2 a **The local police keeps** law and order in the town.
The police are looking for the bank robbers now.

  b **The committee is** meeting again tomorrow.
The committee have all gone back to their homes.

  c **Our athletics team has** won several contests.
The team are driving to Wembley in their own cars.

  d **Our technical staff is** the best in Europe.
The staff go off to lunch between twelve and one.

Members of families, committees, governments, teams, and other bodies can sometimes act separately as individual persons. A collective noun can then take a plural verb.

4 Mass nouns

A Uncountable

1 a We make **bread** with **flour, water** and **yeast.**
  b **Sugar** costs much less than **honey** does.
  c **Cement, sand** and **water** make concrete.
  d Children need good **food**, fresh **air** and **company.**
  e **Steel** is an alloy of **iron** and other minerals.

There are many common things that we do not count in arithmetical numbers, eg **butter, flour, honey, meat, milk, rice, salt, sugar, tobacco, water; air, cement, gold, leather, oxygen, *petrol, silver, smoke, steel, weather.** These are not count nouns (▶ **Chapter 3, E**); we call them *mass nouns* or *non-count nouns.*
  *petrol (Br) = gasoline (Am)

2 a **Salt preserves meat** and **fish.**
  b **Rice grows** well in warmer countries.
  c **Petroleum rises** from the ground or sea-bed.
  d **Honey costs** much more than sugar does.
  e **Time is money** but **money isn't time.**

We do not use **one, two, three, four** etc before mass nouns, so they do not have number in their grammar; they are generally singular in form and in meaning. When mass nouns are subjects, their verbs are singular.

3 a Drive to the garage. The engine needs **some oil.**
  b Get **some petrol** too, at the same time.
  c I've bought **some glass** for a broken window.
  d I had **some** bad **luck** with a tennis ball.

Mass nouns are always singular but do not go with **a, an** or **one.** They can go with **some = an indefinite amount.**

4 a **Wisdom** does not always come with **age.**
  b **Beauty** either grows or goes with passing years.
  c **Politeness** costs nothing but matters very much.
  d Without **health**, what is **wealth?**
  e **Love** makes the world go round.
  f **Life** without **love** is an egg without **salt.**

Mass nouns can name abstractions and personal feelings, eg **anger, beauty, charm, diplomacy, goodness, happiness, health, hunger, imagination, jealousy, kindness, optimism, politeness, rudeness, tact, wealth, wisdom.**

B Measurement

1 a I bought **two kilos of butter** and **some flour.**
  b We drink about **three litres of milk** a week.
  c You'll need **three metres of cloth** for a suit.
  d **Two and a half metres of cloth** would do for me.

Mass nouns do not take numbers but we can measure parts and amounts of a mass. We measure by weight (**grams, kilograms, ounces, tons** etc), by volume (**litres, gallons, cubic metres** etc) or by length and area (**metres, kilometres, miles, yards, square metres** etc). Naturally, we cannot measure the items

e The well holds **ten cubic metres of water.**

f We use it after **a** long **period of dry weather.**

g Is **a litre of water** heavier than **a litre of oil?**

2 Mix **five handfuls of flour, two spoonfuls of oil, a pinch of salt, a cupful of water, ten drops of lemon juice** and **one tablespoonful of yeast** to make **dough** for pizza.

3 a I like just **a little oil** in a salad.

b There's still **a lot of gold** in South Africa.

c Little children always have **lots of energy.**

d They have **lots of fun** with their schoolmates.

e You need **a great deal of patience** with them.

f Ten thousand pounds is **a great deal of money.**

g **Most money** is round to go round and flat to pile up.

4 a Captain Grey has over **thirty years' experience** at sea.
My father does not talk about **his experiences** in the war.

b Mother takes **pleasure** in meeting my friends.
It was **a pleasure** for me to meet her.

c The general served the country **with honour.**
The president gave him the highest **military honours.**

d Think! Use your **reason,** man!
There are **several reasons** for my decision.

e **Duty** to family and friends must be done.
I have **a pleasant duty** to perform today.

f **Chocolate** always **makes** him thirsty.
Too many **chocolates have made** me fat.

in **A4,** above, in these ways (▶ **B3** below).

Practical measures can also go with mass nouns,
eg **handfuls, spoonfuls, cupfuls, a pinch** (of salt), **ten drops** (of medicine), **a large packet** (of tea), **a small bottle** (of soda water), *a tin (of baked beans) (Br) = a can (Am).

Indefinite measure: nouns like the ones in **A4** above and all other mass nouns can have **some** before them (▶ **A3** above). We can also have **a little** + *mass noun,* for a small amount; **a lot of** + *mass noun,* or **lots of** + *mass noun* in conversational English, for a large amount; **a great deal of** + *mass noun* in more formal English for a large amount. The nouns without plural in **Chapter 4, F,** above, can also have these indefinite measures.

Count noun or mass noun? Some nouns usually name abstractions and other uncountable things and they are mass nouns, but they can also be count nouns. The most usual ones are:
chocolate/a box of (small) **chocolates**
cloth/a cloth for cleaning the floor
hair (on the head and body)/**a hair** (on my coat collar)
iron/an (electric) **iron** (for pressing clothes)
fire/a fire (for heating or cooking)
light/a light = a lamp or a match
sight/a sight (on a gun), **the sights** of London
sound/the sounds of the city
speech/a speech in Parliament
We also have:
difficulty/a difficulty
duty/a duty
experience/an experience
honour/an honour

15

pleasure/a pleasure
reason/a reason
trust/a trust (eg for raising money for charity).

5 **a** The hardest **form of carbon** is a diamond.
   b **Many kinds of tea** grow in India.
   c I used **four sorts of wood** to make this table.
   d There were **ten brands of soap** in the shop.
   e Lactose is **a type of sugar** found in milk.

We have seen in **A1-3** above that there are ways of measuring for mass nouns. We can also mention types, kinds, sorts, forms and brands with mass noun. There can be more than one kind of happiness, more than one type of coffee, more than one sort of steel, wood, intelligence, humour etc.

5 Numbers and measures

A Indefinite plural numbers in count nouns

few a few	boys, dogs, books, friends, days, houses, garages, hotels
several some	eggs, tomatoes, men, girls, children, oranges, bottles
enough	potatoes, teachers, horses, matches, pencils, trees
more most	workers, doctors, lemons, soldiers, policemen, nurses
many a great many	hospitals, factories, ships, students, streets, cars
*each every	Monday, afternoon, holiday, child, woman, door, table
**all	vegetables, animals, stories, reports, parents, children
(informal) a lot of lots of	apples, buses, cows, donkeys, workmen, schoolgirls, glasses

Indefinite measures in mass nouns

little a little	money, pleasure, hope, information, flour, sugar
some	milk, coffee, interest, gold
enough	time, heat, ambition, water
more most	nonsense, interest, tea, happiness, light, kindness, news, noise
much a great deal of	need, energy, discussion, excitement, butter, wine
each kind/sort of every type/form of	metal, carbon, wood, cloth, paper, soap
all	petroleum, fear, opposition, wheat, knowledge, mankind, doubt, food
a lot of lots of	money, information, coffee, time, water, paper, energy, cloth

*A singular count noun follows **each** and **every**. We can also say: **each of** the boys, **every one of** the boys.
All can come directly before count and mass nouns at all times.

When **the, this, that, these, those** or *possessive adjectives* (**my, your, his** etc) go with a noun, we add **of** to numbers and measures that do not already have **of**. All can also take an **of** phrase: **all (of) my friends** etc.

count nouns			
All		the	bottles were full.
A few Several Some Enough More Most All	of	these their my the those our her	glasses are clean. ships sail to Naples. friends are coming. apples are ripe now. peaches are in the fridge. students work hard. stories amuse me.
Every one Each one	of of	my these	dogs has a name. houses is for sale.

mass nouns			
All		the	money comes from trade.
A little Some Enough More Most Much All	of	this that my your the our their that	meat is deep-frozen. success was well-deserved. affection for him remains. best cloth is very dear. time was spent abroad. business is with Brazil. information was false. timber is from Finland.

B Few, a few; little, a little

  a **Few men** live to be over a hundred years old.

  b We'll invite **a few friends** to spend **a few days** here.

  c John has **little spare money** so takes **few holidays.**

  d Can you give me **a little ink** to write **a few words?**

  e We've had **little rain** this year and **few falls** of snow.

  f Our wells contain **little water — a few hundred litres** only.

With count nouns, **few** = **a very small number**; **few** emphasises the smallness of the number and can be almost negative in meaning. **A few** = a (very) small but positive number.

  With mass nouns, **little** = a very small amount, a very small measure, and can be almost negative. **A little** = a (very) small but positive amount or measure.

C Some; any

1 a **Some girls** gave us **some yellow** roses.

  b I bought **some bread** and **some sugar** today.

  c Take **some money** and get **some potatoes** too.

2 a I haven't **any eggs** or **any flour** to make cakes.

  b You mustn't give **any food** to these monkeys.

Some and **any** can both go with count nouns and with mass nouns to mean either an indefinite but not high number or an indefinite but not large amount or measure. We use **some** in *affirmative* statements.

We use **any** instead of **some** when the noun is an object or complement of a *negative* verb. (▶ also **Chapter 6, B**).

c There wasn't **any fresh news** on the radio.

d There aren't **any good films** on TV this week.

3 a 'Has Mary **any** elder **brothers?'** 'No, only one sister.'

b 'Is there **any mail** for Grandma?' 'Yes, three postcards.'

c 'Have you made **any coffee?'** 'No, but I will.'

d 'Would you like **some coffee?'** 'Yes, I would.'

e 'Shall I put **some cream** in it?' 'Yes, please.'

f The children sent me **some postcards.**

g There weren't **any stamps** on them!

We use **any** in questions with verbs in the *interrogative* form. The reply to the question can be either affirmative or negative: **Yes, I do./No, I don't.** etc. The questioner may expect a negative reply. We use **some** when the questioner expects an affirmative reply.

D Many; much

a **Many people** from other countries live in Britain.

b There weren't **many guests** at Stella's wedding.

c She hasn't got **many relatives** in England.

d **Much of my salary** is taken for income tax.

e We have **not much money** for luxuries.

f Keep quiet! Don't make **so much noise.**

g Does she spend **much time** abroad?

h Peter talks **too much nonsense** for my taste.

Many = a high number and goes with count nouns.
Much = a large amount or measure and goes with mass nouns.
Much usually takes **of** + *noun phrase* after it, or **not, so, very,** or **too** before it. We do not say \She eats much chocolate\ or \The tickets cost much money.\ Instead of **much** in these cases we prefer **a great deal of** + *mass noun* or, informally, **a lot of / lots of** + *mass noun:* **lots of chocolate/money/fun** etc.

More; most

a Shall I make **more sandwiches** for you?

b No, but I'd like **more coffee,** please.

c **Most boys** like outdoor games in summer.

d There are two here and **more policemen** are coming.

e **Most petroleum** comes from the Middle East.

f Empty barrels make **most sound.**

More and **most** go with both count and mass nouns.
More = an additional number, and an additional amount or measure.
Most = a majority, a high number, and a major proportion, a major amount or measure.

F All

a **All the houses** and **all the furniture** belong to him.

b We sold **all the horses** and banked **all the money.**

c They ate **all the food,** then washed **all the plates.**

d **All steel** has some iron in it.

e **They all** belong to him. **It all** belongs to him.

f We sold **them all** and banked **it all.**

g They ate **it all,** then washed **them all.**

h **It all** has some iron in it.

i They are **all his. It is all his.**

j We were **all** young once. We aren't **all** old yet!

k **The men / They** can **all** rest here for an hour.

l **Our soldiers / We** will **all** be going home soon.

m **They / The houses** might **all** belong to me one day.

n **It / The furniture** would **all** need repairs.

o 'Can they read music?' 'The girls **all can / They all can.'**

p 'Do they like football?' 'The boys **all do / They all do.'**

All = the entire number with count nouns (**a-c**).

All = the whole amount or measure with mass nouns (**a-d**).

All can go with a pronoun; it follows personal pronouns (**e-h**).

When the verb is **be,** we place **all** after it (**i-j**).

When the verb contains auxiliaries, and **all** modifies the noun or pronoun subject of that verb (**k-n**), we place **all** after the first or only auxiliary. **All** can go before its noun in the same way as in **a-d** above, but not before the pronoun.

G With pronouns

few of us/them
a few of you/us
some of them/us/it
more of you/them/it
most of us/you/it
many of them/us
all of us/them/it
a lot of us/them/it
lots of us/them/it
enough of you/us/it
several of us/you/them

When the only verb in a short sentence is an auxiliary, **all** comes before it (**o-p**) but can also come before the noun (**a-d**)

We often use pronouns in place of nouns, usually to avoid repetition. The numeraters (for indefinite numbers) and the quantifiers (for indefinite amounts and measures) in **A-F** above need **of** when they stand before pronouns. The pronoun is in the object form.

6 Negative of nouns

A No

a Robert has **no brothers and sisters.**
b **No mail** arrived by the afternoon post.
c **No news** is good news, some people say.
d **No** sensible **man** really believes that.
e There's **no reason** to be upset about it.
f You shouldn't worry **for no good reason** (but you do worry . . .).
g Work for **no pay** is waste of a day.

No comes before nouns and makes them negative. When subjects or objects are negative in this way, verbs are in their affirmative forms (**a-e**).
  No + *singular count noun* (**e-f**) makes an emphatic negation.
  No + *noun* can be the complement of a preposition (**f-g**), except **without**, which is negative in meaning.

B Not any

a I **haven't any money** in that bank.
b There **weren't any** girls at our school.
c There **isn't any** fresh coffee in the jars. .
d Mary **didn't buy any** groceries yesterday.
e I **won't have any** time for shopping today.
f Good heavens! There **won't be any** fish for the cat!

Here, **not** makes a verb negative; **any** comes before the negative noun (▶ **Chapter 5, C**). When the verb is negative, we do not use **no** with nouns, we use **any** for the negative. **Not any** is not usual before subjects (▶ **A** above and **C** below).

C None of + defined noun phrase

a I have **none of my money** in that bank.
b **None of those girls was** at our school.
c **None of the coffee** in the jars **is** fresh.
d John has eaten **none of this cake.**
e We spoke to **none of our friends** about our plans.
f **None of our friends have** motor-bikes.
g **None of those apples are** ripe enough.
h **None of the pupils go** up and down in the *lift.
  *lift (Br) = elevator (Am)

A noun phrase contains a noun and one or more other words that normally go with a noun and make sense. We can define a noun with **the** (article), **this/these, that/those** (demonstrative) and **my, your, his, her, our, their** (possessive adjective) — ▶ also **Chapter 5, A.** When we define a noun we cannot use **no** immediately before the phrase; we use **none of.** The verbs are in the affirmative form and, in formal style (**b**), should be singular (**none** = not one); informally, **none of** + plural noun as subject often takes a plural verb (**f-h**).

D Neither/nor

a **John** and **Mary were not** at home last week.
  Neither John **nor** Mary was at home last week.

And joins two nouns or pronouns in a phrase
eg John **and** Mary
  iron **and** coal

b We don't export **iron** and **coal** to America.
We export **neither** iron **nor** coal to America.

c **Oranges** and **lemons** don't grow in England.
Neither oranges **nor** lemons grow in England.

d He doesn't ask **for advice or for help.**
He asks **neither** for advice **nor** for help.
He asks for **neither advice nor help.**

oranges **and** lemons
I **and** he
The verbs are in the affirmative form.
Neither goes before the first noun to make it negative; **nor** goes before the second noun to make it negative, without **and.** When **or** joins the two nouns, the negative is **nor** (**d**). The nouns can be complements of prepositions (**d**). The preposition can govern both nouns and **neither** can follow it (**d**).

E Neither + singular count noun; neither of

a 'Peter and Charles will run in the 5,000 metre race.'
'**Neither boy** will win at that distance.'

b 'Could we meet on the ninth or tenth of May?'
'**Neither date** suits me, I'm sorry to say.'

c 'You should watch TV at eight and ten tonight.'
'**Neither programme** interests us very much.'

d 'She would like a St Bernard or a Great Dane.'
'**Neither dog** could live in our small flat.'

e 'It would need lots of food and space.'
'We could provide it with **neither basic need.'**

Two items of the same kind,
eg **Peter** and **Charles** = boy and boy
Monday and **Wednesday** = day and day
six o'clock and **ten o'clock** = time and time
Neither of + *defined noun phrase* (▶ **C** above): in **a-e** opposite we could also have:
a Neither of **my boys** . . .
b Neither of **those days** . . .
c Neither of **the programmes** . . .
d Neither of **these dogs** . . .
e . . . neither of **its basic needs.**
The nouns are plural; the verbs are affirmative.

F Neither of

a **Neither of them** will win the race.
b **Neither of these** suits me, I'm sorry to say.
c **Neither of you** can run 5,000 metres.
d She spoke about **neither of us/you/them.**
e **Neither of them** could turn round in our tiny rooms!

Neither of can stand before a pronoun that represents an entire noun phrase.

7 Articles with nouns

A Indefinite article: a, an

1

> an apple, **an** orange, **an** example; **a** horse,
> **a** baby, **a** cat, **a** child, **a** dog; **an** ugly
> building, **an** old man, **an** ancient city, **an**
> exciting story, **an** easy job, **an** open door

The indefinite article goes with singular count nouns only. We use **an** when the next word begins with a vowel sound and **a** before consonant sounds. The article stands before adjectives that come before the noun. Some adjectives begin with a vowel sound.

> **a** uniform, **a** union, **a** university, **a** useful
> tool, **an** hotel (or **a** hotel), **an** hour, **an**
> honest man

The spelling of some words has **u** as the first letter, but the sound is /j/ as in **yes.** Others begin with a silent **h**; the first sound is a vowel.

2 **a** We have daughters. We don't have **a boy.**
  b Eat cherries instead of **an apple.**
  c He went to the war and lost **a leg.**
  d **A waiter** dropped **a plate.**
  e There was **a whole chicken** on it.
  f There are two children, **a son** and **a daughter.**
  g You can take **an apple** — one apple, not six.

An or **a** before a noun shows
• that it is a count noun
• it is singular
• we mention the noun in indefinite terms, eg **a boy** amongst all other boys; **a leg** does not define which leg he lost.

A and **an** do not mean the same as **one** (1); **one** is a definite number between zero (0) and two (2).

3 **a** John's father is **a farmer.** I'm **an engineer.**
  b Mary intends to become **a mathematician.**
  c **An architect** plans new buildings.
  d Peter has been **a teacher** for many years.
  e Jane works as **a typist** for **a politician.**
  f He's **a friend** of **a friend** of mine.
  g I know **a man** who loves London buses.
  h He says there isn't **a better way** to see London.

We use a and **an** with singular count nouns that name a person's profession, job, nationality, rank, religion, political beliefs. He or she is one of a type or category. Plurals take no article, eg My uncles are **doctors.** (▶ **B** below.)

4 **a** Petrol costs about **twenty-five pence a litre.**
  b I paid **fifty pence a kilo** for good apples.
  c She bought carbon paper at **twenty pence a sheet.**
  d Our postman walks **about twelve miles a day.**

A and **an** = **per** in phrases that mention cost, price, speed, time, informally.

e I was driving at **over sixty miles an hour.**

f We offer a salary of **ten thousand pounds a year.**

g **An apple a day** keeps the doctor away.

h You can't rent a car for **£10 a day.**

5 **a** There was **a mass of people** in the town square.

b **A man** in **the crowd** kicked me, by accident.

c **The fellow** didn't even say he was sorry.

d Once, I hired **a camel** for **a journey.**

e **The animal** wouldn't let me get on.

f It laughed at me, **the** nasty **beast!**

We have mentioned a noun once, with **a/an,** without defining it. If we again mention the same **man, camel,** or whatever the noun is, we define it with **the**

eg We talked to **a man** in the street. **The man** was a complete stranger.

Often, a second and later mention of a noun can be a synonym (a word or phrase of similar meaning). The synonym can also add meaning, sometimes.

B Plural

a **Children** love playing games.

b Dr Jones says that I shouldn't eat **oranges.**

c **Factories** often pollute **rivers** and **lakes.**

d Mary likes **animals** but doesn't keep **pets.**

e We grow **flowers** and **vegetables** in the garden.

f **Lemons** are sour but ripe **cherries** are sweet.

g **Some boys** don't like football.

Plural count nouns do not take articles when we mention the noun in general terms. **Children** = all children; children, generally speaking. **Some** in **g** does not identify; it does not say who the boys are.

C Definite article: the

1 **a** **The man** in **the shop** is **the owner** of it.

b **The girls** beside **the boys** are my sisters.

c **The tea** that she made was too weak.

d Perhaps **the water** she used wasn't boiling.

2 **a** You can get **salt** by evaporating **sea-water.**

b **Brazilian coffee** has a good, strong taste.

c **Honesty** is the best policy, always.

d We wish you **peace, health** and **joy.**

e **Egyptian cotton** sells at a good price.

f They use **oil** for making **soap.**

g **Life** is what you make it, **happiness** is where you find it.

In English, **the** is the only form of the definite article. **The** can go with singular and plural count nouns and also with mass nouns. However, there are times when we use **the** and other times when we do not, as we shall see below.

Mass nouns do not take the definite article when we use them in a general sense: **salt, soap, happiness, anger, morocco leather, stainless steel, China tea** are examples of whole categories (▶ also **B** above).

h Count up to ten! Don't speak in **anger.**

i I shall give Tom a wallet made of **morocco leather.**

j **Stainless steel** costs less than **silver** does.

k I like **China tea** without **sugar** or **lemon.**

D Defined nouns: count and mass

1 a **The man** with the red beard **is my father.**

b **The girl** in the corner **looks like Mary.**

c **The house** by the post office **belongs to us.**

d **The coffee** in the pot **is still quite hot.**

e **The intelligence** of the youngsters **surprises me.**

f **The box** on the left **contains the money for Kate.**

g **A girl** with no shoes **is walking on the *pavement.**

h **His father is a man** with **a beard.**
*pavement (Br) = sidewalk (Am)

We use the definite article **the** when phrases after nouns describe and identify them as particular persons, animals, things, or as particular examples or samples of mass nouns. In these examples, we have prepositional phrases.

If we do not use **the,** a phrase after a noun can describe it but does not always define it (▶ **D 2** and **3** below). We do not know who the girl is in **g**; in **h** we learn that **his father is a man** (no different from every other father) and **has a beard** (like thousands of other beards). Compare the examples **a** and **h** opposite.

2 Description

a **A musician who directs an orchestra** is a conductor.

b **People who live in glasshouses** shouldn't throw stones.

c **Machinery that makes work easier** is useful.

A relative clause can follow a noun and either describe it or define it. A *clause* is a group of words that go together with a verb. (▶ **Chapter 12** for relative clauses).

3 Definition

a **The conductor** who directs this orchestra **is Tom Mack.**

b **The people** that I mention **criticise their neighbours.**

c **The machinery** that we use **is quite modern.**

The goes before all nouns that have any kind of defining phrase or clause after them.

4 The environment

a We usually have breakfast in **the kitchen.**
Pass **the butter** please, John.
I'll put **the coffee** on **the stove** to keep warm.
Father is still shaving in **the bathroom.**
The postman hasn't rung **the bell** yet.

The sun, **the** moon, **the** sky, **the** stars, **the** sea are all unique elements of **the** environment of **the world** we live in.

The defines the things around people in the home, at the office, in the street, on the table, ie in the environment. Generally, there is only one item of the kind in the environment: it is **unique** in its environment.

b

> the Houses of Parliament, the White House, the Eiffel Tower, the Senate, the Politburo, the Kremlin, the Tower of London, the Unknown Soldier, the Parthenon, the Colisseum, the Aswan Dam, the Statue of Liberty

These are examples of things which are unique in the environment. There are millions of houses but only the House of Lords; millions of unknown soldiers but the Unknown Soldier is *the* one we all know about. God is unique but takes no article; 'a god', 'the god' is one of a number of gods, eg Zeus, Jove, Odin.

c

> in/at church, in hospital, at school, at college, at university, in jail or in prison, at home.

These nouns do not have the. People are at or in these institutions because of what happens there — prayer, cure, education, punishment, family life etc. The comes before these nouns: they are then buildings or places. People are at the church, at/in the prison, for any other reason, eg. The priest went to the prison to talk to some of the prisoners. A/The Home for Orphans/Old Soldiers is the name of a particular institution. The nouns in this box are probably unique or almost unique in a local environment.

E Nouns with and without 'the'

1 Proper nouns

  a **Mary** and **Peter** went to **London** in **September.**
  b The capital of **Spain** is **Madrid.**
  c I was in **Athens** until **Sunday,** the second of **June.**
  d I speak **Greek** but my boss speaks **English** only.
  e Many **Swiss** people speak **French** and **German.**

Proper nouns are: the names of persons, the names of countries, towns, villages and names of mountains, rivers, continents and so on. We can recognise a proper noun; it begins with a capital letter. In English, the names of days, months, nationalities and languages are proper nouns and must begin with a capital letter. The seasons of the year are not usually proper nouns; religious feasts and seasons are: **Christmas, Easter, Lent, Ramadan, Passover** etc.

2 Personal names without 'the'

  a **Mr Cox** and **Mrs Fox** both teach English.
  b **Miss Brown** and **Dr Scott** are getting married.
  c **General Breck** and **Professor Grey** are cousins.
  d **Lord Cloe** and **Bishop Jones** have just arrived.
  e **Liz, Mary, Peter** and **Tom** are John Cox's pupils.

Personal names can have a title before them. We do not use the before a person's name, whether there is a title or not. There is one exception: the **Reverend** Harold Clark is a clergyman, ie a priest or minister of a church.

> Queen Elizabeth; **the** queen/**the** Queen
> President Reagan; **the** president/**the**
> President
> Ambassador Fry; **the** Ambassador (to
> Peru)
> **The** Duke of York, **the** Prime Minister,
> **the** Bishop of Oxford, **the** Professor of
> Biology

Personal titles without personal names usually take **the.** A title often names a position in the army, police, diplomatic service etc. The title is often unique — for one person at a time.

3 Place names without 'the'

> Africa, Asia, America, North America,
> South America, Europe, Australasia,
> *Antarctica
> *Argentina, Brazil, China, England,
> France, Germany, India, Japan, Poland,
> Russia
> Madrid, Paris, Stockholm, Turin,
> Vladivostock, Warsaw, Tokyo, Pekin,
> Athens *See opposite

The ordinary geographical names of continents, countries, cities, towns and villages do not take **the.** There are some exceptions: **the Arctic,** and instead of **Antarctica** we can say **the Antarctic;** instead of **Argentina** we can say **the Argentine.** Other exceptions are: **the** Netherlands, **the** Congo, **the** Sudan, **the** Ukraine; **the** Hague is the capital of **the** Netherlands.

4 Place names with 'the'

> **the** Republic **of France/Italy/Greece/
> Finland,** **the United States of America,**
> ****the** United Kingdom **of Great Britain
> and Northern Ireland, the** Kingdom of
> **Jordan,** *****the** Union of **Soviet Socialist
> Republics**
> **the USA or **the** United States**
> ***Britain or **the** UK**
> ****Russia or **the** USSR or **the** Soviet**
> Union

The political titles of states and countries generally have an **of** phrase in them; **the** comes before the title.

> **the** Far East, **the** Crimea (in Russia), **the**
> Levant, **the** Punjab, **the** Rhineland, **the**
> Riviera; **the** Home Counties, **the**
> Midlands (in England)

Also, **the** comes before a few nouns that name large areas, eg **the Middle East.** Also, desert areas take **the,** eg **the** Sahara, **the** Sind, **the** Gobi, **the** Kalahari.

5 Waters and waterways

> **the** Atlantic (Ocean), **the** Pacific (Ocean),
> **the** Indian Ocean, **the** Black Sea, **the**
> Red Sea, **the** Mediterranean (Sea), **the**
> English Channel, **the** Bering Straits, **the**
> Dardanelles, **the** (river) Nile, **the** (river)
> Danube, **the** (river) Thames, **the** Panama
> Canal, **the** Suez Canal, **the** Manchester
> Ship Canal

Oceans, seas and most parts of the sea that have a geographical name take **the** before them. Rivers and canals also take **the.** Lakes do not take **the. Lake** is usually the first word but can be at the end of some names: Silver Lake, Swan Lake, Forest Lake. **The Lake District** is in England, **the Great Lakes** are in North America. When **Bay** is the last word in the name, do not use **the,** eg Hudson's Bay, Goose Bay, Whitley Bay.

> the Sea of Marmora, **the** Sea of Azov,
> **the** Bay of Biscay, **the** Bay of Bengal,
> **the** Gulf of Mexico, **the** Gulf of Finland,
> **the** Straits of Gibraltar

Some geographical names have an **of** phrase; **the** comes first.

6 Mountains and islands

> **the** Alps, **the** Himalayas, **the**
> Appalachians, **the** Blue Mountains, **the**
> White Mountains, **the** Sierra Nevada, **the**
> Sierra Moreno
> **The** Azores, **the** Dodecanese, **the**
> Hebrides, **the** Seychelles, **the** West Indies

Ranges of mountains and hills and groups of islands take **the**. We usually mention these without the words **mountains** and **islands**. We do say **mountains, islands** when the name is an adjective eg **the Blue** Mountains, **the Balearic** Islands, **the Channel** Islands. ▶ **5** above — **the Red** Sea etc.

> (Mt) Everest, (Mt) Fujiyama, (Mt)
> Olympus, (Mt) Snowdon, (Mt) Hymettus
> Britain, Ceylon, Jersey, Ireland, Lewis,
> Madagascar, Rhodes, Trinidad, Sardinia,
> Sicily, Malta, Crete, Cyprus.
> **the** island of Rhodes, Malta, Majorca
> **the** Isle of Man, (**the** Isle of) Capri, (**the**
> Isle of) Sheppey, (**the** Isle of) Skye: these
> are the usual titles for these islands

The name of a single mountain takes the word **Mount** (Mt) before it, without **the**. We can mention a well-known mountain by its name, without **Mount** usually, if the name is not an adjective; then we generally have, eg **Red Mountain, Thunder Mountain, Strawberry Hill**. A single island takes its name without **the**. We can also say: **the island of** + its name but not before an adjectival name: **Devils' Island, Lonely Island, Long Island, Pearl Island** stay as they are.

7 Stars and planets

> **the** Great Bear, **the** Southern Cross, **the**
> Little Bear, **the** Plough, **the** Archer, **the**
> Seven Sisters, **the** Milky Way, Charles's
> Wain, Cassiopeia's Chair, Orion's Belt

Groups of stars (constellations) take **the** before their names except when the first part is a possessive noun.

> Betelgeuse, Polaris, Sirius, **the** North
> Star, **the** Pole Star, **the** Dog Star, **the**
> Evening Star

Single stars with a name do not take **the** except when we have **the** + *adjective* + **star**.

> Jupiter, Mars, Mercury, Neptune, Pluto,
> Saturn, Uranus and Earth

We say **the sun, the moon, the earth** (or **Earth** if we name it as a planet). Other planets have personal names so do not take **the**.

NOTE the English names for parts of the Zodiac all take **the**, eg **the** Fish (Pisces), **the** Bull (Taurus), **the** Twins (Gemini). The Latin forms for these do not take **the** when English-speakers use them, and they often do this.

8 Public places

> the Odeon Cinema, **the** Artists' Club, **the** Albert Hall, **the** Astoria Hotel, **the** Carnegie Library, **the** Pasteur Hospital, **the** Golden Lion Restaurant, **the** New Century Bookshop, **the** Palladium Theatre

> Albert's (Restaurant), Claridge's (hotel), Saint Mary's (Cathedral), St John's (Church), Selfridge's (Department Store), Ann's Kitchen (a restaurant); **the** Hilton Hotel

> the Prince's Feathers, **the** Dutchman's Pipe, **the** Soldiers' Return, **the** Sailors' Rest

A public place is a cinema, club, concert hall, hospital, hotel, inn, library, market, museum, park, public house (pub), restaurant, shop, theatre, or other place that serves the public. Most of these places have names; they all take **the** before the name.

We can omit **cinema, hotel, pub, restaurant** informally, among people who know the place and what it is. The possessive form of a person's proper name does not take **the**; the ordinary form does.

The names of inns and pubs and some other places have a possessive noun before a second noun. We then use **the** eg **the King's Head** Inn, **the Robin's Nest** Café.

9 Streets and roads

> Regent Street, Park Avenue, Sun Crescent, Moon Terrace, Port Gardens, North Lane, Red Lion Square, Belmont Circle, Ludgate Circus, Orchard Way, Cambridge Road

> the Cambridge **road, the** Oxford **road, the** London **road**

A street in a town, city or village can be ... Street, ... Avenue, ... Crescent, ... Terrace, ... Gardens, ... Lane, ... Square, ... Circle, ... Circus, ... Way and ... Road. They all take their full names without **the** and with a capital letter at the beginning of each word.

A road goes from one town to another: **Cambridge Road** is a street in London; it does not go to Cambridge; but **the Dover road** is **the** road that goes to Dover.

10 Ships, trains, aeroplanes

> the Queen Mary, **the** Mary Celeste, **the** Bounty, **the** Explorer, **the** Dolphin
> the Flying Scotsman, **the** Blue Train, **the** Cornishman, **the** Brighton Belle
> the Flying Dutchman, **the** Tasmanian

Ships and boats nearly always have names. Some special trains and passenger aeroplanes can also have names; **the** comes before the name. NOTE **the** Queen Mary, **the** President Jackson, **the** Margarita are ships; without **the** they are people.

11 Newspapers and magazines

> the Daily Telegraph, **the** Evening News, **the** Morning Post, **the** Saturday Messenger, **the** Weekly News, **the** Farmers' Journal, **the** Woman's Weekly, **the** Readers' Digest, **the** Annual Review Collier's Magazine, Harpers', Blackwood's Magazine, Old Moore's Almanac, Stubbs' Gazette

We usually place **the** before the title of a newspaper or magazine. If the title already has **the** (eg **The** Times) we do not repeat it.

When the title of a magazine is a personal name with possessive ending ('s or s') we do not use **the**.

12 Musical instruments and games

Dick gave us a tune on		mouth-organ. piano.
My brother plays		violin. drums.
Mary performs well on	the	cymbals. trumpet.
I'd like to play		flute. guitar.
You could learn (to play)		banjo.

We talk about someone who plays **the flute, the violin.** We usually put **the** before the name of the instrument. We mention **the piano** etc in a general sense; we do not mean **this** or **that** particular piano.

The boys played	chess/dominoes/darts.
He's interested in	cards/poker/bridge.
I seldom win at	bowling, ping-pong.

People play games. We do not put **the** before the names of the games, whether they are indoor or outdoor games.

Rain, rain, go away,
Come back some other day.
Now the children want to play —
football/cricket/baseball/tennis/
cowboys/hide and seek.

13 The calendar

the Sunday	before last
the Monday	after next
*the autumn	of 1984
(**the**) Tuesday	of that week
(**the**) August	of the previous year
the Eve	of St John's Day
the first Friday in October	
*autumn (Br) = fall (Am)	

We say **the previous Sunday** and **the following September** but **next Sunday, next September, last Monday, last June** without **the.** The names of days, months, seasons and the number for the year do not take **the** except when a defining phrase or clause follows them. The date usually takes **the,** it is the date (of the month). We can write eg **19th March** but we say **the nineteenth of March** or **the nineteenth** (of the month).

a 'Do you remember **the Sunday** (that) we went to Bangor?'
'It was **the day** (that) a wheel fell off the car.'

b 'Do you know **the year** (that) they were married?'
'It was **the last Friday** in **the summer** of 1975.'

Relative clauses can follow nouns and often define them (▶ **D2** and **3** above).

F Plural class nouns: 'the'

1

the rich, **the** poor, **the** sick, **the** able-bodied, **the** strong, **the** weak, **the** homeless, **the** deaf, **the** blind, **the** helpless, **the** living, **the** dead, **the** wounded, **the** injured, **the** needy

A *class noun* names an entire class of people; it places them in a category. The noun has exactly the same form as an adjective; the adjective defines the class eg **the young** = all young people, a **The strong have** no right to bully **the weak.**

b **The rich are** few, **the poor are** many.

c Books for **the blind** are written in Braille.

d **A poor man** went to **a rich person** for help.

e **The rich person** was **a very deaf man.**

f He couldn't hear **the poor man's voice.**

as a general category. The most common class nouns appear in the box at the bottom of page 30.

Class nouns are always singular in form but plural in grammar. They take a plural verb and, always, **the.**

We can, of course, mention one or more persons: *adjective + noun* does not name the whole class or category.

2

> **the** British, **the** Dutch, **the** English, **the** French, **the** Irish, **the** Scots, **the** Spanish

The adjective that states the nationality of the people in a country is often also the class noun for the whole nation. From each example in **2**, we can make a singular or plural count noun: **two Dutchmen, an Englishman, three Frenchwomen, four Irishwomen** etc, **a British/Spanish/French** person (woman, child, boy, girl, man).

3

> **the** Swiss, **the** Burmese, **the** Chinese, **the** Japanese, **the** Portuguese

In **3** we change the article to **a** or a number for count nouns, eg **a Swiss, three Japanese.** If we are not referring to men, we can make it clear: **three Chinese women, five Japanese boys.** In **2** and **3** the class (nationality) nouns all end in sibilant sounds — /ʃ/, /tʃ/, /z/ and /s/.

4

> **the** Americans/**an** American; **the** Russians/**a** Russian; **the** Egyptians/**an** Egyptian; **the** Iranis/**an** Irani; **the** Iraqis/**an** Iraqi; **the** Germans/**a** German etc

Class nationality nouns with **the,** and count nouns that are the same form as the adjective.

5

> **the** Danes/**a** Dane; **the** Finns/**a** Finn; **the** Greeks/**a** Greek; **the** Poles/**a** Pole; **the** Swedes/**a** Swede; **the** Turks/**a** Turk

Some nationality words are ordinary count nouns, with a capital letter at the beginning.

6 Families and names

a **The Browns** live next door to **the Smiths.**

b Shall we invite **the Macmillans** to the party?

c Have you met **the Johnsons** before?

We refer to a whole family with **the** + *the plural of the surname* (family name).

d Look at his face! He's **a Cameron,** for sure.

e She's **a Nelson,** just like her mother was.

f We do business with **one of the Johnsons.**

g That little girl is **one of the Rockefellers.**

h We met **some of the O'Gradys** at a wedding, recently.

7 Meals

a The family were all at **breakfast,** early.

b None of them come home for **lunch.**

c They have **lunch** in the canteen on working days.

d I sometimes watch TV after **dinner.**

e Shall we go to **the Nature Lovers' Lunch?**

f I've got two tickets for **the Hunters' Dinner.**

g We can't afford **the lunch** and **the dinner.**

h I generally have **a light breakfast.**

i Of course, I take **a good lunch** at midday.

j Jane prepares **a tasty supper** most evenings.

The singular with **a(n)** usually means that a person has the strong characteristics of the family.

We can mention a person as a member of a family but not which member, by name: **one of the** + *plural surname.* **NOTE** personal names ending in **-y** take **-s** for the plural not **-ies** as in **lady/ladies** etc: eg· There are two **Marys** in our office.

Breakfast, lunch, tea, dinner and supper are our daily meals at home, at a friend's home, in a restaurant or café; we do not use **the** before the noun for a meal.

Clubs, committees and similar groups sometimes arrange meals for special purposes. Generally, we have to buy tickets for them. The noun takes **the.**

The indefinite **a** comes before *adjective + noun;* the adjective describes the meal.

8 The possessive case

A The apostrophe ('s, s') with nouns

1 a John plays **Mary's old jazz records.**
  b **John's records** are mostly classical.
  c **The doctor's car** is parked at **Tom's house.**
  d **Tom's house** is next door to **Dr Gray's.**
  e They make **girls'** bikes different **from boys'.**
  f **Boys' things** are for boys, **girls'** for girls, of course.

A person has something eg a house, a car, a dog, a farm, shoes, keys: he or she owns a house etc. The house belongs to **Mr Long**; it is **Mr Long's house.** The house belongs to **Mrs Long**; it is **Mrs Long's house.** When the owner is a singular noun, we add **'s**; for plural owners, we add **s'** to show that the nouns are in the possessive form. Only possessors (owners) take the apostrophe (**'s or s'**) forms. The things they own (possessions) do not change form in any way. A possessive noun can stand alone when the speaker does not wish to repeat the name of the possession (**d-f** opposite).

2 a Women sometimes say: 'It's **a man's world.'**
  b **Women's lives** are not the same as **men's.**
  c **Men's lives** are generally shorter than **women's.**
  d I'm making a shelf for **the children's books.**
  e **The children's dog** bit the **postman's leg.**

Some nouns do not make the plural with **-s** eg a man / some men (▶ **Chapter 3, C1).** Add **'s** to them for the possessive form, singular and plural.

3 a We get our bread at **the baker's** in Main Street.
  b **The baker's** is next door to the *****chemist's.**
  c There's **a grocer's** opposite the supermarket.
  d **Roscoe's** didn't have any shoes I liked.
  e Try **Conway's** or **Penman's.** They're good shops.
  f No more shops today. My feet are killing me.
  ***chemist's** (Br) = pharmacy (Am)

*The name of a shop is generally a possessive noun that says what the shopkeeper is, or a proper noun that says who the shopkeeper is, without the word **shop.**
*shop (Br) = store (Am)

4 a **Tony's** away. He's having a holiday at **Grandma's.**
  b **Uncle John's** is a great place for a holiday.
  c Mary didn't go home. She went to **Jenny's** (**her sister's**).

We mention familiar people's homes and professional people's places in the same way — **the doctor's, the dentist's** etc. These are all places we go to / come from / visit / stay at for one or other purpose.

d I'm going to **the architect's** about our new house.

5 | a **dog's** nose / **dogs'** noses; a **cow's** horns / those **cows'** tails; a **cat's** paws / **cats'** paws; a **horse's** head / **horses'** heads; a **lion's** den / a **lions'** den

Possessive nouns with apostrophes can stand for people and well-known, common kinds of animals.

6 | **Achilles'** heel, **Hercules'** labours, **Socrates'** words, **Venus'** beauty
Charles' or **Charles's**, **Marcus'** or **Marcus's**, **Dolores'** or **Dolores's**
Strauss's music, **Mr Cross's** office; **the Crosses'** house, **Tess's** father

Personal names that end in **-s** in the singular often make the possessive with an apostrophe without an extra **-s**. They are mostly classical names; other names can take one or other form in writing, but in spoken English they generally have the extra, unstressed syllable, /ɪz/. When a name ends in **-ss**, its possessive form is always **'s** (singular) or **-es'** (plural).

B Possessors and possessions

1 **a** Are you a member of **the Men's Institute?**
  b Yes. I teach **a beginners' class** there.
  c **The Women's Society** meets on Mondays.
  d **Kate's family** were all here yesterday.
  e Kate's father is head of **the Veterans' Legion.**
  f **John's employer** pays fair wages.
  g **John's union** has never called a strike.
  h **The teachers' study room** is opposite my classroom.

We used the term possessive in **A** above. The examples mention people and animals that own something: something belongs to them. We also use the possessive noun with a difference in meaning: **the Girls' High School** — the girls do not own the school, the school does not belong to the girls; in fact, the girls belong to the school. It is the **High School for Girls.** In a family, the members all belong to the family and to one another (**d**).

2 **a** **Mary and Tom's** son is called Bob.
  b **Smith, Dunn and Company's** prices are high.
  c **Brown and Sons'** prices are lower.
  d **Tom and Jerry's** tricks amuse me.
  e **Mary's girl and Jane's** are cousins.
  f **Mary's** and **Jane's** girls are cousins.

When there are two or more possessors of the same possessions, the apostrophe goes with the second or last. **A firm, company** etc can be singular (**b**) or plural (**c**).

The apostrophe on each possessive noun (**e, f**) shows separate possessors of separate belongings or possessions.

3 **a** **Mary's husband's** brother lives in Brazil.
  b A thief took **John's grandfather's** gold watch.
  c **A neighbour's child's** ball broke our window.
  d This looks very like **our son's ball.**

There can be two possessive nouns. The first owns the second, and the second owns the next.

C Idiomatic and common phrases

1
> for **goodness'** sake, for **heaven's** sake,
> **money's** worth, in **harm's** way, out of
> **harm's** way, a **stone's** throw, at my **wits'**
> end, in the **mind's** eye

Some common idiomatic phrases have a possessive noun in them.

2
> **two hours'** work, **ten minutes'** walk, **a**
> **good night's** sleep, **a month's** *holidays,
> **six weeks'** wages, **a fair day's** pay, **a hard**
> **day's** work
> *holidays (Br) = vacation (Am)

Some common expressions of time have a possessive noun in them. When there are numbers of minutes, hours, days etc we can also have,
eg **a two-hour job**
a ten-minute walk
a five-year contract.

D Of + possessive noun

1

1	2	3	4
A/An	friend	of Harry's	arrived.
	cousin	of Jane's	left.
One	aunt	of the Browns'	came.
	uncle	of Mary's	sang.
A few	cousins	of Bill's	danced.
Some	colleagues	of the twins	helped.
Two or three	fellow-students	of Miss Lee's	stayed.
Several	relations	of father's	called.

The nouns in the table (column 2) all mention one or more persons. These belong to a larger group. Most people have more than one friend, uncle, colleague etc.

some friends of Harry's = **some** of Harry's **friends; a cousin** of Jane's = **one** of Jane's **cousins.**

One to one relationships, eg **John's father / eldest son / youngest sister / mother / car / home / wife / oldest friend** etc. are unique relationships. We cannot use the pattern in the table **a mother of Harry's**, as **one of Harry's mothers** makes physical and grammatical nonsense. We can have: **the** mother of Harry / **the** father of the family etc (▶ **E** below).

2 a **That dog of Tom's** is a proper nuisance.
   b **Those children of the Browns'** seem nice kids.
   c I won't listen to **these silly friends of Jim's.**
   d **That old grandfather of Jane's** looks half his age.

We can express admiration, anger, criticism, amusement, humour and other feelings about persons and all other things in unique relationships by using demonstrative adjectives (**this, that; these, those**) before the possession (for notes on demonstrative adjectives, ▶ **Chapter 10, B**).

E Possessor + of + possession

1

the **boy's** the **boys'**	teacher/sister/sisters/father
the **girl's** the **girls'**	hair/clothes/brother/brothers
the **dog's** the **dogs'**	legs/paws/eyes/claws

In the box opposite, the written examples of singular and plural possessive nouns are clear: **'s** and **s'**. In spoken English, singular and plural possessive nouns sound exactly the same, and because **the** goes with both singular and plural nouns, the meaning is not always clear.

2

the father/teacher/sister(s)	**of**	**the boy/girl**
the hair/clothes/brother(s)	**of**	**the boys/girls**
the legs/paws/eyes/claws	**of**	**the dog**
	of	**the dogs**

We can make it clear; the pattern can also be *possessor* + **of** + *possession*. There is no apostrophe.

3 Parts of larger things: part + of + larger thing

a A tornado damaged **the roofs of many buildings.**

b **The tops of these mountains** are always white.

c **The chimneys of the factories** here have filters.

d There are filters on **the tips of cigarettes.**

Generally, we do not use apostrophe forms when the first noun names a part of a larger thing, eg the roof of a/the house; the top of a/the mountain; a part of a/the sentence; a branch of a/the tree etc. The nouns stand for things that are not animate, ie not persons or animals, and so without life; neither noun could possess the other; they just belong to each other.

e the funnel **of a ship / a ship's** funnel; the wings **of an aeroplane / an aeroplane's** wings; the end **of the day / the day's** end; the work **of the day / the day's** work; the scent **of a flower / a flower's** scent

A few familiar phrases can be in this pattern or with apostrophe.

4 Smaller parts of a/the part

the bridge **of the** nose, **the** scruff **of the** neck, **the** joints **of the** fingers, **the** calf **of the** leg
the panels **of the** door, **the** shaft of **the** piston, **the** base **of the** cylinder
the veins **of the** leaves, **the** hairs **of the** roots, **the** petals **of the** flower

There are many nouns that name parts of persons' or animals' bodies; other nouns refer to parts of buildings, engines, machines, plants and everything else: the leg, the arm; the door; the piston, the cylinder; the roots, etc. When we mention a smaller part of a part, we use an **of** phrase. Parts of parts of the human body take **the** with both nouns, usually.

The smaller parts of other things take **the**; the larger part, if it is a count noun, can take **a** or **the**, eg **the** head of **an** axe; **the** handle of **the** kitchen door.

Some parts of parts of the body can be like the examples above but are more often one-word nouns:

eardrum, eyeball, knee-cap, eyebrow, eyelash, eyelid, fingernail, toenail

F Own with possessives

a **John's own car** broke down. He borrowed Jim's.

b All the pupils in this school have **their own books.**

c How a man spends **his own time** is **his own affair.**

d **Tom's own opinion** is that you waste time.

e He thinks you should earn **your own living.**

f Would he risk **his own money** to give me a start?

g Let's not pay the rent! We'll buy **a home of our own.**

h Aunt Mary has no children **of her own.**

i She takes care of Billy as if he were **her own son.**

Own can come between possessive nouns or adjectives and the possession. **John's own car** points out that John is the real owner. **His own money** — not a loan from the bank.

We can also have *possession* + **of** + **own** possessive phrase: **money of his own, a car of her own.**

G Possessive adjectives

1 I'm Tom Brown. She's Jane Brown, **my daughter.**

I'm Jane, He's **my father.**

I'm Jim Brown. I'm **your brother.**

I'm **your little sister.**

That's Jim. I'm **his sister.**

That's Jane. I'm **her brother.**

This is the family car. I'm **its driver.**

The possessive adjectives are:

	singular	plural
1st person	**my**	**our**
2nd person	**your**	**your**
3rd person (male)	**his**	
3rd person (female)	**her**	**their**
3rd person (common)	**its**	

Third person singular: our choice depends only on the sex of the possessor. We use **his** when the possessor is male (**man, boy** and other words that can mean man or boy); **her** when the possessor is female (**woman,** or **girl** and other words that can mean woman or girl). **Its** is the possessive adjective for all nouns that name inanimate (non-living) things and for animals when their sex is not known or does not matter to the speaker.

eg I saw **a spider. Its** legs were black and hairy.

We are Jane and Jim. They are **our parents.**

We are Mum and Dad. We are **your parents.**

We had **a black bull. Its** horns were a metre in length.
That's **my dog. Her/Its** name is Lassie. **His/Its** name is Bobo.

They are the Browns and this is **their house.**

2 a 'Did you go to **Richard's office?'**
'No, I saw him at **his home.'**

b 'Did he introduce you to **his wife?'**
'No, she was visiting **her brother.'**

c 'Were **their children** with **his wife?'**
'**Their children** were both fast asleep.'

d 'What was **your reason** for going there?'
'**My reason** is **my own affair,** not **your business.** I've nothing more to say. Thank you for ringing. Good-bye!'

A possessive adjective stands before a noun; it cannot stand alone.

H Possessive pronouns

1

	singular	plural
1st person	**mine**	**ours**
2nd person	**yours**	**yours**
3rd person (male)	**his**	
3rd person (female)	**hers**	**theirs**
3rd person (common)	***its**	

*We rarely hear or see **its** as a possessive pronoun; **its** is usually a possessive adjective and stands before its noun.

a With two pullovers, **mine** and **hers,** I soon got warm.

b They hadn't enough cash. **His** and **hers** made £20.

c **Yours** seems to be a big family. **Mine** is too.

Possessive pronouns stands for both the possessive noun and the possession, eg 'Is this **Mary's coat?'** 'No, that's **hers.'** = 'No, that's **her coat'.**
'Our cat loves **fish.'** 'So I see. It has eaten most of **mine** and some of **yours,** too. It was **ours,** for dinner.'
Most of mine = most of my fish
some of yours = some of your fish
it was ours = it was our fish.

NOTE we do not use **own** with possessive pronouns. For **own** ▶ F above.

2 Of + possessive pronoun

a I felt cold. Flora gave me an old pullover **of hers**.

b We lent them **some of ours** to add to **theirs**.

c **A son of ours** (we have four) studies economics.

The possessive nouns with apostrophe in **D1** and **2** above can become possessive pronouns,

eg **A friend of Kate's** is also **my friend**. = A friend **of hers** is a friend **of mine**. Some ex-pupils **of Miss Tring's** are classmates **of the boys**. = Some ex-pupils **of hers** are classmates **of theirs**.

NOTE of phrases of the kind in **E3** and **4** above can have an object pronoun instead of the noun, but not a possessive pronoun

eg **their roofs, the roofs of them; its base, the base of it,** etc.

3 You already know the personal pronouns for subjects and objects. In the third column below you can see the possessive pronouns and in the fourth column the possessive adjectives.

singular	subject	object	possessive pronoun	possessive adjective	
	I	**me**	**mine**	**my**	1st person
	you	**you**	**yours**	**your**	2nd person
	he, she, it	**him, her, it**	**his, hers**	**his, her, its**	3rd person
plural	**we**	**us**	**ours**	**our**	1st person
	you	**you**	**yours**	**your**	2nd person
	they	**them**	**theirs**	**their**	3rd person

The words in the third column are pronouns but in the fourth column they are adjectives and stand before a noun: **my** hat, **your** book, **her** brother, **his** father, and so on.

9 Definers of nouns

A Some definers of nouns

1 Words that show indefinite number in count nouns and indefinite amount in mass nouns ▶ **Chapter 5.**

Words that define negative number and amount ▶ **Chapter 15.**

Articles: **a/an, the** ▶ **Chapter 7.**

Possessive adjectives ▶ **Chapters 8, G; 10, A and 11, B.**

In this section of the book a *definer* is a word that comes before a noun that mentions particular persons and things eg **this man / these men;** not **a man / men** in general terms.

2

for count nouns	for mass nouns
this/that ⟷	this/that
these/those ⟶	*
both ⟷	*
either ⟷	*
each ⟶	*
every ⟷	*all
such (a)	such
enough (plural only)	enough
some	some
any	any

*These definers do not go before mass nouns directly. We can mention measures with mass nouns (▶ **Chapter 4, B**). The measures are count nouns: both **sacks** of corn; every **litre** of milk, each **bottle** of oil, etc.

Definers of nouns do the same work as **the** but add their own meanings, eg **this house** can mean **the house here, the house we are in now; that house** can mean **the house there, the house we were in then.**

Without **the** or any other definer, nouns have a general meaning:

Boys are **boys** and **girls** are **girls** and make the world go round.

'**Money** is the root of **evil.**' 'Perhaps it is but **money** doesn't grow on **trees**'.

With definers, we move the meaning away from the general and towards the particular. **The/My/Those children** are particular children, not **all children** in general terms.

B Demonstrative adjectives

a We live in **this house.** We sold **that** old *flat.

b We got a good price for **that** little home.

c With all **these** children you need **this** big place.

d In **these** times, families are generally smaller.

e Grandma had six children — not many in **those** days.

f **These** apples come from our garden. They're good.

g You're right. **This** apple is delicious.

This, these; that/those are demonstrative adjectives. **This** goes with singular nouns and **these** goes with plural nouns. **This** and **these** refer to **place = here, near the speaker** or to **time = now, at present,** in connection with a noun:

This is my wife

and **these** are our little angels

h It's the first of May today. **This** is Kate's birthday.

i She was born in 1960. We lived in Dover at **that** time.

j In **those** years, Father worked on a ferry-boat.

k Now he's retired. He takes things easy, **these** days.
*flat (Br) = apartment (Am)

That's our house.

Those birds are crows.

That goes with singular nouns, **those** goes with plural nouns and they refer to things **there, then** — a more distant place or time.

With **that/those**, time can be in the past or in the future; **this/these** refer to **now**.

C Either, or; both

1 a Could you be here on **either** Monday **or** Tuesday?

b We can have **either** fish **or** chicken for lunch.

c **Either** Jane **or** John answers the telephone.

d I'm free on **Monday and Tuesday.** We could arrange a meeting for **either day.**

e **Number 18 and number 88** buses stop here. You can get to Marble Arch on **either (bus).**

f **Kate** and **Tony's** car has a very large boot. **Either of them** can drive you with all your luggage.

g '**Either sugar or honey** will sweeten your tea.' 'Thank you. Is **either (of them)** on the table?'

h I shall cook **either potatoes or beans. Either** make a good salad, for the evening.

There are two nouns; **either** goes before the first and **or** before the second noun. **Either . . . or** phrases mean *one of the two,* if the first then not the second; if not the first, then the second.

Instead of repeating the **either . . . or** phrase, we can have **either** + *singular noun* (**a-e**) and we can have **either of the buses, either of them/us** etc (**either of** + *plural noun or pronouns*). The verb is singular either way. Subjects, when the nouns are plural, take plural verbs (**h**).

For **neither/nor** ▶ **Chapter 6, D.**

2 a **John** and **Charles** were born in the same year.
Both (boys) are twelve years old now.

b **Dr Pole** came to talk to **Dr Cane. Both (doctors)** are heart specialists.

c **Coal and oil** come out of the ground. We use **both (of them)** as fuel.

d **Both gold and iron** are minerals. **Both (of them)** are useful in different ways.

e They are **both** useful in different ways. **Both gold and iron** have their uses.

There are two nouns, the first and the other; **both** combines the two nouns, and if they are subjects, the verb is plural (**a-e** opposite). **Both** can stand without a noun to avoid repeating the noun immediately (**a-d, f** opposite).

We can have **both** + **of** + *plural object pronoun* to avoid repeating the noun (**c, d, f** opposite). In **e** opposite, we see *a subject* + *part of* **be** + **both** and **both** + *noun* and *noun*.

f There was an apple for Jim and an apple for Tom. Dick ate **both (apples)/both (of them)**.

D Every; each

Every	man dog child	likes to play games. can learn to swim. needs proper food.

Every one of Every one of Each of	the these our my	men dogs children	has a job. works hard. gets special care. plays games
Every one of		us you them	

a **Both boys** got full marks in the exam. **Each boy** received a different prize.

b **Each child** in a family differs from the others. **Every mother** knows this very well.

c These men are hooligans, **every one of them.** I'd like to see **each of them** in a separate cell.

d An editor sent three reporters to a press conference. **Each** reported the minister's words incorrectly. **Not every minister** has a clear, strong voice.

Every + *singular count noun* is plural in meaning: **every house** in London = all the houses in London; **every woman** = all women, generally and without exception.

Every one of + *defined plural count noun*: this pattern is necessary when **the, this/that, these/those** or possessive adjectives (**my, her, our** etc) already define the nouns in particular terms, eg **Every one of our children** has a job. The nouns are plural in form; the verb is singular. The same pattern is used before object pronouns (eg **every one of us**). Notice too **every member of that family; every gram of their gold; every drop of this liquid,** with collective nouns and mass nouns.

Each + *singular count noun*: **each** is singular in meaning; it mentions a person or other thing as a separate individual but as one of a larger number. The larger number can be two, three or any higher number. **Each one of** or **each of** + *plural noun or object pronoun* can stand before **the/these/my** etc.

E Such, such a

1 a I was lucky. **Such luck** seldom comes twice.

b It's freezing outside. **Such weather** in May is rare.

c They're beautiful. I couldn't grow **such roses.**

d Marry him! Where did you get **such an idea?**

e They're clever. **Such** clever **girls** learn quickly.

Such + *plural count nouns and singular mass nouns* and **such a** + *singular count noun*: in the examples opposite

such luck = luck of this / that sort
such weather = weather like this / of this sort
such roses = roses like this/of this sort/type/quality;
such an idea = an idea like that / of this kind;

f It's too old. **Such an** old **house** needs repairs.

g I can't see clearly in **such** poor **light.**

h **Such a** (fine) **woman** as Mary wouldn't tell lies.

i **Such** (sour) **wine** as this harms the stomach.

j Tom knew nothing of **such** famous **men** as Plato.

such a (silly) idea as this is.
Such (a) + *adjective* + *noun:* often, there is an adjective before the noun (**e**).

2

They don't have	things	**such**	blankets.
We shall need	equipment	**as**	tents.
They have sent	supplies		tools.
I'll provide	items		drills.
He'll transport	goods		clothing.
They sell	stuff		fuel, oil.
There is money for			pumps.
			explosives.

Such (a) + *noun* + (**as** + *noun*) (**h-j** opposite): the noun or pronoun after **as** can name an example; we mention **a fine woman** and define Mary for the example (**h**); **such famous men as Plato** (**j**) means I mention Plato for the example of **such famous men. Such as** often introduces a list of particular examples; the meaning of the noun before **such** can cover all the items in the list, as in the table opposite.

3 a I've worked hard for such money **as I now have.**

b Such young men **as Jane met** were all farmers' sons.

c Such a romantic girl, **as Jane was then,** ignored them.

d Such a Prince Charming **as she wanted** never appeared.

Such (a) + *count or mass noun* + **as** clause. in these, **as** is a relative pronoun and introduces a relative clause, ie a group of words with its own verb. The clause describes the **such (a)** + *noun* phrase.

F Enough

a We haven't **enough boys** to form a football team. We have **too few boys** to form a football team.

b I haven't **enough flour** to bake bread today. I have **too little flour** to bake bread today.

c 'Does he spend **enough time** on homework?' 'Yes. I think he spends **too much time** on it.'

Enough can come before plural count nouns and also before mass nouns (mass nouns are singular). **Enough** = as much / as many as necessary, ie not too much and not too little; not too many, not too few. When **enough** goes with **the/this/these/my/your** etc before a defined noun, we have an **of** phrase, and **enough of** + *object forms of pronouns* is also necessary. After **enough of,** defined nouns can be singular and plural count nouns, and mass nouns.

G Any; some

1 Any + singular count and mass nouns

| Any | man
girl
woman
person | tries to
hopes to
wants to | find happiness.
live in peace.
make a good marriage.
rise in the world. |

| I shall be glad to see you
*Ring me up at home
Bring the children too | any | time you like.
day next week.
time on Friday. |

*ring/ring up (Br) = call (Am)

| Any | news
food
help
equipment | would be better than none.
that we send goes by air.
that gets here is welcome.
goes direct to its destination. |

With **any** + *singular count nouns* — **any man, any dog, any day** etc — we refer to each and every one of them, whoever or whatever he or it may be.

Any + *mass noun* — **any help, any money, any intelligence, any news** etc — refers to each and every sort of / each and every amount of these things.

NOTE **either** of two but **any** of three or more (▶ C above for **either**). So we can also have **any of** + *plural noun*
eg **any of these (three, four) dates** will be convenient.
In spoken English, we often stress **any** in these patterns.

2 Some + singular count noun or mass noun

a 'Who was it on the phone?' '**Some youngster** who asked for Kate.'

b 'What did you tell the youngster?' 'I said she was out at '**some friend's place.**'

c 'Don't you know where Kate is?' 'She's got **some extra job** to finish at work.'

d 'That boy doesn't seem very clever.' 'Every boy has '**some ability** of '**some sort.**'

e 'Why are you hopping about on one leg?' '**Some elephant** trod on my toes.'

f Be careful about water in this area. '**Some water** is unfit for drinking.

With singular count nouns — **some man, some dog, some fool** etc — we mention a person, animal or other thing. We do not and probably cannot define them except by the noun we place after **some.** That noun can show the speaker's displeasure, eg some **idiot**, some **silly fellow; some** generally shows that its noun is anonymous, ie without name or definite identity. With mass nouns, **some** = indefinite quality/sort and amount. We usually stress **some** when we use it like this. (For **some** and **any** with indefinite number and amount ▶ **Chapter 5, C.)**

10 Personal pronouns

A Pronouns

singular	subject	object	possessive	reflexive
1st person	**I**	**me**	**mine**	**myself**
2nd	**you**	**you**	**yours**	**yourself**
3rd (male)	**he**	**him**	**his**	**himself**
(female)	**she**	**her**	**hers**	**herself**
(common)	**it**	**it**	**its**	**itself**
plural				
1st person	**we**	**us**	**ours**	**ourselves**
2nd	**you**	**you**	**yours**	**yourselves**
3rd	**they**	**them**	**theirs**	**themselves**

possessive adjectives
my (+ noun)
your (+ noun)
his (+ noun)
her (+ noun)
its (+ noun)

our (+ noun)
your (+ noun)
their (+ noun)

B Subjects of verbs

A personal pronoun represents a noun that can come earlier or later in a sentence. Here personal pronouns are subjects of **be** and the nouns are the names after **be** in the complement.

1 Singular

Singular = not more than one.

a **I** am Tom.   **I** am Mary.

first person

The first person is the speaker, and can be a boy, a girl, a woman or a man (**I**).

b **You** are Mary.   **You** are Tom.

second person

Somebody speaks to the second person; the second person is the one a speaker addresses. A boy, a girl, a woman or a man can be the second person (**you**).

c **He** is Bob.   **She** is Liz.

third person.

People speak to the second person and speak about a third person. We use **he** for a boy or a man, and **she** for a girl or a woman (▶ **3c**).

2 Plural

a We are Tom and Mary.

first person

b You are
Liz and Bob.

You are Tom and Mary.

second person

c They are girls.

They are men.

third person

Plural = more than one; two, three, ten etc.

First persons are the speakers. **We** can be men, women, boys, girls or a mixture of different sorts of people.

Second persons are the ones that someone addresses. **You** can be men, women, children or a mixture of different sorts of people.

Third persons are the persons that people talk about. **They** can be men, women, children or a mixture of people. In the plural, we do not have one pronoun for females and another for males. **They** is the plural form for **he** (a male), **she** (a female) and for **it** (3a-e).

3 He, she, it

a He's a good dog.
She's a pretty little cat.
It's a very big lion.

b It is an aeroplane.
It is a new book.

c 'Somebody is on the phone, for you.'
'Who is **it?** Do you know?'

d 'Somebody is outside the door.' 'If **it** is Peter, let him come in.'

e Tell me about the new **baby. Is it** a girl or a boy?

We can use **he** and **she** to speak about male and female persons (**B1**) and also for male and female animals when we know them well. **It** is the pronoun we use for an animal, generally.

It is the pronoun we use to speak about anything which is not a person and not an animal; **it** is not a living thing.

We do not know the name of **somebody** or whether **it** is male or female. **It** is a person; **it** is somebody.

The speaker may mention a name — **Peter** — and may be right or wrong.

We say **it** is a **baby** before we know that **he** is a **boy/he** is **Peter** or **she** is a **girl/she**'s **Rose.** The plural for **it** is **they** (**2c**).

C Objects of verbs

1 Singular

In **B1-3** we saw subject forms of personal pronouns. Here, we shall see object forms for them.

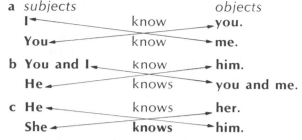

a *subjects*   *objects*
I   know   **you.**
You   know   **me.**

b **You and I**   know   **him.**
He   knows   **you and me.**

c **He**   knows   **her.**
She   knows   **him.**

d **It** costs fifty pounds.
I don't want **it.**

First person: **I** for subject, **me** for object.

Second person: **you** for subjects and objects. **You** is also the plural form.

Third person: **he** for male subject, **him** for male object.

Third person: **she** for female subject, **her** for female object.

Third person: **it** is the form for subjects and objects (**3a-e**).

2 Plural

a *subjects*   *objects*
We   help   **you.**
You   help   **us.**

b **They**   help   **us.**
We   help   **them.**

First person: **we** for plural subjects, **us** for plural objects.

Second person: **you** for plural subjects and for plural objects.

Third person: **they** for plural subjects, **them** for plural objects. **They/them** are the plural forms for **he/him, she/her** and **it/it (1a-d).**

D Uses of object pronouns

               direct   *indirect*

1   John gave **flowers** to **Mary.**
     John gave **them** to **her.**
     John gave **her** flowers.

2   Children swim in **the lake.** I catch fish in **it.**
     Tom is dancing with **Liz.** He's dancing with **her.**

3   'Mary Grey, did you say?' 'That's **her,** at the window.'
     '**A man** wants to see you, sir.' What! It is **him** again.'

The examples in **C1-2** show personal pronouns as direct objects of verbs. A verb with an object is a transitive verb.

Object forms of pronouns can represent direct and indirect objects. Some verbs take an indirect pronoun object first and a direct object with noun follows.

Object forms can come after prepositions; the complement of a preposition — in **it,** with **her,** etc — takes the object form.

Object pronouns can be complements of **be.** In short sentences in informal spoken English, nearly everyone uses the object forms after **be.**

E Reflexive pronouns: -self/-selves

1 **a** The barber shaves Grandpa twice a week. **Father shaves himself** every morning.

All the singular reflexive pronouns have the singular form of the ending **-self**; the plural reflexive pronouns all end in

47

b Jane was cutting carrots with a knife. The knife slipped and **Jane cut herself.**

c Mary dressed little Jenny for the party. **Little Jenny undressed herself** and put on jeans.

d 'What did you say just now, Peter?' 'Nothing. I was thinking aloud, **talking to myself.**'

e I'll help you in every way I can, Tom. But you must do **something for yourself,** too.

f Come on, mother. Let's go away for a week. **We'll give ourselves** a holiday, for once.

-selves. The subject and object of a verb can mention the same person or thing. We use a **-self** or **-selves** pronoun for the object. We do not say: \John fell and **hurt John**\. — we say: John fell and **hurt himself. The -self, -selves** pronouns cannot be subjects of verbs. They are often complements of prepositions (**d, e**) and refer back to the subject.

Notice also: **help yourselves/yourself** (take what you want); **enjoy yourself.**

2

1	2	3
My parents	built this house	by themselves.
Mr Cox	made a fortune	by himself.
You	often stayed here	by yourselves.
I	can't live there	by myself.
Jane and I	did all the work	by ourselves.
Sarah	managed the office	by herself.

a These modern gates open and close **by themselves.**

b Don't call the children. They'll come **by themselves.**

c I didn't touch the switch. The light went out **by itself.**

d Nobody pushed him. The man fell down **by himself.**

e Open the door. The bird will fly out **by itself.**

f But will it fly in again **by itself?**

By myself, ourselves etc can mean *without help; without other people; alone; without company.* In the table opposite, columns 1 and 3 belong together as they stand; each phrase in 2 can go with them.

By itself, themselves etc can mean *automatically;* people do nothing but something happens.

3 a 'Has Smith spoken to **Mother herself** about this?' 'No, he asked us to have a word with her.'

b '**The lawyers themselves** seem not to agree.' 'True. That's why there are so many of them.'

c '**I'll** talk to both of them **myself,** today. **We** had a similar problem **ourselves,** once.'

-self, -selves pronouns can follow a noun or pronoun and emphasise it, eg **The president himself** wrote to her. / She received a letter from **the president himself.** In this way, **himself, themselves** etc mean *in person; directly; personally.*

F Reciprocal pronouns

I help Tom.

He helps me.

Tom and I help

each other.

The children play with **one another.**
They sometimes tease **one another.**
Our girls and boys all like **one another.**

Tom and I often visit **each other's
homes.** In our village, people know **one
another's families.**

Each other and **one another** stand as objects, and after prepositions. They can also be possessive with **'s (each other's, one another's). One another** usually stands for groups of three or more; **each other** stands for two, and can stand for a small group (three or four) conversationally. Each and every person, animal or other thing in a group acts in the same way towards each and every other member. **Each other/one another** are reciprocal pronouns. In English, we do not use reflexive pronouns in this way.

11 Impersonal pronouns

A One; you; they

a **One** has to pay **one's rent** regularly. **One's landlord** needs money as much as **oneself.**

b **You** can't get blood out of a stone, can **you? You** can't earn money if **you** don't find work.

c '**They** say that you have tons of money.' '**They** say! How do **they** know? **They** and their words!'

Impersonal pronouns mention people in a general sense; they do not stand for particular persons.

One (formal) refers to people and the speaker.

You (informal), without stress, can replace **one.**

They refers to people, but the speaker does *not* place himself among them.

Notice **one's** as possessive adjective, and **oneself,** reflexive pronoun.

B One; ones

1 a Of course, we want to have **a big car.** At the moment we can't afford **one.**

b 'Could you draw **a kangaroo** for me?' 'I'll try. I've never seen **a real one.**'

c 'Would you like **a nice ripe peach?**' 'No, thank you. I've just had **one.**'

One stands for singular count nouns and avoids repetition of them. **One** and **ones** are not stressed in speech.

A(n) + *adjective* + **one** can also stand for singular count nouns. In place of **a(n)** we can also have **the, this/that, my/her/our** etc as definers of singular count nouns.

2 a 'How many **balls** were on the billiard table?' 'There were **two white ones** and **a red one.**'

b 'Dick wants **some new shirts** for work.' 'These **cotton ones** are best. **Nylon ones** won't do.'

c 'If you need **an umbrella** take **that one** in the hall.' '**The one on the floor** is **an old one** of Sally's.'

Ones stands for plural count nouns but cannot stand alone. We can use an adjective **red ones;** or a demonstrative **these ones/those ones;** or the phrase or clause after **ones** is a definer: **the ones in the box/on the table; the ones I gave her.**

3 a 'My blue **dress** isn't clean. I'll wear **another one.**' 'Put on **your green one** or **this grey one** of mine.'

b 'Peter is **your youngest son,** isn't he?' 'No, **my youngest one** is Tom. Peter is **the middle one.**'

Possessive adjectives do not come immediately before **one** and **ones;** there must be another adjective: my **red** one; your **old** one; her **best** ones; our **only** one/ones etc.

c 'There's John, Mary's **the next one,** then **the other ones.'** 'So Mary's **the second one** of our four children.'

d 'I need some lemons. May I take **these ones?'** 'Pick **those ones** on that second tree of ours.'

e 'Are these your gloves?' 'No, **those ones** are Jim's. **My leather ones** are in my pocket.'

f Your bottles are all green; Kate's bottles are brown. If you give her **some green ones** of yours, she'll give you **a few brown ones** of hers.

We can also have **of** + *possessive pronoun* after **one/ones** (▶ table in **10A** above):

    a red one of mine
    two old ones of hers
    a few new ones of ours

or possessive noun:

    of Kate's
    of Mrs Clark's.

12 Interrogative pronouns

A Subjects

who ...?	personal subject form
whom ...?	personal object form
what ...?	personal and non-personal subject and object
which ...?	personal and non-personal subject and object
whose ...?	possessive

Interrogative pronouns can begin questions: **Who** wants some ice-cream?

All interrogative pronouns can begin questions about people; each of them asks a different kind of question, as we shall see below.

Nouns cannot immediately follow **who** and **whom**; they can follow **what/which/ whose**, eg **Whose house** is it?

1 Who

Who		caused the damage?
		broke the window?
Which	man	frightened the horses?
Whose	girl	made such a noise?
What	stone	killed Cock Robin?
		hit the target?
What		

'Who broke the window?'
'Bill broke the window.'
'What stone hit the target?'
'A stone from Bill's catapult hit the target.'

Interrogative pronouns do not have separate forms for singular and plural nor for male and female persons.

The **wh-** question words and phrases in the table are subject of their verbs. The questions ask for the name of the subject. The verbs are in the affirmative form, NOT the interrogative.

'Who	made this mess?'	'The boys	
	washed the car?'	'I	did.'
	took the dog out?'	'Kate	
	will help me?'	'That man	
	will cut the grass?'	'Grandpa	will.'
	will lend me a bike?'	'The porter	

Who ...? asks for personal names or for a description that defines a person or persons so that we know who they are. **'Who** are you?' 'I'm Dina Moore. I'm the director's secretary.'

2 What

'What is Jane Glen?'	'She's	a nurse.'
		a friend of mine'.
		a law student.'
		a Scots girl.'
'What is her father?'	'He's	an engineer.'
		a gardener.'
		a civil servant.'

What ... ? asks for information about one or more persons. The questions can ask a person's name, eg **What's his name?** or it can refer to a person's job, nationality, politics, position at work or in society, profession, religion and so on

'What	animals have long necks?' river runs through Egypt?' insects make honey?'	'Giraffes have them.' 'It's the Nile.' 'Bees do that.'
	runs but never walks?' cannot see but has an eye?'	'A river of course.' 'A needle.'

What . . .? can ask for information about animals and all other things. **What . . .?** also asks about activities.

3 Which

'Which	woman **spoke** to you?' boy **is** her son?' girl **left** early?'	'The curly-haired one.' 'The taller of the two.' 'The younger one.'
	bottles **contain** vinegar?' sunglasses **suit** my face?' gloves **seem** warmer	'The other ones.' 'The darker ones.' 'Those on the left.'

Which . . .? asks about persons, animals and all other things. The speaker asks **which . . .?** questions when he knows that only *one* answer is possible, eg 'Which hand do you write with?' 'I write with **my right hand/left hand.**'

When there are only *a few* possible answers, we also use **which**. 'Which cousin married Tom Brown?' 'Aunt Jane's daughter, Kate.' The other words in the question can suggest a limited choice for the answer — **What girl** (of all girls) married Tom? **Which cousin** (of yours) married Tom?
Which can have **of** + *defined plural noun* after it, **Which of the/those/my boys?**

Which of	your friends **was** on the phone? these men **is/are** going abroad? the horses **comes** from France? those buildings **belongs** to us?

NOTE Which/Which of . . . can refer to a singular or plural noun and the verb shows this.

4 Whose

Whose	car crashed on the *motorway? workers will get 10% more money? house is for sale, did you say? mother is coming to stay with them? horse won the Derby last year

Whose . . .? asks for the names or descriptions of personal possessors.
'Whose dog bit you?' 'Peter's (dog) bit me.
'Whose house is that?' 'The Robsons'./It's **the Robsons'** house.'

*motorway (Br) = highway (Am)

B Objects

a **Who(m)** did you take to the zoo?
b **Who(m)** have you invited to dinner?

Interrogative pronouns do not have separate forms for subject and object, except **who/whom**. **Whom** is quite formal

   c **Which (dress)** shall I wear today?

   d **What** would you like for dessert?

   e **Whose (dictionary)** did John borrow?

   Who(m) did you take to the zoo?

                 objects

   We took **Peter and Wendy** (them) to the zoo.

                  objects

   Whose dictionary did John Borrow?

   John borrowed **Tom's dictionary**.

and correct. In spoken English we usually say **who …?** instead of **whom …?** in questions about a personal object (but see **C** below). The **wh-** pronouns stand for objects, the verbs are in the interrogative form NOT the affirmative (▶ **A 1** above).

C Complements of prepositions

   a **To whom** were you speaking on the phone?

   Who(m) were you speaking **to** on the phone?

   b **To whom** shall I address these letters?

   Who(m) shall I address these letters **to**?

   c **For which dictionary** did you pay £50?

   Which dictionary did you pay £50 **for**?

   d **In which** city do you live?

   Which city do you live **in**?

   e **In what country** is Peter working now?

   What country is Peter working **in** now?

   f **Out of what materials** do you make these?

   What materials do you make these **out of**?

The object forms of all pronouns serve as complements of prepositions (▶ **B** immediately above). Formally, the preposition comes before interrogative pronouns. Immediately after a preposition, we must use **whom** not **who** in questions about persons. However, except in quite formal style, the prepositions follow the questions. Prepositions come after intransitive verbs (verbs without objects) and after the objects of transitive verbs.

D Types of question

Where …?	place
When …?	particular time
Why …?	reason
What … for?	purpose; reason

How …?	method, means, manner
How + adjective/adverb?	degree, extent
How long …?	length of time
How often …?	number of times
How much …?	amount, in mass nouns
How many …?	number, in count nouns
How far …?	distance

Where …? and **When …?** questions sometimes have a preposition before them in formal style. Generally, the preposition is in the end position (▶ **C** immediately above):

   From where have they come? *(formal)*

   Where have they come **from?** *(usual)*

   By when must I pay the bill? *(formal)*

   When must I pay the bill **by?** *(usual)*

   Since when have 'you had 'red hair?

As a preposition, **since** usually comes before **when** even when the question is informal in tone and style.

E How

1 + adjective + a count noun

a 'Can you give me **an envelope?**' 'Yes, I can. **How large an envelope** do you need?'

b I won't name **a price. How high a price** would they pay for this old car?

c Can we send ten kilos by post? **How heavy a parcel** will the post office accept?

We could also have:

> **What size of** envelope do you need?
> **What's the highest price** they would pay?
> **What's the heaviest parcel** the post office will accept?

with practically the same meanings. The following sentences,

> 'How old a woman is she?' 'Quite young, about thirty.'
> 'How old is she?' 'She's about thirty.'

just ask a person's age.

2 How . . .?

a '**How** was the examination?' 'Very easy.'

b '**How** do you feel now?' 'Fine, thank you.'

c '**How** do I look in these clothes?' 'Very smart.'

d '**How** did you come home?' 'On the 18 bus.'

e '**How** does Harry drive?' 'Badly and too fast.'

f '**How** will you live?' 'As cheaply as possible.'

g '**How** can she manage him?' 'With tact and humour.'

h '**How** would you deal with him?' 'With a big stick.'

How . . .? questions ask about methods, the ways and means for doing things, manner and style. The answer to a **How . . .?** question often has an adjective, adverb or prepositional phrase in it that expresses method, ways and means, style, manner or the speaker's comment.

3 How long . . .? How often . . .?

| 'How long | have you lived here?'
 has he known us? | 'For twenty years.'
 'Since 1965.' |
| | did she wait?
 shall we be on the plane? | 'For an hour.'
 'Till morning.' |

How long . . .? questions usually refer to a space of time. Often, we use **for** + *period*, eg **for six months,** or **since** + *beginning of the period* eg **since January.** Of course we can also say **How long** is Oxford Street? meaning, **What's the length of . . .?**

'How often	do you play chess?'	'Twice a week.'
	does Sally come here?'	'Almost never.'
	did Tom visit them?'	'Regularly.'
	will you be away?'	'Now and again.'

How often . . .? asks about how many times something happens.

4 How many . . .?; How much . . .?

'How many	eggs do you need	'Five or six.'
	windows did you clean?'	'Just a few.'
	people use these keys?'	'Only one.'
	women work there?'	'About ten.'
'How much	work does he do?'	'Just a little.'
	fuel do you burn?'	'Quite a lot.'
	sugar do you take?'	'Very little.'
	coffee does she drink?'	'Too much.'

How many + *plural count noun*: the questioner asks for an answer with a definite or indefinite number in it.

How much + *mass noun:* the questioner asks for an answer with a definite or indefinite amount/quantity in it.

How much of + *defined singular count noun.* **How much of the/that/your water melon did we eat?**

5 How far . . .?

'How far	is it from here?'	'An hour's drive.'
	do you want to go?	'About ten miles.'
	away is your office?'	'A ten-minute walk.'
	are the nearest shops?'	'Just round the corner.'

How far . . .? refers to the distance between one place and another. The answer can be in kilometres, miles, etc or the time we need to cover the distance. Often **away** follows **How far . . .?**

F Why/What for?

'Why	have you come today?'	'Because	I need advice.'
	couldn't you wait?'		I'm worried.'
	did you see a lawyer?'		I'm in a hurry.'
'What	did she send plasticine **for?**		'To play with.'
	did he take a dog **for?**		'For the girls.'
	are these toys **for?**		'For Jimmy.'

Why . . .? asks for a reason; the answer to **why . . .?** is often a clause with **because**.

What . . . for? means exactly the same as **why . . .?** but is less formal. **What . . . for?** questions also ask for information about the use and purpose of activities, people and all other things.

NOTE **for** never comes before **what** in this pattern.

G Reported or indirect questions

a 'Who lives in the Smiths' old house now?'
She **wants to know** who lives in the Smith's house now.

b 'Which of the diamond rings would you like?'
He **asked** which of the diamond rings I would like.

c 'What did she say about her salary?'
He **asked** what she had said about her salary.

d 'How many loaves of bread do we need?'
Tom **wants to know** how many loaves we need.

e 'How much money have you in your purse?'
He **asked** how much money she had in her purse.

f 'How do you make these lovely toys?'
She **wanted to know** how he made these lovely toys.

Reported or indirect questions are parts of a sentence. The sentence begins with its own subject, of a verb such as **ask, enquire, want to know,** or other verbs such as **inform, tell, let (somebody) know, report** and others of similar meaning. All reported questions are in the affirmative order: *subject + verb*. The original direct question can be in the interrogative order (**B** above) but if we report it, or repeat it indirectly, we use the affirmative. (For reported speech ▶ **Chapter 28.**)

H Interrogatives and 'else'

a 'We met Sally and Jim at Mary's party.' 'That was a surprise. **Who else** was there?'

b 'You have education, youth, health and capital.' '**What else** could a young man ask for?'

c 'We don't want to live in town or in a village.' '**Where else** do you hope to find a house?'

d 'I'm much too busy on Monday afternoons.' '**When else** can you arrange to see me?'

e 'I like gardening and playing the piano.' '**How else** do you spend your time?'

f 'The burglars took all of Kate's jewellery.' 'She didn't say **how much else** they stole.'

g '**Who else**'s house did they break into?' 'The police didn't say **who else's** house it was.'

Else meaning other and different can come after all **wh-** interrogatives, after **how . . ., how many/how much . . .** When **else** follows the interrogative we cannot have a noun too: we can say '**Who else** did you see?' or '**Which/What other people** did you see?'

We do not use **else** when we mean more of the same thing. We then use **more:** 'Would you like **more tea?**' 'No, thank you.' 'Can I get you **something else?**' = something other and different from tea.
The possessive form is **who else's +** *noun.*
NOTE else does not often go with **which.**

13 Exclamations *with nouns and adjectives/adverbs*

A With nouns: What (a) . . .!
Such (a) . . .!

1

What Such	'beautiful 'music we heard there! 'splendid 'players the musicians were! 'lovely 'clothes the singers wore!
What a(n) Such a(n)	'clever fellow Tom has become! 'interesting 'film we saw last night! 'price they paid for that old house!

What + *plural count noun or a mass noun* / **What a** + *singular count noun:* the speaker makes a short exclamation or strong comment and expresses all kinds of feelings and criticism about the noun that follows. **What (a)** + *noun phrase* comes first in the exclamation. There can be an adjective before the noun; we generally stress it.

The **What (a)** phrase as an exclamation often has nothing after it except a noun.

2 'The manager *sacked me for one little mistake.' 'Poor girl! **What a 'pity! What a 'shame! What a 'scandal! What un'-fairness!'**
*to sack an employee (Br) = to fire an employee (Am)

3 a We heard 'such 'beautiful music there!
  b The musicians were '**such** 'splendid players!
  c Tom has become '**such a** clever fellow!
  d We saw '**such an** 'interesting film last night!
  e They paid '**such a** 'price for that old house!

Such (a) follows the same patterns as **what (a)** but does not stand alone as a phrase; **such a** can follow *subject + verb* and still be an exclamation or strong comment, eg It is **such a pity!** It seems **such a shame!** It's **such unfairness!** The word **such** is usually stressed.

B With adjectives/adverbs:
How . . .! So . . .!

1

How	**lovely** the singers' clothes were! **splendidly** the musicians played! **interesting** that film was last night! **cleverly** Tom solved our problem!

How + *adjective or adverb:* the speaker makes an exclamation or strong comment and expresses feelings and criticism. By means of an adjective he describes a person or anything else; or by means of an adverb he describes the manner or quality of someone's doings.

a Tom solved our problem 'so 'cleverly!
b Last night's film was 'so 'interesting!
c They paid 'so 'high a price for that old place!

2　**a** **How very** kind of you! Yòu are **so 'very** kind!

　b **How** silly of me! I'm **'so** silly, sometimes.

　c **How** forgetful of him! He's **'so** forgetful these days.

　d **How** thoughtful of Kate! She's **'so** thoughtful!

So follows the same patterns as **How** in exclamations. **So ...!** phrases can come at the beginning of an exclamation; **How ...!** phrases cannot come anywhere but at the beginning in exclamations.

Very can be used in either **how** or **so** exclamations: How **very nice** to meet you! It's so **very nice** to meet you!

14 Relative pronouns

A Non-defining relative

1 **who**   personal subject form
  whom   personal object form
  which non-personal subject or object form
  whose possessive form

In a complete sentence we can have a noun or noun phrase and immediately after it a relative pronoun; it refers back to the noun: eg **An uncle, whom I have never met,** lives in Texas. The noun **an uncle** before its relative pronoun is the *antecedent*. Relative pronouns have one form only which serves as both singular and plural; **who/whom** go with both male and female antecedents.

2 **a** An uncle lives in Texas. I've never met **him.**

  An uncle, **whom** I've never met, lives in Texas.

b My husband hates garden work. **He** isn't lazy.

  My husband, **who** isn't lazy, hates garden work.

c Tom met Jane in Spain. **She** writes novels.

  Tom met Jane, **who** writes novels, in Spain.

d Dr Coe took my appendix out. **He** loves dogs.

  Dr Coe, **who** loves dogs, took my appendix out.

e John's sister Suzy came to tea. **She's** great fun.

  John's sister Suzy, **who** is great fun, came to tea.

f Someone told her all. I shall not name **him.**

  Someone, **whom** I shall not name, told her all.

A clause contains a number of words that make sense together, and has its own verb. A *relative pronoun* stands immediately after its antecedent and is the first word in a *relative clause*. We can make one longer sentence instead of two (or more) short ones by using relative clauses. We use **who** or **whom** for persons as subjects or objects in their relative clauses. Antecedents can be subjects or objects but their relative pronouns can have a different role in *their clauses*. In **C** opposite, we have an object (**Jane**) and a relative subject (**who**), for example.

  Non-defining relative clauses are usually more or less interesting comments about the antecedent; the information in a non-defining clause is separate and different from the information in the main clause. We use commas to separate the clauses. Sometimes, the antecedent is a defined noun and needs no more definition (**b-e** opposite).

3 **a** Expensive gifts, **which I don't want,** arrive every week.

b Beef, **which we never eat,** is good for children.

c I put my shopping, **which was heavy,** into the car.

Which is for non-personal antecedents and can be subject or object in its clause. In **a, b, d** opposite, **which** is the object in its clause: I don't want **them.** We never eat **it.** I like **it** too. In **c** and **e**, **which** is subject in the relative clauses:

d He drinks tea, **which I like too,** at breakfast.

e Your dog, **which I won't have in the house,** has dirty paws.

4 a Your secretary, **whose name I didn't catch,** rang me.

b Mr Doe, **whose contract ends soon,** is leaving us.

c The boss, **whose disappointment is obvious,** wants you.

d Our firm, **whose business is growing,** needs good men.

e Her horse, the saddle **of which** was white, won the race.
Her horse, **whose saddle** was white, won the race.

f My firm, the name **of which** is good, is honest.
My firm, **whose name** is good, is honest.

g He had a clock, the parts **of which** were on the bench, to mend.
He had a clock, **whose parts** were on the bench, to mend.

5 a **I love Tom very much,** which may surprise you.

b **He tells me silly lies,** which annoys me.

c **She makes the children's clothes,** which saves money.

d **We earn a few pounds apart from our pension,** which makes life a little easier.

He told me a lie, which shocked me. = **The fact that he told me a lie** shocked me.

He told me **a lie that shocked me.** = **It was a shocking lie** that he told me. The lie shocked me, not the fact that he told a lie.

My shopping — it was heavy. **Your dog — it** has dirty paws.

Whose is possessive and can go with personal subject and personal object nouns.

Whose can go with any noun to avoid **of which** possessive phrases. Some people prefer **of which** for non-personal possession, especially in formal styles. Some others (mistakenly) keep **whose** for personal nouns only.

Which can refer back to a whole sentence or clause. The **which** clause makes a comment on all the information in the antecedent clause. The verb in a **which** clause of this kind is singular, eg **We grow our own potatoes and other vegetables. This saves money / This makes sure they are fresh / This means that they have no harmful chemicals in them.** In these sentences, **this = which.** A comma between the clauses is necessary. **That** refers to the antecedent noun only, not to the whole sentence.

B Defining relative pronouns

1   I know │a man◄─►This man/He│ has a
                                  Rolls Royce.

    = I know │a man   who│ has a
                              Rolls Royce.

    antecedent   *relative pronoun*

A defining relative clause tells us something about the antecedent in direct terms. When you say **'Tom is a man,'** you give very little information; **Which** Tom? **Which** man?

Tom is	a man a friend a cousin somebody	that drives a bus. that went to Canada. that lives nearby. that works beside us. that has a Rolls Royce.

That as a defining relative pronoun can take the places of **who, whom** and **which. Who/whom** can come after antecedents that clearly name people but **that** is also correct.

2

who	subject form for people
whom	object form for people
which	subject and object form for everything except people
***that**	subject and object form for people and for everything else
whose	possessive (▶ 6 below)

***that** cannot come immediately after prepositions as complement (▶ 8-9 below).

Defining relative pronouns come at the beginning of a clause
eg a man **who has a Rolls Royce**
   the girl **that danced with Harry**
   the cow **that jumped over the moon.**

3 a He's **an uncle of mine that lives** in Brazil. Do you know **my uncle John who lives** in London?

b 'A girl that says she knows Dick is on the phone.' 'It was **the Browns' daughter who** rang me up.

c 'I don't know **a/any Harry Gray that rides horses.'** 'Jack Gray who sells bikes plays tennis.'

d '**Some men that work in offices** need more exercise.' **Those younger men who work here** often go jogging.'

Compare these pairs of sentences containing **who** and **that.** We can use one or the other of these as subjects. The antecedent can be a noun in the unique sense — it can mention persons who are the only ones of their kind eg my father; his sister Kate; your uncle John; my cousin Rachel. For these and for other clearly named particular persons, we generally use **who. That** or **who** are used for all other sorts of people.

	objects		*subjects*	
Do you know	my uncle John? my uncle John	He who	lives there. lives there?	

I have	a good friend.	She	helps me.
I have	a good friend	who	helps me.

Antecedents can be subjects or objects in their own clauses. Relative pronouns can also be subjects or objects in relative clauses and we use **who** and **whom** as subject and object. They do not accord with the antecedent.

4 a Dr Tabb has a patient (**that/whom**) he can't help.

b Jane won't invite people (**that/whom**) she dislikes.

c Are you one of the people (**that/whom**) she likes?

We use **that** and **whom** for persons. **That** and **whom** can both be objects in defining clauses. We say and write **whom** for the relative pronoun, when we use it in an interrogative form. Generally, we use **that. Whom** can go with particular persons with names, or

d Tom is a boy (**that/whom**) I shall not forget.

5 **a** He's a member of a club **that** is only for men. There are organisations **that** accept women only.
  b 'The butter **that** you sold me has a funny taste.' 'I shall return the money **that** you paid for it.'
  c Dial the number **that** I gave you yesterday. Book seats on the Concorde **which** leaves tomorrow.
  d I can't show you the dog **that** bit me. The dog **that** bit me died next day.
  e The party **which** you represent will never govern.
  f Mary's father founded the club **which** you mentioned.
  g I am the owner of the house **which** is for sale.

6

a We found a little bird a wing **of which** was broken.
b They will build a new factory the chimneys **of which** will be sixty metres high.
c A car **of which** the brakes are out of order isn't safe.

a We found a little bird **whose wing** was broken.
b They'll build a new factory **whose chimneys** will be sixty metres high.
c A car **whose brakes** are out of order isn't safe.

a We found **a little bird with a broken wing.**
b They'll build **a factory with chimneys** sixty metres high.
c Cars with brakes out of order aren't safe.

with titles or definitions as good as names; **that** is also correct.
  For object clauses without relative pronouns, ▶ **7** below.

That and **which** can both stand for all non-personal nouns. We generally use **that**; some people prefer **which** for non-personal nouns that have proper names or other clear definition, eg the United Nations Organisation; the Ministry of Education; the Concorde, the Blue Train and other particular or unique things.

NOTE institutions or groups of people such as a committee, (social) class, (political), party, club, government, society, sometimes take **that** or **which** as particular non-personal nouns (▶ **e-g**).

However, as a defining relative, most people use **that** at all times. (▶ also **10 below.**)

Of which/whose: non-personal nouns do not usually own things; the various parts of an animal, a house, a tree, a machine etc are not possessions, but they belong to an animal, a house, a tree, a machine as parts of them. We can have: *antecedent* + *part* + **of which** or *antecedent* + **of which** + *part* eg **A house the walls of which** were made of glass would not suit most families. or: **A house of which the walls** were made of glass . . .

Whose can replace **of which; whose** comes immediately after the antecedent. Some people (mistakenly) use **whose** for personal antecedents only.

  There is another way to avoid **of which: with** + *complement,* eg **a radio of which the switch is green = a radio with (that has) a green switch.**

d The landlord **whose house** we rent is very helpful.

e I know the men **whose names** are on this list.

f The girl **whose bike** I borrowed knows you.

Whose goes with all *personal possessors*. The pattern is *possessor* + **whose** + *possession*.

NOTE prepositional phrases using **with** often mention a personal characteristic, eg **a girl with red hair/a pleasant voice/a kind face** = a girl who has/had red hair = a girl **whose hair is/was red** — **whose voice is/was pleasant** etc.

7 a I met the girl **who/that** married Jack Kay.
I met the girl (**that/whom**) Jack Kay married.

b We sent them a telegram **that/which** never arrived.
The telegram (**that/which**) we sent had the wrong address.

c We've just had an exam **that/which** lasted three hours.
The longest exam (**that/which**) we've ever had went on for three hours.

Defining relative clauses without **that, whom, which**. When **that** is the object in its own defining relative clause, we can use it or not, as we wish (▶ **4** above). Similarly, when **whom** and **which** are objects in defining clauses, we can use them or not. But **whom** and **which** can be complements after prepositions; and then they must appear in the clause (▶ **8-9** below).

In the pairs of examples opposite, the first shows subject relative pronouns; the second shows object relative pronouns that we can use or leave out of the sentence.

8 a **The women with whom** Ann works are all married.

b **A man to whom** we spoke answered in Spanish.

c **The car in which** he came home was mine.

d **The day for which** we fixed a meeting was Friday.

e **The family at whose farm** we camped were friendly.

f **The official in whose hands** your papers are, is out.

The object forms of all pronouns also serve as complements of prepositions. Some pronouns have only one form that serves as subject, object and complement eg **you**. In relative clauses, both defining and non-defining, **whom, which, whose** can follow prepositions immediately as complements in clear, formal style; **that** cannot take a place immediately after a preposition.

9 a The women (**whom**) Ann works with . . .

b A man (**whom**) we spoke to . . .

c The car (**which**) he came home in . . .

d The day (**which**) we fixed a meeting for . . .

e . . . whose farm we camped at . . .

f . . . whose hands your paper are in . . .

g The women (**that**) Ann works **with** are all married.

Prepositions can come at the end of an object relative clause. They come after verbs which have no object or complement of their own, and after the objects and complements of verbs that have them. **NOTE whose** + *noun*.

When the preposition is in the end position, **whom** and **which** can stay or

h A man (**that**) we spoke **to** answered in Spanish.

i The car (**that**) he drove home **in** was mine.

j The day (**that**) we fixed a meeting **for** was Friday.

k The club (**that**) she's president **of** is the other one.

l The New Street Club is the one (**that**) she's president **of**.

m These are the tools (**that**) I do my work **with**.

go out, as you wish, in ordinary conversational style. **That** can replace **whom/which** and often does; but **that** can go out too, and the clause can stand quite correctly without object relative pronoun, with a preposition at the end.

10

a **The only person that drives** this car is you.

b **It's the oldest boneshaker that runs** on wheels.

c **The first person that called** was Kate's sister.

d **The next person that rang** said 'Wrong number'.

e **The last horse that passed** the post was mine.

f **The cleverest students that took** the test passed.

g **The best thing that happened** was meeting you.

h Tell me about **the worst thing that happened.**

a The only person to drive this car is you.

c The first person to call was Kate's sister

e The last horse to pass the post was mine.

f Tell me about the worst thing to happen.

That is the relative pronoun for all antecedents when a superlative adjective (tallest, greatest, cleverest, most intelligent etc) describes the antecedent, or when the antecedent has an ordinal number with it (first, second twenty-ninth etc) or **only, last, next. That** is the subject in its clause in all the examples opposite.

We often use an infinitive instead of a **that**-clause in sentences of this kind.

11

pronouns:	**who**	**whom**	**what**
adverbs:	**when**	**where**	**why**

12a We buy **what we need** at the village shop.

b We sometimes disagree about **who goes** to the village.

c It's an open letter **to 'whom this may concern'.**

d Read it and tell me **what it is all about.**

Relative without antecedents: **What** can stand for all kinds of things, and all sorts of doings. **What** does not need an immediate antecedent and never has one; **what = the thing(s) that ... the action(s) that ...** We can say **A fresh apple** is **what I like best. Who** and **whom** can stand also without antecedent, meaning *the person(s) that ...* in a general sense. The speaker may or may not have particular persons in mind.

e You can't do **what you like** all the time.

f I have promised **what I will do**, I'll do **what I've said.**

g You can't have **what you'd like** so try to like **what you have.**

13 Our general manager decides **who travels** abroad on business, **whom the traveller should meet** and **what they should discuss.** The traveller writes to customers. He mentions **when he** will be in their neighbourhood, **where they** can reach him by telephone and **why he** wishes to meet them.

Relative adverbs do not normally take antecedents. The speaker or writer can have a particular time, place and reason in mind, or not.

14 The traveller writes to customers and mentions **when he will be there.** He mentions **the time at which / the date on which / the dates between which** he will be there etc. He mentions **where** they can find him — **the place / the address / the hotel / the office** etc **at which** they can find him or leave a message. He also mentions / tells them / informs them of **the reasons for wishing to meet them.**

If we have an antecedent noun we should not follow with a relative adverb. *Prepositions + relative pronouns* stand after antecedent nouns. (▶ also **8-9** above.)

15 We buy food in the village and get **what else** we need in town.

The family and **who else** they invite spend weekends at their country place. John was there on Sunday. **When else** he was there I don't know. **What else** he does and **where else** he goes are his own affairs.

Else meaning *other and different persons, things and doings* can follow relative pronouns and adverbs (▶ **Chapter 12, H**).

C Universal relatives

1 Pronouns/adverbs

pronouns:		
whoever	**whatever**	**whichever**
adverbs:		
however	**whenever**	**wherever**

'Somebody's on the phone, sir,' '**Whoever** it is, say I'm busy.' 'It's Mr Lock, Exports Manager, sir,' '**Whoever** and **whatever** he is, tell him I'm busy. I can't see him today, **whatever** he wants.' 'I'll tell him **just whatever you say**, sir,'

Relative pronouns and adverbs ending **-ever** have no antecedents in their sentences: **whoever** = anybody, no matter who he, she, they might be. **Whoever** does not stand before nouns.

Whoever/whatever = anybody, no matter what his importance, high or low, may be. **Whatever** = anything, any activity, idea, thought etc of any kind. **Whatever** can stand before a noun.

2 **Whatever** we decide today is final. We shall discuss **whatever new ideas** you

Whichever = anything, no matter which thing, activity (etc) it is, from a small

may have. There are several ways of handling our problem. **Whichever** we choose will cost money. So, our firm must first find money **wherever** we can get it and **however** we handle our problem.

3   **However** I hurry to the station from **wherever** I happen to be in town on Fridays, I always miss the early train. **Whenever** I take a taxi there's a traffic jam, **whenever** I go on foot somebody stops me for a chat. It seems that I get home late, **whatever I do.**

4   'You owe Mary an apology.' 'Apology! **What ever** for?' 'You were rude to her.' 'Not me.' '**How ever** could I be rude to Mary! **Who ever** put that idea into your head! **When ever** did this happen, will you tell me! **Whatever** it was, it's none of your business, anyway.'

selection. **Whichever** can stand before a noun. **Whichever** can have an **of** + *defined person phrase,* eg **Whichever of our daughters is at home prepares lunch.** (either Kate or Jane or Mary).

Adverbs
Wherever = any and every place, no matter where or what that place is; everywhere, without exception.
However = in any and every way/style/ manner; by any and every means and method; no matter how we do it.
Whenever = at any and every time without exception; no matter when it may be.

Ever: what ever . . .! who ever . . .! where ever . . .! etc as two words. Here **ever** emphasises the relative word, very often in an exclamation. **Ever** = in God's name; for heaven's sake etc.
    What ever is that dog eating!
NOTE **else** can come after all the forms in **C1-3** above (▶ **B15** above).

15 Pronouns: every-/any-/some-/no-

A Persons, non-persons and places

1 For persons

> everyone/everybody; anyone/anybody;
> someone/somebody; no-one/nobody

2 For non-persons

> everything; anything; something; nothing

3 Places

> everywhere; *anywhere; *somewhere;
> nowhere
> *any place; *some place (informal Am.)

4 a **Everybody** in our team **tries** hard and **plays** fair. **Anybody** who **breaks** the rules **loses** his place.

b Locusts eat **everything** that **grows** in fields. They leave **nothing** behind them.

c **Everywhere** in London **seems** full of visitors this summer. **Nowhere else** in the world **attracts** so many tourists.

d **Everybody's name begins** with a capital letter. Do we use capital letters for **anything else?**

e '**Somebody was saying** that Bermuda is good for holidays.' '**Anywhere** warm, sunny and cheap enough **suits** me.'

f 'Let's go **somewhere** today.' '**Somewhere** by the sea **would be nice.**'

Every-/Any-/Some-/No: the endings **-one** and **-body** mean exactly the same; some people say **somebody**, others say **someone** and practically **everybody** uses both of them.

The words in the boxes are all *pronouns;* they can be subjects, objects and complements in sentences. Adjectives, when we use them, follow these pronouns; **else** can also follow.

The possessive ending (**'s**) on the pronouns for persons — **everybody's, nobody's, anyone's, someone's,** — marks a possessor and a noun can follow, eg. **somebody's head, nobody's dog** etc. Also the possessor can stand as a possessive pronoun, eg. The world isn't **mine,** it's **everybody's. Everybody's parents were** at the meeting. — note the *plural subject + plural verb.*

These pronouns are all singular, always. When they are subjects, their verbs are in the singular form (when there is one) and *third person.*

No- forms are negative; their verbs are affirmative (**c** opposite).

The same words (**3**) can be adverbs, and are not then subject or object. **Somewhere** in the first sentence of **f** opposite is an adverb, but in the second sentence it is a *pronoun* and the subject of a verb.

B Every-/any-

a **Anyone** would be glad to have Jane as his wife. **Everyone** would be glad to have a wife like Jane.

b **Everyone** gets off the bus at the corner of Tap Lane. **Anyone** will show you the way to our new house.

c **Everywhere** in Scandinavia is cold in winter. **Anywhere else** in Europe is warmer, usually.

Every- refers to the total number of people, things, places as a whole.
Everybody = 100% of people collectively.
Anybody = each and every person, as an individual.
Everywhere = the whole place, the entire area;
Anywhere = each and every part of the place.

d 'Something that Exe said is worrying me.'
'Anything that Exe says needs a pinch of salt.'

C Any-/some-

'Is your brother at home?' 'No, he's **somewhere in France** on holiday.' 'In Paris?' 'No' he's touring on a bicycle. He could be **anywhere between Calais and Toulouse** at the moment. He and **somebody else** went away together. At nights, they camp **anywhere they happen to be.** They'll probably stay **somewhere** over the weekend. Tom's a good fellow. He gets on well **with anybody. Nothing** that people do **seems to bother him** very much.'

Pronouns in **any-** are quite indefinite, eg **Anybody, no matter who the person is,** can learn a foreign language, by one or another method. Pronouns in **some-** are *definite* but do not name or identify, eg '**Somebody is asking** for Tony on the phone.' 'Who is it?' 'How would I know? Tony gives our number to **anybody (any girl)** he happens to meet.'
(▶ also **Chapter, 5, C** and **Chapter 6, B** for **some** and **any**.)

D No-/none (of)

a **None of** these boxes is made of plastic.

b We expected visitors but **none of** them came.

c **None of** that cream is fresh enough to eat.

d **None of** your land is good for growing corn.

e **Nothing** that we sell is made of plastic.

f **Nobody** visited the castle that day.

g **Nowhere** in this area is for growing corn.

h **Nobody's pupils go home** before 3.30 pm.

In addition to **nobody, no-one, nothing** and **nowhere**, we can also have **none of** + *defined plural count nouns* and **none of** + *defined mass nouns*. Verbs after **no-** and **none of** (as subjects) are singular, except when a possessive, eg **nobody's, everybody's,** has a plural possession (**h** opposite).

E Not

a **Not everybody** is as lucky as we are. We are luckier than most people are.

b **Not everything** here costs twice the price.
Some of the local goods are quite cheap.

c '**Anybody** in his right mind would accept my offer.' '**Not 'anybody,** Charles. **Not 'everybody** believes that they can get **something** for **nothing.**'

Not everybody, not everything, not everywhere, = not 100% of people, things, places etc. So, **not all,** but a good many, a high proportion.

F 'Everybody' etc and personal pronouns

a **Everyone** who works in this coal mine has **his/their** own locker and **his/their** own tools. (all men)

b **Everyone** can do as **they like,** within the law.

c **Anyone** with red spots on **his/her/their** back should go to a doctor at once.

d **Everybody** on the nursing staff in this hospital has **her/their** own private bedroom. (all women)

e **Nobody** dislikes hearing that **their/her/his** friends are happy and well.

In **A1** above, the pronouns for persons can have *personal pronouns* and *possessive adjectives* that refer to **everybody, anybody, somebody, nobody.** Very formally, the **he** set of pronouns is used (**he, him, his** etc). Generally, we use the **they** set (**they, them, theirs, themselves** and **their**) (▶ Chapter 10) In modern times, if **everybody** refers to a totality of women and girls, the **she** set is sometimes used.

16 Finite verbs

A The parts of regular verbs

In English, there are two main types of verbs. They are auxiliary verbs (▶ **Chapter 24**) and finite verbs. A finite verb is a verb that can form all the usual past, present and future tenses and can have its own subject.

Regular verbs all form their parts in the same way. We add **-ed** to the base verb to form the past tense and past participle; if the spelling of the base verb ends in **-e** we add **-d** only. The past tense and past participle of the regular verb look and sound exactly the same. We add **-ing** to the base verb for the **-ing** participle. If the base verb ends in a *consonant* + **-e** we drop the **-e**, eg (**love — loving**). Other names for **-ing** are the progressive participle and present participle.

1

base verb	past tense	past participle	-ing participle
talk	talk**ed**	talk**ed**	talk**ing**
cook	cook**ed**	cook**ed**	cook**ing**
wait	wait**ed**	wait**ed**	wait**ing**
love	lov**ed**	lov**ed**	lov**ing**
try*	tried	tried	try**ing**

*base verb ends in *consonant* + y: change **y** to **i**, except for **-ing** participles.

2 Double consonant before -ed and -ing

'rob	rob**bed**	rob**bing**
per'mit	per'mit**ted**	per'mit**ting**
re'fer	re'fer**red**	re'fer**ring**
'stop	stop**ped**	stop**ping**
'ban	ban**ned**	ban**ning**

The only or last syllable of the base is stressed and ends with a single consonant (b, d, t, r, m, n, etc.). The vowel in that syllable contains only one letter (a, e, i, o, u). The spelling of the words needs a double consonant before **-ed** and **-ing**: They **robed** the Archbishop. = They dressed him in his robes. They **robbed** the Archbishop. = and left him without a penny.

The sound of **-ed** is /id/ after **t** and **d** (eg **waited, wanted, landed, loaded**). After /b/, /g/, /d/, /m/, /n/, /ŋ/, /r/, /v/, /z/, and /ð/, /ʒ/, the sound of **-ed** is /d/. After /f/, /k/, /i/, /p/, /s/, /ʃ/, /θ/, the sound is /t/.

There are a good many finite verbs that do not follow the patterns in **1** and **2** opposite, to make their past tense and past participle. We call them irregular verbs. Every finite verb is regular in the **-ing** participle. Some of them, eg **begin — beginning** follow the spelling rule given in **2** opposite.

B Base verb

to	+	base verb	=	infinitive
to	+	**look** **walk** **dance** **fly**	=	**to look** **to walk** **to dance** **to fly**

simple present	
We don't	**write** to them.
He doesn't	**walk** to work.
I do	**like** ice-cream.
Does she	**know** the lady?
simple past	
Did she	**make** good coffee?
We did	**want** to play cards.
He didn't	**get** up early.

Finite verbs can be regular or irregular. The four parts of any finite verb do the same work as the same parts of any other finite verb — they have the same functions. For the parts of regular verbs ▶ **A**; for irregular verbs ▶ **Chapter 17**.

We use the base verb after **do/does** in the negative, interrogative and emphatic forms of the simple present and after **did** in the same forms of the simple past tense (▶ **Chapters 18 and 21**).

We use the base form after some other auxiliary verbs (▶ **Chapter 24**). The base form also makes the imperative: **Go! Stop! Run!** etc (▶ **Chapter 2, A**).

C Past tense form

simple past	
He **closed**	a window.
She **opened**	a door.
If they always **opened** both we'd all catch cold. *(unreal condition)*	

The past tense form is used in the affirmative form only of the simple past tense and of some unreal conditions and wishes (▶ **Chapter 21** and **Chapter 23, F**).

D Past participle

perfect tenses		
Everyone Tom They	has had will have have	**arrived.** **finished.** **gone** away **stayed** there.

some passive voice forms		
The book	was will be is has been	**written.** **printed.** **sold.** **burned.**

With parts of **have (have/has; had)** before a past participle we have perfect tenses: present perfect and past perfect (▶ **Chapters 20 and 22**).

Passive voice: **be** (or any part of **be**) + *past participle* = a verb in the passive voice (▶ **Index**).

E -ing participle

some progressive forms	
I am	**reading**
She is	**writing.**
He was	**working.**
We were	**doing** a job.

The **-ing** participle follows **be** or any part of **be** in progressive (or continuous) tenses (▶ **Chapters 18 and 21**). Past participles and **-ing** forms can also be used some other ways; here, they are parts of verb tense forms.

17 Irregular verbs

You can see the parts of most irregular verbs in the columns below. They are: *base verb, past tense, past participle* in that order, for each verb. The **-ing** *participle* is never irregular (▶ **Chapter 16, A2**). Verbs such as **put, set, hit** are the same in all three parts; others are irregular in the past and again in the past participle; some have one form for past tense and participle, as regular verbs do.

In the lists below, verbs marked *R* also have *regular* forms, without change of meaning.
*****Fell** is a regular verb, and has an object, eg **I felled a tree** (with an axe).
*****The past participle **gotten** is quite common in speech in Am.
*****The regular verb **lie** means **tell a lie, say something untrue.**
*****Hang,** as a regular verb, means **kill someone by hanging.**
   Some verbs show two forms of past participle. Generally, the one in brackets is used as an adjective, eg **a lighted candle.**

List of irregular verbs

base verb	past tense	past participle
arise	arose	arisen
awake	awoke	awoken (awaken is usually *R*)
be	was/were	been
bear	bore	borne
beat	beat	beaten
become	became	become
befall	befell	befallen
begin	began	begun
behold	beheld	beheld
bend	bent	bent
bereave	bereft	bereft *R*
bet	bet	bet *R*
bid	bid	bid (= offer a price)
bid	bade	bidden (= request, greet, etc)
bind	bound	bound
bite	bit	bitten
bleed	bled	bled
blow	blew	blown
break	broke	broken
breed	bred	bred
bring	brought	brought
broadcast	broadcast	broadcast *R*
build	built	built
burn	burnt	burnt *R*
burst	burst	burst
buy	bought	bought
cast	cast	cast

base verb	past tense	past participle
catch	caught	caught
chide	chid	chid (chidden) *R*
choose	chose	chosen
cleave	cleft (clove)	cleft (cloven) *R*
cling	clung	clung
come	came	come
cost	cost	cost (= calculate the cost of : *R* and transitive)
creep	crept	crept
cut	cut	cut
deal	dealt	dealt
dig	dug	dug
do	did	done
draw	drew	drawn
dream	dreamt	dreamt *R*
drink	drank	drunk
drive	drove	driven
dwell	dwelt	dwelt *R*
eat	ate	eaten
fall	*fell	fallen
feed	fed	fed
feel	felt	felt
fight	fought	fought
find	found	found
flee	fled	fled
fling	flung	flung
fly	flew	flown
forbear	forbore	forborne
forbid	forbade	forbidden
forecast	forecast	forecast *R*
forget	forgot	forgotten
forgive	forgave	forgiven
forsake	forsook	forsaken
freeze	froze	frozen
get	got	got (*gotten)
give	gave	given
go	went	gone
grind	ground	ground
grow	grew	grown
*hang	hung	hung
have	had	had
hear	heard	heard
hide	hid	hidden
hit	hit	hit
hold	held	held
hurt	hurt	hurt
keep	kept	kept
kneel	knelt	knelt *R*
know	knew	known

base verb	past tense	past participle
lay	laid	laid
lead	led	led
lean	leant	leant *R*
leap	leapt	leapt *R*
learn	learnt	learnt (learned) *R*
leave	left	left
lend	lent	lent
let	let	let
*lie	lay	lain
light	lit	lit (lighted) *R*
lose	lost	lost
make	made	made
mean	meant	meant
meet	met	met
mislead	misled	misled
mistake	mistook	mistaken
misunderstand	misunderstood	misunderstood
mow	mowed	mown *R*
outdo	outdid	outdone
outgrow	outgrew	outgrown
outrun	outran	outrun
overcome	overcame	overcome
overdo	overdid	overdone
overfeed	overfed	overfed
override	overrode	overridden
overrun	overran	overrun
overtake	overtook	overtaken
put	put	put
quit	quit	quit *R*
read	read	read
rid	rid	rid *R*
ride	rode	ridden
ring	rang	rung
rise	rose	risen
run	ran	run
saw	sawed	sawn *R*
say	said	said
see	saw	seen
seek	sought	sought
sell	sold	sold
send	sent	sent
set	set	set
sew	sewed	sewn *R*
shake	shook	shaken
shear	sheared	shorn *R*
shed	shed	shed
shine	shone	shone (shine = polish is *R*)
shoot	shot	shot
show	showed	shown *R*

base verb	past tense	past participle
shrink	shrank	shrunk (shrunken)
shut	shut	shut
sing	sang	sung
sink	sank	sunk (sunken)
sit	sat	sat
sleep	slept	slept
slide	slid	slid
sling	slung	slung
slink	slunk	slunk
slit	slit	slit
smell	smelt	smelt *R*
sow	sowed	sown R
speak	spoke	spoken
speed	sped	sped *R*
spell	spelt	spelt *R*
spend	spent	spent
spill	spilt	spilt *R*
spin	spun (span)	spun
spit	spat	spat
split	split	split
spoil	spoilt	spoilt *R*
spread	spread	spread
spring	sprang	sprung
stand	stood	stood
steal	stole	stolen
stick	stuck	stuck
sting	stung	stung
stink	stank	stunk
stride	strode	strode (stridden)
strike	struck	struck (stricken)
string	strung	strung (stringed)
strive	strove	striven *R*
swear	swore	sworn
sweep	swept	swept
swell	swelled	swollen *R*
swim	swam	swum
swing	swung	swung
take	took	taken
teach	taught	taught
tear	tore	torn
tell	told	told
think	thought	thought
thrive	throve	thriven *R*
throw	threw	thrown
thrust	thrust	thrust
tread	trod	trodden
unbend	unbent	unbent
unbind	unbound	unbound
undergo	underwent	undergone
understand	understood	understood

base verb	past tense	past participle
undertake	undertook	undertaken
underwrite	underwrote	underwritten
undo	undid	undone
unwind	unwound	unwound
uphold	upheld	upheld
upset	upset	upset
wake	woke	woken *R*
wear	wore	worn
weave	wove	woven
wed	wed	wed *R*
weep	wept	wept
wet	wet	wet *R*
wind	wound	wound
withdraw	withdrew	withdrawn
withhold	withheld	withhold
withstand	withstood	withstood
wring	wrung	wrung
write	wrote	written

18 Verb tenses: *present time*

A Simple present

Affirmative

I You We They	**work** **live** **study**	there. here. at home. in London. upstairs.
Tom Kate He/she	**works** **lives** **studies**	

The base form of verbs serves for all persons except third person singular; add **-s** to the base form for this.

Interrogative

Do	I/you we/they	**work** **live** **study** **stay**	downstairs? there? here? in London? at home?. upstairs?
Does	Tom/Kate he/she anybody		

Auxiliary **do** comes before the *subject + base verb,* for all persons except third person singular; we use **does** + *base verb* for this. We place a question mark (?) at the end of a complete interrogative sentence.

Negative

I/You We/They The Browns	**do not** **(don't)**	**work** **stay** **live** **study**	here. in London. at home. upstairs. next door.
Tom/Kate He/She My sister	**does not** **(doesn't)**		

We place **does not** between the *subject + base verb* for third person singular and **do not** in the same position for all other persons. In familiar speech **do not** is usually **don't** and **does not** becomes **doesn't**.

Interrogative-negative

Don't	you/they I/we Peter	**work** **stay** **live** **study**	here? at home? upstairs? in London? next door?
Doesn't	Jane anybody		

We place **doesn't** before *third person singular subject* + *base verb*, and **don't** before other subjects. More formally, **not** comes after the subject and before the verb:
   Do they **not** study?
   Does he **not** live here?

1 **a** John **lives** at 10, Green Street.
   b We both **work** for Dunn and Company.
   c I **know** John very well.
   d Spring **comes** and summer always **follows.**
   e Children **grow up** and **become** men and women.

We think of time in general and of what happens; the present is part of all time, *not* a moment of today. The examples opposite mention happenings or doings that are true for today, for before today and after today in the present time, speaking generally.

f The earth **goes** round the sun.

g Living things **need** food, drink and air.

h The city of Rome **stands** on the Tiber.

i The sun **rises** in the east and **sets** in the west.

Often, in the simple present, we mention happenings that belong to the whole of time; we refer to facts and happenings that are permanent and constant.

2

	frequency adverb		
I	**often**	write to	old friends.
You	**sometimes**	talk about	our parents.
We	**seldom**	meet	Jack.
They	**never**	mention	them.
Susan	**hardly ever**	visits	Aunt Mary.
Her brother	**rarely**	sees	the old folk.

I go to my dentist	**twice a year.**
We take a holiday	**now and again.**
She stays over the weekend	**once in a while.**
They write to us	**from time to time.**

When things happen from time to time, more or less often, or as matters of habit, custom, routine, we use the simple present; often there is an adverb of frequency, ie an adverb which can answer the question **How often . . .?** or **How many times . . .?**

There can be a phrase at the end of the sentence to express frequency.

3   *cause*   *effect*

I **write** things down and **remember** them.
Rain **falls** in spring and **fills** the wells.
You **press** a button and the door **opens.**

We mention something that always happens (or generally happens) and the immediate result or effect. Both cause and effect are in the simple present.

4

The ship	**gets** to	Rio	tomorrow night.
My train	**reaches**	Naples	at 10.30.
The plane	**arrives** at	Caracas	at noon, local time.
John	**leaves** for	London	in two hours' time.
	leaves from		

Simple present and future time: things may happen as parts of a programme, time-table, or because they have their place in a routine. We use the simple present when we mention future happenings of this kind. Often, there is an adverb or phrase that shows future· time in the sentence.

a Tony **leaves** school **next year, when he's eighteen.**

b He **goes** into the army **a year later.**

c Ann **takes** the final exam **in three weeks.**

d If the rules **don't** change, Father **retires in two years.**

e He **gets** a pension **when he becomes sixty-five.**

We can have personal subjects. They do whatever they do and things happen in the future because of the law, the rules, customs, routines that already exist now.

B Present progressive

Affirmative

singular	
I am (I'm)	reading.
You are (You're)	writing.
He is (He's)	learning.
She is (She's)	trying.
It is (It's)	eating.
plural	talking.
We are (We're)	swimming.
You are (You're)	running.
They are (They're)	

The present forms of the auxiliary **be** + **-ing** *participle* make the present progressive tense, affirmative form. Familiar speech forms are in brackets.

Negative

I am (I'm) **not**	flying.
You/We/They are **not** (aren't)	crying.
He/She/It is **not** (isn't)	trying.

Place **not** between auxiliary and **-ing** participle,
eg You are **not** reading.
    She is **not** writing.
Except for **I am** or **I'm**, we often shorten the negative in familiar speech —
You/We/They **aren't** and He/She/It **isn't** + **-ing** participle.

Interrogative

Am I	eating?
Are you/we/they	speaking?
Is he/she/it	cooking?

Move the auxiliary to come before the subject:
    Am I reading?
    Are they reading? etc.

Interrogative-negative

Am I **not**	waiting?
Are you/we/they **not**	playing?
Is he/she/it **not**	going?
or:	
Am I **not**/**Aren't** I	dancing?
Aren't you/we/they	asking?
Isn't he/she/it	working?

Formally, we place the auxiliary before subjects and place **not** before **-ing** participles:
    Are you **not** listening?
    Is Tom **not** reading? etc.

In familiar style, we place **Aren't** and **Isn't** before their subjects:
    Aren't they coming?
    Isn't Ann swimming?

1

We **are studying** your problem	now
I'm **giving** it my full attention	at this moment.
We're all **trying** to find a solution	at present.
We're **doing** everything we can	at this time.

We refer to happenings and activities that are actually in progress now, while we are speaking about them. They have no connection with other parts of general time. The present progressive mentions only a part of time — now.

2 a The sun **rises** in the east. *(a fact of nature)*
Look! the sun **is rising** over the horizon.

b Dogs **bark**. *(a fact of nature)*
Listen! The dog **is barking** again. Why?

c Tom **works** in a bank as head cashier.
Painters **are working** at the bank. Mind your clothes!

d Spring always **comes** after winter.
Spring **is coming** very slowly this time.

3

Kate**'s writing** poetry
She**'s doing** very well
They**'re having** a
  holiday
We**'re taking** a rest
He**'s working** at full
  speed
	at the moment.
	at present.
	these days.
	for a change.
	now there's a
	  chance.

a **We usually go away** on holiday in August. **This year,** as you see, **we're staying at home.**

b **I teach English** but **I'm taking** a history class today. Their regular teacher **is attending** a seminar.

c **Peter always works hard** and **never feels tired. He's overdoing things now** and **he's getting tired.**

4 a **She's making** bread and **Tom's helping** her.

b The boss **is dictating** a letter, **I'm writing** it.

c **Rain is falling** and **everything's getting** wet.

d **When I'm expecting** an international call, **I don't allow** anyone to use the telephone.

e **While we are working** together on business, **we seldom mention** personal matters.

f **The postman comes** while **we're having lunch.**

g Why **do you interrupt** when **I'm speaking?**

The present time can be a moment or a longer period, but it is not permanent. The present comes and goes; it is a temporary moment or period. The present progressive contrasts with the simple present in this way (▶ **A1** above). For example in **c** opposite, Tom **works** in a bank. (that is his job, his permanent place of work); Painters **are working** at the bank (now, temporarily). Where they were painting before, and where they will go to work later, we do not say.

Temporary happenings and activities in the present time: the present progressive is used for happenings and activities which are in contrast with what usually happens; they are exceptions to the normal, usual, general, more or less permanent routines, habits, customs. In the examples opposite, Kate **is writing** poetry. tells me that Kate's usual activities are different, eg She **operates** a computer in an office.

Happenings and activities can take a moment of time or a length of time. Two activities can go on together for the same length of time, give or take a little. We use the present progressive for both; things are happening now. We can see or hear what is happening during this present length of time.

One activity is going on. During the length of one activity, a shorter or momentary happening takes place. Use the present progressive for the longer one and the simple present for the momentary or shorter one. The whole sentence can refer to now in particular or to now in general terms.

5

Whenever	I see him	he's always eating.
Every time	we visit	she's watching TV.
No matter when	you go	he's doing nothing.
	I pass by	he's always doing something.

Frequency adverbs do have their place with simple present verbs (▶ **A2** above). Because of their meanings, we do not use frequency adverbs with the present progressive; temporary time cannot sensibly be **always/never** etc. Activities that are characteristic and happen again and again during a length of present time can have **always/never** and adverbs of similar meaning with the present progressive.

6 Future time

a The morning train for Scotland **leaves** at 10 am. **It's leaving** at 11 tomorrow because of the holiday.

b Dr Ross **sees** patients at the hospital on Sunday. He **isn't seeing** anyone next Sunday. He's going away.

c We usually **celebrate** Jane's birthday at home. Next time, we**'re all going out** to a restaurant.

d The ship **is due** in Colombo next Saturday. The ship **is actually arriving late,** on Sunday.

e I'm **not going home** this evening. My wife **is coming here** and **we're going** to the cinema.

f Our conference **starts** next Monday in Mexico City. We **leave** for there tomorrow. We don't know yet **when we're coming back.**

We see in **A4** above that when standard programmes, rules, time-tables, routines, regulations operate normally, we can use the simple present for future happenings. We can also use the present progressive for future happenings; these happenings are usually exceptions to normal routine etc. They can be appointments, plans or arrangements for one or a few occasions at some future time. The speaker already knows about them now.

19 Non-progressive verbs

1

> believe, desire=want; detest, dislike, doubt, forgive, guess (Am)=suppose=think (Br); hate, know, mean, prefer, realise, recognise, remember, satisfy, understand, want, wish=want.

We can use most English verbs in progressive forms in connection with temporary activities and states. Some verbs do not take progressive forms because their meanings would not make sense in connection with temporary time periods, eg **I know** your father (at all times); X**I am knowing your father**X (but just for today?). Clearly, the progressive form is absurd. Similarly, Kate **has** blue eyes; and there is nothing temporary about them, while she lives. The verbs in the box opposite seldom or never appear in progressive forms.

2

> appear=look, seem (**it appears easy,** etc).
> *appear=become visible, present oneself; *be, belong to, contain, *depend, deserve, equal, *feel, fit (**these shoes fit me**); have=own, possess, *hear, like, love, matter, mind (**do you mind?**); own, possess, remain, require, resemble, seem, *smell, sound, *taste.
> *These verbs have more than one meaning

Most of these are stative verbs = verbs whose subjects do not actively perform the action of the verb: eg The dog **belongs** to me. (by no action of its own); This soup **tastes** funny.

The verbs marked * in the list opposite are usually stative, but can have other meanings with an activating subject, eg The cook **is tasting** the soup (perhaps it needs more salt). Some examples are given in the second box. Stative verbs do *not* appear in progressive tense forms.

stative	not stative
This bed **feels** hard.	**I'm feeling** better.
He **appears** worried.	**He's appearing** on TV.
She **doesn't hear** well.	**The judge is hearing** our case tomorrow.
My key **fits** that lock.	Then **I'm fitting** a new lock.
Your roses **smell** sweet.	The dog **is smelling** the tree.

3 a Bob **is being** very helpful this evening.
  b Then why **are you being** so unkind to him?
  c **I'm being silly,** I suppose. I'm not cruel.
  d **He's being patient,** but for how long?
  e **He's just being deaf** and keeping quiet.

Be is usually a stative verb:-
  He's deaf, poor man. (constant characteristic);
  She's a helpful girl.
  He's a polite man. etc.

A person can be deaf/helpful/polite etc, *on purpose;* **be** can then take progressive forms.

20 Verb tenses: *present perfect*

A Present perfect

Subject + (**have/has** + *past participle*)
Something   has happened.

Affirmative

I/You We/They	**have**	**prepared** **finished**	a meal. lunch.
He/She/It	**has**	**ordered** **eaten**	something. nothing.

Negative

I/You We/They	**have not** **(haven't)**	**prepared** a meal. **finished** lunch.
He/She/It	**has not** **(hasn't)**	**ordered** anything. **eaten** enough.

Interrogative

Have	I/you we/they	**saved** any time? **ordered** anything?
Has	he/she/it	**forgotten** the keys? **lost** money?

Interrogative — negative

Haven't	I/you we/they	**ordered** anything? **saved** time?
Hasn't	he/she/it	**lost** enough money?

Have I/you/we/they **not ordered** . . .? **Has** he/she/it **not saved** . . .?

We use parts of auxiliary **have** in all perfect tenses. Here, **has** is for third person singular and **have** with all others, before any past participle. The forms of the present perfect appear opposite. In the negative, **haven't** and **hasn't** are usual in familiar, informal spoken English; in the interrogative-negative, the first examples are of familiar, informal speech and the second ones (**Have we not saved time?**) are more formal.

The present perfect refers to time before now and to happenings and activities in the time before now. It is a present tense, not a form of past tense. We do not refer to particular past time and do not use adverbs and phrases that mean = that time in the past. The present perfect refers to before now: something has happened before now; because it has happened there is some effect, interest, outcome at this present time. The present perfect connects a previous activity with a present outcome.

I Present perfect (previous activities + present outcomes)

a **I've seen** all these old films on TV.
   (I don't want to go to the cinema. / I can tell you about them. / Let's try the other channel.)

b **We haven't eaten** anything all day.
   (We're very hungry. / I feel quite weak. We have splendid appetites now.)

c '**Have you heard** the news today?'
   ('That's why I'm so worried. / I can give you the main points. / We're discussing it now.')

2 'Since' and 'for' + present outcomes

a We've lived here **for a very long time.**
We've lived here **since June 1970.**
(Everybody here knows us. / We don't want to go away now. / We are almost natives of the place.)

b Ann has phoned me three times **since midnight.** She has woken me up three times **in four hours.**
(I'm annoyed. / She worries me. / I can't fall asleep again. / That's why the phone is disconnected.)

c His parents haven't seen Tom **since September.** They haven't seen him **for several months.**
(They don't know exactly what he's doing now. / They're glad he's home again. / They are anxious to see how he looks now.)

Since/for: a previous time can have a beginning; **since** marks the beginning of a period of pre-present time (**pre** = before). **For** marks the total length of a period of pre-present time. We can have: . . . **since last Sunday** (beginning) and **for six days** (length/duration) of a period of time. The activity can continue from beginning to end of a *since* period; it can happen once, twice, or more often, at different points in the pre-present period. We use **in** or **during** (not **for**) once/twice in the last week or once/ twice during the last few weeks etc.

3 With frequency adverbs + present outcomes

I/You Jane and I Our friends	have	often sometimes rarely	taken a holiday. asked for help. come in a taxi.
Bob Susan	has	hardly ever always almost never	sent telegrams. borrowed books. had a problem.

Frequency adverbs can go with the present perfect: **I have never met** your family. Frequency adverbs come after **have** and before the past participle. There are very many combinations in this table, each with a number of probable outcomes at the present moment, eg I have often taken a holiday so I know some places quite well.

4 'Still/yet' + present outcomes

a 'Have you answered that letter **yet?'**
('No, I haven't found time **yet.')**
'Has Mr Ray come back from London **yet?'** ('If he has, he hasn't come here **yet'.)**
'Have the other girls gone out to lunch **yet?'** ('Yes, **they are still out.** I haven't had lunch **yet.')**

b 'Have you **still not answered** that letter?'
('No, **I still can't find time** for it.')
'Has Mr Ray **still not come back?'** ('Well, **he still hasn't come** to the office.')
'Have you **still not had lunch?'** ('No I'm

Still/yet with present perfect: we use **yet** in questions that ask whether a happening has already taken place; we refer to any point in pre-present time. **Yet** also comes into negative replies to questions, and into negative statements generally.

Still: we ask a question and receive a negative reply:
    'Have they sent the money **yet?'** 'No, **they haven't sent** it **yet.'**
Later, we ask again, and receive a reply that says the negative situation has not

still waiting. The others **still** haven't returned.')

changed; it is still the same as it was:

'**Have they still not sent** the money?'
'**No, they still haven't.** We're still waiting.'

5 Ever, just, already

Has anyone		been in Lisbon?
Have I		told someone a lie?
Has he	**ever**	known what hunger is?
Have you		been in love?
Have they		won a lottery prize?

Questions that begin **Have you ever . . .? Has he ever . . .?** refer to the entire period of previous time:

Has he ever seen a real whale? (at any time in his life)
Have you ever been to Australia? (at any time in your life)
Have you ever ridden on a camel **before?** = Is this the **first time in your life?**

Yes, I've		come back from Lisbon.
You've	**just**	asked a silly question.
He has		ended a five-day fast.

Just with the present perfect refers to a time that is very near the present moment; just a little time has passed since something happened:
eg **Your brother has just gone out** — you'll catch him up, if you hurry.

a We have built a fine ship and they've launched it **already.**

b We have **already** given the boys some extra pocket money. Have they spent that too, **already?**

c Where have June and Bob gone? Have they gone home **already?**

d It isn't really winter yet but it has become very cold **already.**

We use **already** with the present perfect when somebody has done something before the present moment, perhaps sooner than is necessary, or faster, earlier than we expect:
eg Don't forget to do your homework, Bob.' **I've already done** it, except for English.'

6 Adverbs of present time

We've watched TV	most Saturdays	this summer.
They've been here	at weekends	this year.
Uncle Joe has come	now and again	since Easter.

Has anyone	asked for Tom	this morning?
They haven't	been anywhere	this week.
He hasn't	come late again	today.

Today and parts of today (**this morning, this afternoon, this evening**) can all be adverbs of present time, as lengths or periods of time. In the same way, **this week, this month/year/century** are present. The 20th is the present century. We use the present perfect to mention happenings in the previous part of a time period, eg **this morning, this century,** when a fixed day, date, year or hour is not given.

NOTES

1 The time period can begin with **all,** in which case we do not use **for:** eg She has lived there **all her life / all the time since then.**

2 In negative sentences, **for** can be ambiguous (can have two meanings) eg Tom hasn't worked there **for two years.** = Tom hasn't completed two years yet *or* It is two years since he stopped working there. The use of **in** makes the second meaning clear: He hasn't worked there **in two years.**
*for/in (Br); in (Am) generally

3 **has gone; has been**
They have gone (to the cinema, Paris, work etc) = they are not here, they are somewhere else.
They have been somewhere (to the theatre, the dentist's, Athens etc) = they are not there now — they are here, or they have left the first place and have gone to another.

4 **He has gone** + **for** *time phrase:* after **gone,** a **for** time phrase states the total length of the period from beginning to end:
eg **They've gone** to Spain **for a fortnight** — they'll be back in ten days. (some of the time has passed already, some is still to come)
He has been in Italy **for a week.** (seven days have passed, in Italy).

5 We do not use the present perfect with adverbs and phrases that mention definite times in the past such as **yesterday, last night, in 1950, five minutes ago, nine o'clock** etc. Happenings at definite past times take a past tense. So we can say **I have written** to my brother **this week** (*present period*): **I wrote** to him **yesterday** (*defined past*).

3 Present perfect progressive

Affirmative

I/You We/They	have been	**lying** in the sun **playing** on the beach	all day. until now.
He/She/It	has been	**sitting** on the grass	for hours.

Subject + **have/has** + (**been** + **-ing** *participle*): this form of the verb needs two auxiliaries: **have/has** (perfect) and **been** with **-ing** (progressive). Some verbs do not normally take progressive tense forms (▶ **Chapter 19**).

Negative

I/You/We/They	have not	been lying in the sun.
He/She/It	has not	been sitting on the grass.

Interrogative

Have I/you/we/they	been sleeping . . .?
Has he/she/it	been playing . . .?

Interrogative-negative

Haven't I/you/we/they	been sleeping . . .?
Hasn't he/she/it	been playing . . .?

Have I/you/they	not been playing . . .?
Has he/she/it	not been sleeping . . .?

When there are two or more auxiliaries we place **not** after the first. Here, **have** is the first, in the negative and affirmative forms, **have** and **has** often become **'ve** and **'s**, informally, eg **I've been . . . He's been . . .** etc.

The first auxiliary, when we have more than one, takes its place before the subject.

In familiar, informal spoken English, **haven't** and **hasn't** come before the subject.

More formally, **not** comes between subject and second auxiliary.

1 Continuous activities

John's Sally's The man's We've They've	been	**writing** reports **typing** them **help**ing him **working** hard	all day. for hours. since noon. since lunch.

An activity that began at some time before this moment and has continued, practically speaking, until now, is present, perfect and progressive.

2 From time to time

We've		**meeting**	twice a week	for a year.
They've	been	**having** lessons	regularly	since April.
You've		**seeing** him	now and again	since then.
Ann's		**coming** here	on Fridays	for ages.

Activities have taken place from time to time, more or less often, during a period of previous time = time before this time.

3 Unfinished activities

We've		**living** here	for at least five years.
They've		**working** there	since last summer.
Ann's	been	**writing** a book	for quite a long time.
Bob's		**using** these tools	since Father retired.

Ann's been living here **since she was a baby.** = She has lived here, lives here now and will live here, on into the future.

We've been working there **for five years.** = We have already worked for five years, we work there now and (most probably) we shall continue on into the future.

Generally, the perfect progressive mentions time before now and happenings during that time. We measure the time between **then** (when it began) up to **now** (as far as this moment / day etc),
eg **for five minutes / years,**
    since April / last summer / six o'clock
The activities that have been going on up to now will probably continue after now and go on in future, too, until they come to an end.

4 Comparison between present perfect and present perfect progressive

a **She has written** a book. Buy it and read it.
She's been writing a book. It isn't finished yet.

b **We've discussed** this matter. Here's our decision.
We've been discussing it. We need more facts yet.

c **She has knitted** a pullover. I'm wearing it now.
She's been knitting a pullover. She needs more wool.

d **She has studied** hard. She's ready for the test.
I've been saving my pocket money. I've got £75 now.

In these pairs of examples, the first mentions activities and previous time: both have come to end about now or before now. There is at this time a result, consequence, outcome of more or less interest or importance to the present speaker (▶ **A** above). In the second example in each pair, the activity is not yet complete; it will go on and become complete (or not) at a later time, after now (▶ **3** above). There may or may not be a present outcome (▶ **d** opposite).

21 VERB TENSES: *past time*

A Simple past

Affirmative

I/We	arrived	yesterday.
You/They	left	last Monday.
He/She/It	returned	last night.

The simple past tense of regular verbs appears in **Chapter 16** and of irregular verbs in **Chapter 17.** These show affirmative forms only; there is only one form and it serves for all persons, singular and plural.

Negative

I/We	didn't	arrive	yesterday.
You/They	did not	leave	last Monday.
He/She/It	didn't	return	last night.

Did, the past tense of **do,** is the auxiliary verb for all persons, singular and plural. We place **did not** between the subject and base form of the verb to make the negative of the simple past. The base forms of verbs appear in **Chapters 16** and **17.** Conversationally, **did not** often becomes **didn't.** To ask a question in the simple past, we place **did** before the *subject + base verb* for all persons, singular and plural.

Interrogative

Did	I/we	go	that day?
	you/they	arrive	at that time?
	he/she/it	leave	last Monday?
		return	yesterday?

Interrogative-negative

Didn't	I/he/she/it we/you/they		go arrive	last night? at that time?
Did	he/she they/we you/it	not	return leave work	last Monday? then? in 1980?

Didn't comes before the *subject + base verb* in familiar, informal speech. Formally, we can have **did** + *subject* (+ **not** + *base verb),* eg **Did** they **not** arrive yesterday?

1

I met	Peter	last weekend.
He **saw**	them	**every day last week.**
We **phoned**	you	**after lunch yesterday.**
She **wrote** to	Mary	**several times**
Ann **asked** for	him	last month.

A plane for Tokyo **left**		at six o'clock.

The simple past tense is the one we use for happenings and activities that took place at any defined time in the past, eg yesterday
 last week
 any day or date
 any hour or time, in the past.

2

Jane	**played** tennis	**on that day.**
Charles	**went** to the cinema	**on Saturdays.**
We/You	**drove** to the seaside	**every day that week.**
The girls	**used** my boat	**often.**
Everybody	**swam** in the river	**in those days.**
I	**worked** overtime	**last weekend.**

We also use it for happenings and activities that took place once or a few times; regularly, often, or constantly in the past. Frequency adverbs often go with the simple past.

3

Mother's grandparents	**lived** here **all their lives.** **brought up** a large family. **farmed** this land **for fifty years.** **went** to the village school. **could read** and **write** well.

The simple past is for happenings and activities that, practically speaking, were routine, regular or permanent during a period of past time.

4 Time phrases

a He **always** preferred tea.
He has **always** preferred tea.

b They worked here **for thirty years.**
They have worked here **for thirty years.**

c We **often** met **in the evenings.**
We have **often** met **in the evenings.**

d I knew old Bob **for ages.**
I have known old Bob **for ages.**

e It rained heavily **all day.**
It has rained heavily **all day.**

Time phrases such as **all their lives, for fifty years, every day, during the winter/evening/morning** etc can refer to past, present or future time;
eg **I have lived** here **all my life.** =
present (perfect) verb + present life
He lived here **all his life.** = *past verb + past life;* we mention a dead man.
In the examples opposite, the first one of each pair mentions the past time: verbs, adverbs and time phrases all refer to happenings and activities that began and finished in the past. In the second sentence of each pair, the verb refers to now and a period of time before now, in the present perfect; the time adverbs and phrases include the present moment. So:
I knew old Bob **for ages** — he **was** a good man; **I've known him for ages** — he **is** a good man.
For present perfect tense ▶ chapter 20.

5 Time period + ago

When	did you arrive?' did he ask for me?' did you ring them?' did you post the letter?' did she start work?'	**'A few days ago.'** **'Half an hour ago.'** **'About an hour ago.'** **'Two weeks ago.** **'Five minutes ago.'**

The time period can be any length from a few seconds up to millions of years. The speaker defines a time in the past; he counts backwards from now to then in the past, eg Mary is now 18 years old: Mary was born **18 years ago.** The simple past is the tense we use.

6 a You weren't in your room a minute ago.

b I didn't see anybody here five minutes ago.

c You spoke to me here **not very long ago.**

d Dr Cole left the hospital **not ten minutes ago.**

e Ann's brother went to Brazil **not quite a year ago.**

f They wrote to us **not more than a fortnight ago.**

When the verb is in the negative form we have a normal negative sentence (**a-b**). The verb can be affirmative with **not** before the time phrase (**c-f**); **not** = not even, not as much as, not as long as.

7 a Dr Cole **left** the hospital half an hour ago. **He has taken a long time. / He hasn't arrived yet.**

b Tom **went** to Brazil about a year ago. **He's written** to us regularly. **/ He hasn't come back.**

c They **sent** us a letter about a fortnight ago. **We've given it** to the police. **/ We haven't replied.**

d Liz **started** work less than a fortnight ago. **She has made** a good start. **/ She hasn't seemed tired.**

e I **phoned** them about an hour ago. **They've rung back twice. / They haven't rung back yet.**

f **We played** tennis together a few weeks ago. **We've met twice in the meantime. / I haven't seen her since then.**

8 a 'I met your sister Susan on the way **this morning.**' 'Did you? I didn't see her **until this afternoon.**'

b 'Didn't she mention me at all **this afternoon?**' 'Susan and I didn't talk much **at tea-time.**'

c 'I hope she didn't mind meeting me **today.**' 'Well, she said nothing to me **this afternoon.**' 'Did you exchange telephone numbers?'

In the meantime (f) is a phrase that means during the period between two points in time. Happenings and activities took place some time ago, a long time ago, a year ago, in past time. People count back between now in the present and then in the past. Very often, this brings them to thoughts in the opposite direction — between then in the past and now in the present. They talk of what has happened or has not happened in the meantime. The examples with **ago** are in the simple past — they took place at definite times in the past. The examples that refer to the meantime, between then and now, are in the present perfect.

Today/this morning/this afternoon/this evening etc can sometimes appear with the simple past. The speaker mentions something that happened in an earlier part of **this** morning etc; it has no effect on anything that is happening now. There is no present outcome. The speaker's words may or may not interest others.

B Used to /juːst tʊ/

1 a Mary's grandparents **used to live** here.
b We **used to go** to the village school.
c He **used to prefer** tea to coffee.
d My brother **used to work** in London.
e I **used to visit** old Bob on Saturdays.
f We **used to play** cards or dominoes.

The simple past tense can refer to activities and happenings during a period of past time. They were constant or often repeated activities or they were matters of custom and habit during a past time. Happenings and activities began and ended in the past (▶ 3-4 above). **Used to** + *base verb* also refers to the same kind of happening and activity.

2 a He **always** used to ask for tea.
b I **often** used to meet Bob in the park.
c We **never** used to talk about politics.
d He always asked for tea.
e I often met Bob in the park.
f We never talked about politics.

Generally, **used to** does not go with **since** and **for** phrases that measure the length of the past time period and others such as **all his life** etc. Sometimes, in familiar, conversational style, we can use a frequency adverb (**How often . . .?**) but more formally, the simple past.

3 a Tom **used not to drink** coffee. He does now.
He **didn't use to drink** coffee.

b We **used not to play** cards. Nowadays we do.
We **didn't use to play** cards.

c People **usedn't to be** so stressed. They are now.
People **didn't use to be** so stressed.

d **Used** your brother **to work** in London? He is in Dublin now.
Did your brother **used to work** in London?

e **Used** Dr Brown **to smoke** a pipe? He doesn't now.
Did Dr Brown **use to smoke** a pipe?

f Bill's father **used to be** a champion runner.
Used to be, of course — he's nearly sixty now.

g **Didn't** Liz **use to live** here?
Usedn't she **to be** a close friend of Bob's?

Negative: formally, we place **not** between **used** and **to;** informally, we can have **did not/didn't use to** in familiar speech (**a-c**).

Interrogative: formally, **used** comes before the subject; informally we can say **did he use to . . .?** (**d-g**). **Used to** very often appears in questions and statements that compare the past with the present and show them to be different. Things **are not now** the same as they **were/used to be,** then in the past.

There are two forms of negative-interrogative — informal and formal (▶ **g**).

NOTE there is no present time form of this idiomatic **used to.** In **He is used to hard work.** we have quite a different meaning; hard work doesn't bother him, he is accustomed to it.

C Past progressive

Affirmative

I He/She/It	was	working. playing running. singing.
We/You/They	were	

We have the past tense of **be** + **-ing** *participle of a finite verb.* The parts of auxiliary **be** are: **was** for first and third person singular; **were** for all other persons, as in the tables opposite.

Negative

I He/She/It	was not (wasn't)	working. playing. running. singing.
We/You/They	were not (weren't)	

Was not and **were not** are very often **wasn't** and **weren't** in normal conversations. Generally, we do not shorten **was** and **were,** and we do not stress them at all, except for emphasis. The negative form takes **not** between auxiliary **was/were** and **-ing** participle.

Interrogative

Was	I he/she/it	working? playing? running? singing?
Were	we/you/they	

The auxiliary **was/were** before the subject makes the interrogative form.

Wasn't/Weren't . . .? are most usual in spoken English. **Was I not . . .? Were you not.?** are most formal, in speech and in writing.

Interrogative-negative

Wasn't		I he/she/it		working? playing?
Weren't		we/you/they		running? singing?
Was Were	I he/she/it we/you/they		not	sleeping? travelling? doing that?

1 a We **were spending** more money than we **were making.**

  b In those days we **were living** in that huge old house.

  c I **was working** as a salesman at that time.

  d We **were running** at a loss until **business improved.**

  e That old place **was ruining** me before I **sold** it.

  f Before I **became** manager I **was working** as a salesman.

2 a Ann **was wearing** slacks, which surprised me. (Ann always **wore** a skirt or a dress.)

  b We wondered why the Smiths **were having** tea that day. (They usually **asked** for coffee at breakfast.)

  c Our pupils **were having** an extra holiday that day. (Generally, they **were** at school on Mondays.)

3 a While **I was preparing** to go out, **Liz came in.**

  b **I was writing** a letter when **the lights went out.**

  c Tom **hurt** his foot while **he was playing tennis.**

  d While **Jane was talking** on the phone, **they cut her off.**

  e **The phone rang** again while **I was having lunch.**

  f While **I was waiting** for a bus **it began to rain.**

Some verbs do not take progressive forms because their meanings are not suitable you can see them in **Chapter 19.**

The past progressive refers to happenings and activities which were in progress, for a longer or shorter period of time, in the past.

The activities and the periods of past time in **d-f** finally came to an end in the past. Often, some other happening or activity put an end to them; this generally takes the simple past — it happened once, then at a definite time.

The past progressive mentions interruptions and exceptions to normal habits, customs, routine, time-tables, programmes etc. The general, usual activity is in the simple past (**A3-4** above); the exceptional happenings and interruptions were only temporary and take the past progressive tense.

During a period of past time, an activity or happening was in progress. While it was happening, at any point during that time, something else happened. The longer activity is in the past progressive, the momentary happening is in the simple past.

4 **a** **Tom was driving** and **Mary was sitting** next to him when I saw them.

b **She was talking** to him but **he wasn't paying much attention. He was keeping** his eyes on the road and **minding** the traffic until he **parked** the car.

Two activities (or more) can progress together during a period of past time.

Both activities take the past progressive.

5 **a** 'Hello, Bob! I thought you were in Italy.' 'I **'was planning** to go, that's all.'

b 'Have your relations arrived yet?' 'They **'were coming** yesterday, but couldn't get seats on the plane.'

Was/were with stress can often mean that someone intended to do something, in the past, but there is uncertainty about whether he did it or not, or changed his mind.

22 Verb tenses: *past perfect*

A Past perfect

Affirmative

I/He/She/It We/You/They	had stopped. had started. had left.

The past perfect tense takes auxiliary **had** (past tense form of **have**) and the past participle of a finite verb, for all persons, singular and plural. **Had** is often **'d** in familiar conversation.

Negative

I/He/She/It We/You/They	hadn't had not	stopped. started. left.

We make the negative in the usual way, by placing **not** between the auxiliary (**had**) and the past participle; **had not** is often **hadn't** in conversational style.

Interrogative

Had	I/he/she/it we/you/they	stopped? started? left?

The interrogative takes the auxiliary (**had**) before the subject, in the usual way.

Interrogative-negative

Hadn't	I/he/she/it we/you/they	stopped? started? left?
Had	I/he/she/it not we/you/they not	agreed? spoken?

For the interrogative-negative form, in normal conversation, we put **hadn't** before the subject. Formally, **had** comes before the subject and **not** between subject and past participle.

1 The past in the past

earlier happenings (perfect)	later outcomes (simple)
She **had done** her work.	She was free to leave.
Everyone **had gone** home.	Nobody was there.
I **had written** my letters.	I *posted them at once.

*to post letters (Br) = to mail letters (Am)

Ann went home **after she had done her shopping. Tom had already come home** before Ann arrived. **He had prepared lunch** so Ann laid the table. They sat down to eat **after Ann had laid the table. When they had finished**, Tom went back to work.

The past perfect refers to earlier happenings in past time; they had an effect, consequence or outcome at a later time, also in the past. An activity, further back in time, affects a second activity not so far back.

2 Since and for with past pefect

a That tree **had grown** there for two hundred years, then a flash of lightning **killed** it.

b Ann **had known** Joe for less than a month when he **asked** her to marry him.

The length of a time period between then in the past and a point further back in past time usually has **for** + *time period*:
eg I had worked **for a week** so I asked

c I **had known** him since the time we **were** in the army together and at university.

d My car **had stood** there since nine o'clock until the police **took** it away. They **said** I **had left** it in a 'No Parking' area for two days.

3 Negative past perfect and time periods

a I hadn't smoked a cigarette **for a year / since 1st January.**
It was a year since I'd smoked a cigarette.

b I hadn't earned any money **for six months / since June.**
It was six months since I'd earned any money.

c The men hadn't shaved **for a week / since the previous Sunday.**
It was a week since they had shaved.

d Ann hadn't worked there **for six months / since the summer.**
It was six months since Ann had (last) worked there.

e She hadn't written to us **for ages / since before Easter.**
It was ages since she'd (last) written to us.

4
a **It is** three months since we (last) **saw** John.
It was three months since we **had** (last) **seen** John.

b **It is** a year since **I did** any real work.
It was a year since **I had done** any real work.

c **It's** almost two years since **we** last **had** a free weekend.
It was almost two years since **we had had** a free weekend.

5 After, before, when

a I paid the driver **before** I got out of the taxi.

b **After** I heard the news I turned the radio off.

c People left the hall **before** the meeting ended.

d **When I had slept,** I felt a little better.

for my wages that Saturday.

We connect the beginning of the period to its end point in later past time with **since:**
eg I had worked every day **since the previous Monday** so on the Saturday I asked for my wages.

We can have a negative verb in the past perfect with a **for** or **since** phrase, just as we can with any perfect tense.

For cannot introduce a clause; **since** can introduce a clause.

We can make a negative sense with **It was** + *time phrase* (without **for**) and then **since** + *past perfect clause,* affirmative as in the examples opposite.

Last before or after the past participle makes it clear that the speaker refers to the beginning of a period of negative happenings.

Compare the examples with: I haven't heard from him **for six months.** = **It is six months since** I heard from him. (in **4** below).

In these pairs, the first sentence refers to present time:
a We haven't seen John for three months.
b I haven't done any real work for a year.
c We haven't had a free weekend for almost two years.

The second sentence in each pair refers to past time, as in **3** immediately above.

These can introduce time clauses. One thing happened before another but did not affect it in any way. Both clauses can be in the simple past, or if you wish, the first in time can be in the past perfect.

e **After I had paid** the driver he helped with my bags.

f She went to town **after she had received** an invitation from someone.

B Past perfect progressive

Affirmative
subject + **had been** + *past participle*

I/You John/Mary The dog We Tom and Jane	**had been**	**waiting** there. **swimming** in the sea. **running** after a ball. **eating** something.

Affirmative **had** is often **'d** in conversational English.

Negative

I/you He/She/It We/They	**had not been**	**waiting** there. **swimming** in the sea. **running** after a ball.

There are two auxiliary verbs: **had** and **been; not** comes after the first auxiliary; **had not** often becomes **hadn't** in conversational style.

Interrogative

Had	I/you he/she/it we/they	**been waiting?** **been eating** something? **been swimming?**

The first auxiliary (**had**) comes before the subject.

Interrogative-negative

Hadn't	I/you he/she/it we/they	**been waiting** there? **been swimming?** **been running?**
Had	I/you not he/she/it not we/they not	**been sleeping?** **been reading?** **been having** fun?

Usually, **hadn't** comes before the subject in normal conversations. Formally, **had** comes before the subject and **not** comes between subject and second auxiliary (**been**).

NOTE some verbs do not appear in progressive tenses because their meanings cannot go sensibly with phrases such as **for the time being, during that time only, for a while** etc ▶ **Chapter 19** for these verbs.

1 a Ann came back yesterday. **She had been visiting** her parents **for a few days.**

b Tom became impatient. **He'd been waiting for an hour** and nothing had happened.

c I woke up to reality. **I'd been dreaming** that I'd won the national lottery.

d **It was** time for a change. **They'd been living abroad** and (they'd been) **working there since their children were babies.**

A period of past time began, continued, then came to an end, at a later time in the past. Happenings and activities took place during that period, continually or repeatedly. We measure the length of a period of pre-past time with **since** and **for** phrases; the activities and happenings did not necessarily stop when time periods ended. In **b** opposite, **Tom had been waiting for an hour** — and probably continued to wait for some time.

2 **a** I **had read** your book.
  I**'d been reading** your book.
 b Corporal Coe **had served** for ten years.
  Corporal Coe **had been serving** for ten years.
 c She **had written** a new modern play.
  She**'d been writing** a new modern play.

Often, there is no outcome or consequence at a later past time, but there can be sometimes. Generally, we measure the length of a pre-past period; the activity during the period can finish at the end of the period or go on after that.

In the first sentence of each pair, the activity and the time period are both complete. Possible outcomes might be: **a** I knew your opinions. **b** the corporal left the army. / They made him a sergeant. **c** She was looking for a theatre or a publisher or a producer.

In the second sentence of each pair, the activity was not complete; it most probably went on into later time.

23 Verb tenses: *future time*

A Simple present tense

1 a Christmas Day **falls** on a Friday next year.
  b Today's Monday. The Weekly Magazine **comes** tomorrow.
  c We **pay** the whole year's taxes next March, as usual.

2 a **John's coming** to lunch next Saturday.
  b **He's bringing** a friend with him, this time.
  c **We are all going** to the zoo, afterwards.

3 a Peter says **he's going to buy** a new car.
  b **I'm not going to make** an offer for his old car.
  c **We're goint to plant** more roses next year.
  d **Tom's going to dig** the garden for us, in the spring.
  e **Aren't you going to plant** in the autumn?
  f What **are you going to use** as fertilizers?

4 a Don't feed the dog all the time. **It's going to get ill.**
  b It's getting warmer. **The river is going to thaw** soon.
  c Look at Mrs Rae! **Is she going to have a baby?**
  d She tells me **she's going to have twins.**
  e Look out! **That tree is going to come down.**
  f It's such a strong wind. **It's going to cause damage.**
  g If I pass the exam, Father's **going to give me £20.**
  h **What's he going to do** if you don't pass?

5 a **We were just about to go out** when you rang.
  b **Ann's about to put on her hat** and I'm ready.
  c **The plane is about to leave.** We are just in time.
  d **They are about to get married** but have no furniture.

We can express future happenings with the simple present tense. Present programmes, time-tables and routines are for now and for the future too (▶ **Chapter 18, A4**).

The present progressive tense refers to arrangements, appointments and so on. The speaker knows now about a future occasion, and mentions it (▶ **Chapter 18, B**)

Going to + *base verb:* the speaker expresses his or her own intentions, in the first person (**I/we**) and, with other subjects of **going to**, the speaker expresses the subject's intentions for a future time.

Going to + *base verb:* the speaker has good reason for saying that something is sure to happen in the future — very soon or at some time in the future. What the speaker sees, hears and understands now gives him good reason for saying that **something is going to happen,** sooner or later.

Be about to + *base verb:* we use the present tense of **be** with **to** and the base verb (the full infinitive). The subject of the verb is on the point of doing something in the very near future — within the next few seconds or minutes, or very, very soon.

e Why is he standing there? **What is he about to do?**

f Let's watch. Perhaps **he's about to sing a song.**

B Shall/will

1 a 'I **shall** be eighteen next birthday,' Mary said.

b Tom **will** grow as tall as his father in a year or two.

c You **will** all come to school next Monday.

d We **shall** see one another then, after the weekend.

e Our children **will** become parents themselves, one day.

f We **shall** have a new generation of young people.

Shall and **will** serve as future tense auxiliaries, but have other non-future uses too (▶ **Chapter 24, B18-19**).

Shall/will + *base verb* = *the plain future.* **Time will pass** and as a result **something will happen.** Neither speakers nor subjects of verbs can make any difference to the work of time; whatever will be, will be. We use **shall** with first persons and **will** with all others. Very often, **shall** and **will** become **'ll** after personal pronouns, in familiar conversations.

2 a **I will give you** all the help that you need.
You shall have money and time for experiments.

b **We will pay** the costs for materials and time.
They shall receive salaries, starting next month.

c **He shall not come** into my house ever again!
I shall call the police. **I shall set** the dog on him.

d **We shall do** everything we can to avoid wars.
Our countries shall live at peace, as good neighbours.

Will/shall + *base verb:* **the coloured future.** This form of the future is coloured by the speaker's intentions towards the subject of the future time verb. The speaker expresses a promise, a decision, a threat, a firm intention about what will happen to the subject. We use **will** for first persons (they are both speaker and subject) and **shall** for all other persons. **Will** and **shall** do not become **'ll** in the coloured future.

NOTE speaker/subjects very often use **shall** to express determination.

3 Negative

a **I shall not / shan't go** to the office tomorrow.

b It's Sunday. **You will not/won't go,** either.

Not comes between the auxiliary (**shall** or **will**) and the base verb. **Shall not / will not** often become **shan't / won't** in conversational style.

4 Interrogative

a **Shall I** be happy, **shall I** be rich?

b **Will the sun** always shine on us?

The auxiliary comes before the *subject* + *base verb.*

5 Interrogative-negative

a **Shan't we all** grow old, as time goes by?

b **Won't you and they** become pensioners?

c **Shall we not have** grey hair too, some day?

d **Will you not remember** your good old times?

Shan't (= shall not) or **Won't** (= will not) comes before *subject + base verb*. Formally, **shall/will** comes before the subject, and **not** comes between subject and base verb.

C Progressive future

1 a At this time tomorrow **I'll be flying** to Paris.

b What **will you be doing** in ten years' time?

c **Will you still be teaching** English here?

d **We shall be staying** in Madrid till Sunday.

e **I shall be marking** students' tests till bed-time.

f **We won't be watching** TV after seven thirty.

2 a **I don't think Tom will be here** on a Saturday. **He'll be spending the weekend** at his parents' place.

b That's true. He often does that. **He'll be driving back** late on Sunday, as usual.

c **'You'll be travelling** as usual, I suppose.' 'Yes. **We shan't be meeting again** before Friday.'

d Today's the twenty-ninth. **I shall be getting** my salary. **They'll be paying** it into my bank, as always.

e How's Grandma? Is her rheumatism better? **She'll be taking medicine** for it, I suppose.

An activity or happening is in progress now, at present, and will come to its end at a point in future time: *subject +* **shall/will** + **(be** + **-ing** *participle*), eg **I shall be working** until midnight. = I'm working now and I shall continue/shall not stop until midnight. The starting point of the activity can be before now or after now; the end of a progressive activity is at a definite point in the future.

We know people and their ways so well that we can say, with more or less certainty, what they are probably doing now, and probably will be doing at a future time. We assume that what we say is highly probable, because of our own experience of people and happenings. The progressive future can mention assumptions for present and future times.

D Future perfect

I'll/We'll You'll/They'll He'll/She'll It'll/It will	have	arrived left finished appeared	before mid-day. by Saturday. before then. by 11 am.

Shall/will be + **(have** + *past participle):* activities and happenings will become complete at or before a definite time in the future. When the activity began does not matter; it began at any time before its future completion.

E Future perfect progressive

We'll She'll I'll You'll They'll	have been	working teaching operating studying writing	for two years for a year for six weeks	soon. by June on Friday. in the meantime. before that time.

Shall/will + **have been** + **-ing** *participle:* activities can begin at any time and continue up to a definite future time. The activities may or may not continue beyond that future time.

F Future-in-the-past

1 **a** Christmas Day **fell** on a Friday the following year. (▶ **A1**)

 b John **was coming** to lunch the following Saturday. (**A2**)

 c Peter said **he was going to buy** a new car. (**A3**)

 d I **wasn't going to make** an offer for his old car. (**A3**)

 e Mrs Rae told me **she was going to have twins.** (**A4**)

 f He warned us that **the tree was going to fall.** (**A4**)

 g **Ann was about to put** her hat on and I was ready. (**A5**)

 h **The plane was about to leave.** (**A5**)

2 **a** Mary said **she would be** eighteen on her next birthday. (**B1**)

 b He promised **he would give** all the help we needed. (**B2**)

 c He said that our countries ***should/would live** at peace. (**B2**)

 d **I would be flying** to Paris at that time, the following day. (**C1**)

 e She thought **he'd be spending the weekend** at his parents'. (**C2**)

 f I assumed **she'd be taking medicine.** (**C2**)

 g They said that **they'd have arrived** by 11 am. (**D**)

 h **We'd have been working** for two years by that Friday. (**E**)

The future-in-the-past is often a form of reported speech. Someone spoke and mentioned future time, as it was then, eg **Napoleon said, 'I shall be master of all Europe'. = Napoleon said that he would be master of all Europe.**
The personal future of Napoleon, among millions of others, is now in the past and we use a future-in-the-past tense when we mention it now.

The past forms for **shall** and **will** are ***should** and **would,** in all future tenses shown in **B-E** above. Other tenses that can refer to the future take their usual past tense forms when they refer to future-in-the-past.

***Should** as an auxiliary verb has a number of different uses; in one of them **should = ought to.** This can cause misunderstanding, sometimes, so many people use **would** only in the future-in-the-past. **Should/would** are often **'d** in spoken English; notice that **had** is also **'d.**

24 Auxiliary verbs

Auxiliary verbs are verbs that combine with a subject and a part of a finite verb. They can show the tense of a verb and that it is a simple, progressive or perfect tense. We call them *tense auxiliaries*.

Other auxiliaries, which we call *modal auxiliaries* combine with a subject and a part of a finite verb and show some other effect such as permission, probability, habit, advice in connection with the finite verb and someone's activities.

Auxiliary verbs follow the same patterns of word order in connection with finite verbs.

Affirmative

I	will	help her.
They	would	talk to him.
We	can	go to the cinema.
You	must	try a little harder.
	ought to	tell somebody.

Auxiliary verbs follow the subject and come before the finite verb.

Negative

I	will not	speak to him.
They	would not	go to the cinema.
We	cannot	do anything at all.
She	must not	tell anybody.
You	should not	waste time.

*Subject + auxiliary + **not** + finite verb:* when there are two or more auxiliaries, **not** comes after the first one.

Interrogative

Will	she	talk to them?
Can	he	drive the tractor?
Should	you	do that too?
Do	they	go by train?
Could	I	stay out late?

The first or only auxiliary comes before the subject.

Interrogative-negative

Won't	she	watch the TV programme?
Can't	he	drive the tractor?
Mustn't	we	stay out till midnight?
Couldn't	I	go for a walk today?
Shouldn't	they	ask a few questions?

Formally, the first or only auxiliary comes before the subject and **not** follows the subject. Informally, a negative short form comes before the subject.

NOTE There can be more than one auxiliary in a verb phrase: modals come before perfect tense auxiliaries, which in turn come before progressive tense auxiliaries, and passive auxiliaries come after any other auxiliary
(▶ Chapter 25)

A Tense auxiliaries

be: am, are, is; was, were; been

do: do, does; did

have: have, has; had

shall, will

should/would

used to (+ base verb)

Be: we use parts of **be** as auxiliary verbs in progressive tenses and also as the auxiliary for the passive forms of verbs.

Do: this is the auxiliary verb for the simple present (**do, does**) and simple past (**did**).

Have is the auxiliary verb with perfect tenses; the present perfect takes **have/has; had** is for the past perfect tenses.
As tense auxiliaries, **shall** and **will** appear in **future tenses.** Usually, they do not appear in **conditional** clauses.

As tense auxiliaries, **should** and **would** appear in **future-in-the-past** tenses, as past forms of **shall** and **will.**

This idiomatic auxiliary phrase can sometimes appear instead of the simple past tense (▶ **Chapter 21, B**).

B Modal auxiliaries

Modal auxiliaries have this name because they add meaning to other verbs and show a mode or style in activities and happenings, eg **may** refers to permission or to probability.

1 Can/could + base verb

a Tom's a fast worker. **He can do** two men's work.
b Ann's clever. **She can learn** a language quickly.
c I'm free tomorrow. **I can stay** at home with you.
d 'Can I borrow your bike?' 'No, **you can't,** today.'
   NOTE negative **can't = cannot**

Could is the past form of **can.** We use these to mention:
● physical or other personal ability
● personal opportunity to do something
● permission (in familiar spoken English).
Be able to: except for permission (see above) parts of **be able to** can replace **can/could.**

2 'Be able to' and 'could'

a Tom **is / was able to do** two men's work, sometimes.
b Ann **is / was / will be able to learn** quickly.
c I **am / was / will be able to stay** with you.

Could is the past tense form of **can;** sometimes, with opportunity, **could** is conditional in sense:
b Ann is clever. **She could learn** the language quickly — **if she gets the opportunity / if she wants to** (etc).
c I'm free tomorrow. **I could stay** at

d We'll be able to afford a longer holiday next summer.

e When I'm in town tomorrow, **I'll be able to visit you.**

f Tom **could do** a lot more work — but will he?

g Ann **could learn to drive** a car if necessary.

h We **could afford** a longer holiday if we stayed in a tent.

i I **could visit you** tomorrow, if that suits you.

home with you — **if you like / if you don't mind / if you are at home too** (etc).

We use **be able to** + *base verb* when we mention opportunity without conditions, as actual happenings that took place or will take place.

3 Be able to

a Your broken leg will take six weeks to heal. **You'll be able to walk** without a stick, then.

b 'When **shall I be able to play** football again?' 'You **won't be able to kick** a ball before Christmas.'

c 'What a noise! I wish he could play the guitar properly.' **'He'll be able to play quite well** in a few months' time.'

We use **can** or **be able to** forms when we mention a person's abilities at present. Ability, physical or mental, that a person does not have now but will have at some future time, generally appears as **shall/will be able to.**

4 Can/could

a Even a professor **can make a mistake,** sometimes.

b Rex is a very friendly dog usually, but **he 'can bite.**

c They say that **any good soldier can become a general.**

d August is the warmest month and **can be wet,** too.

e Grandma was easy-going. She **'could be strict,** if necessary.

f She loved us all though **we 'could annoy her** sometimes.

We mention happenings and activities that are improbable or quite unusual, but not impossible — such things 'can happen, sometimes. We often stress **can** or **could,** in this sort of statement.

5 Permission

a **'Can I eat** this piece of cake, mother?'

b 'No, **you can't.** It's almost lunch-time.'

c **'You can have it** later, if you want it.'

d **'Could I see you** for a few minutes, please?'

e 'Of course. **You could come** to my office at ten.'

f He said that **I could see him,** so I went there.

Can and **could** often appear in connection with asking and giving permission in familiar, informal styles (**a-f**). Both **can** and **could** can refer to present and future time. **Could** sometimes seems a little more polite and respectful than **can.**

NOTE could also refers to past time.

g 'It's very late! **May I stay** with you overnight?'

h 'Of course **you may. You can sleep** on the sofa.'

i '**Might I use** your razor?' 'Well, yes, **you may.**'

j Ann **may not drive my car** while she still has L plates.

k He said that **I might not drive his car** yet.

l Our guest asked whether **he might stay** overnight.

m The manager said that **I might see him** and I did.

n I wanted to know whether **I might take a few days off.**

o He said that **I mightn't,** unless it was really necessary.

May, might in connection with asking and giving permission (**g-o**) are formal and we use them when familiarity and informality are not suitable.

Both **may** and **might** refer to present or future time; **might** often appears when someone feels that he is asking for too much. **Might** is also the past form of **may.** The spoken short form **mightn't = might not** is quite usual; **may not** generally has no shorter form, nowadays.

6 Possibility and probability

a This child **might become** president of our country, one day.

b You **might get** a good pension in forty years from now.

c I might. However, **I might not survive** till then.
Peter won't tell a lie but **he might refuse to answer.**

d I might be a millionaire next time we meet.

e You might — and **pigs might fly.**

f Sell the house in spring. You **may get** a better price.

g Jane **may change** her job if she finds a better one.

h We're very busy. I **may work** late this evening.

i I'll let you know later. I **may be** home for supper.

Nothing is impossible, everything is, in some very small degree, possible and probable. We use **might** to express ideas of this kind (**a-e**).

May expresses a reasonable degree of probability or possibility (**f-i**). Probability and improbability are almost equally balanced.

7 Compulsion

I must finish this work even if it takes all night.
We must hurry or we'll miss our train.
You must pay all your taxes before 5th April.
I must **not stop** before I finish this work.

Must expresses compulsion and obligation of all kinds. In the examples opposite we see

a self compulsion; it is a personal matter, the feeling of compulsion comes from oneself;

b the obligation to hurry comes from

e We must hurry. We must **not miss** our train.

f You must **not delay** your tax payments.

g People must **not bring** dogs into this shop.

h Pupils must **not chew** gum in class.

8 'Must' and 'have to' + base verb

a I'm not rich. **I have to work hard** for a living.

b Look at the time! **You'll have to run** to the bus stop.

c My phone is out of order. **I'll have to get it fixed.**

d '**Must you leave us** so early?' 'No, **we don't have to go** home yet but **Charles has to call** at the office on the way.'

e Our babysitter **doesn't have to wait up** for us. She goes to bed with the children. **She has to get up with the children too.**

9 'Must' or 'be to' + base verb

a My dentist says **I am not to eat** sweets.

b **John is to appear** before a judge tomorrow.

c **You are to start** work at nine o'clock exactly.

d **Nobody is to come** late. Latecomers **are to be fined.**

e This is secret information. **They are not to see it.**

f **We are to keep it** under lock and key, here.

g **We are not to talk about this to anyone.**

10 'Must' and past time

a My dog was ill. **I had to take him** to the vet.

b The vet was busy. **We had to wait** a long time.

c The dog **didn't have to take medicine.**

d **I had to keep him** without food for two days.

e **He didn't have to go** there again.

f She said **you weren't to eat sweets.**

g **People weren't to bring dogs** into the shop.

some outside source, (a railway time-table, for example);

c obligation and compulsion come from some person or office that has a right to say what others must do.

In all of these **must** + (**not** + *base verb*) states commands and obligations **not to do** certain things (**d-h**).

We often use **have to / has to** instead of **must** when obligation is not by someone's command; it is the outcome of circumstances. The negative **don't have to / doesn't have** to means there is no obligation — do this or not, as you wish (**d-e**).

In **7** above we saw that persons and offices and other authorities can have a right to compel or oblige others to obey using **must**. Instead of **must** we can have: **I am to / you are to / he is to** + *base verb*. The negative forms **you are not to** etc mean the same as **must not**, ie a command NOT to do something. Often it is the person who receives a command, or knows about it, who refers to it with **be to**.

The modal auxiliary **must** has no past form of its own. We can use **had to** as the past tense of **have to** (▶ **8** above) and **was/were to** as the past tense of **be to** (▶ **9** above). As modal auxiliaries **have, has, had** do not often take the short forms **'ve, 's, 'd.** The negative form is **didn't have to** = was/were not obliged to; didn't need to.

h **We were to pay our taxes** before 5th April.

i **John was to appear** before a judge that day.

11 Certainty of opinion

a Nobody has answered the phone. **Ann must be out.**

b Aunt Flora's the eldest. **She must be over sixty.**

c Dick lives very well. **He must have a good income.**

d Coffee at ten pounds a cup! **That must be a mistake.**

e Go swimming in January! **You must think I'm mad.**

f She bakes bread every day. **That must keep her busy.**

g Go swimming in mid-winter! **You can't mean it.**

h Coffee at such a high price! **This can't be right.**

i You want £1,000 for that car. **You can't be serious.**

j He spends too much. **He can't go on like this.**

k They never open a book. **They can't know the lessons.**

Must states the speaker's absolute opinion. The facts of the matter, as the speaker knows them, all point to one affirmative opinion,

eg A baby that is not a girl **must be a boy.**

If yesterday was Monday, **today must be Tuesday.**

Can't or **cannot** also state an absolute opinion. The facts, as the speaker knows them, all point to one negative opinion.

12 Advice and recommendations

a '**You ought to wear a coat** in this cold weather.' 'Yes, I suppose **I ought to.** I will, tomorrow.'

b '**Jenny shouldn't give half her dinner** to the dog.' '**The dog shouldn't be** in this room. Put it out.'

c **Passengers shouldn't talk to me** when I'm driving. **They shouldn't expect me** to talk and drive.

d John ought to take more care of his health. **He ought to have a check-up** once a year.

Should/ought to + base verb: there is no difference in meaning between **should** and **ought to.** We can use one for the other at all times. We do not order anyone to obey (as we can with **must**) but give a word of advice; others may follow this advice or not, as they wish. **Should not** and **ought not to** are often **shouldn't** and **oughtn't (to)** in familiar conversational style.

13 Opinions

a I am on my way. **I should be home** in an hour.

b That's a good shop. **They should have** what you want.

Opinions can be expressed with **should** and **ought to.** The speaker has some information already and on that basis, he supposes or presumes the outcome but not in absolute terms (▶ **11** above).

c Ask your teacher. **She ought to know** the answer.

d Carlos speaks Spanish. **He should be able to** translate this.

e The tenth is a Sunday. **They shouldn't be** at work then.

14 a **You should finish your homework** before you watch TV.

b **We shouldn't leave today's work** for tomorrow.

c **He oughtn't to let people** take advantage of him.

d **He ought to pay more attention** to his own advantage.

e **I should write to Tom** more often than I do.

15 a It's a small shop. **They wouldn't have what you want.**

b Tom doesn't speak Spanish. **He wouldn't be able to translate.**

c Don't ask her. **She wouldn't know the answer to that.**

d It's a working day. **They wouldn't be at home,** then.

16 a Peter left long ago. **He'll be home by this time.**

b Joe spent years in Mexico. **He'll know Spanish well.**

c Mary studies hard. **She won't fail the examination.**

d It's the biggest shop in London. **You'll find everything there.**

e Go by bus. **It won't take long at this time of day.**

17 Must; can't; should/ought to

The tall man in the middle is wearing a gold chain. **He must be the Mayor.** The pretty girl on his right **can't be his wife** — she's too young. **She must be his daughter,** I suppose. Some people think that our Mayor **ought to have the President's position.** Certainly, **he ought to have a place** in the government. **They should make him a minister,** in my opinion. Who knows? Perhaps they will, probably they won't.

The speaker's opinion expresses recommendations to himself or someone else, about an obligation or a duty; someone **is not doing** what he **should do** or he **is doing** something that he **should not do.** This is firm advice or a strong reminder about an obligation.

In **13** above, affirmative opinions can be with **ought to** and **should** as in the examples. We can state a negative opinion with **wouldn't** or **would not** to avoid **shouldn't** and **oughtn't to** when we do not mean to confuse this meaning with a negative obligation as in **14** above.

Will, won't (will not): will is often **'ll.** With **should, ought to** and **wouldn't,** speakers do not mean that what they say is quite certain; they mention probability and leave room for doubt or error.

Will and **won't** express opinions more definitely, with more certainty; the speaker feels little or no doubt about what he or she says.

All of these can express opinions with certainty. **Must** and **can't** express absolute opinions; the speaker refers to the facts of the matter (**11** above). With **should** and **ought to,** speakers refer to non-fact; they recommend, advise that non-fact should become fact, but often with no expectation that this will happen.

18 Offers and requests for services

Shall I
Shall we
	make some fresh coffee for you?
	look after Billy for them next
	  week?
	return these books to the library
	  for her?
	post your letters in town for you?

Will you **Would you** **Could you**	make some fresh coffee, please? look after Billy next week? return Mother's books to the library? post these letters in town for her?

Shall, will, would, could: first persons, singular and plural, offer a service to someone usually by way of a question with **Shall . . .? Can . . .?** is informal but not necessarily familiar in manner: **Can I help you** madam? in a shop, for example.

A more or less polite request for a service begins with **Will** and more politely with **Would** or **Could:**
eg **Would it be possible** for you to do this, please?
Without these *auxiliary* + *subject* phrases, the sentence is imperative, ie an order, more than a request.

19 Acceptance of offers of service

If you will please **If you would please** **If you could please**	make some coffee. look after our dog. post these letters.

If you will/would/could: when the speaker accepts an offer of service, he often answers with an **if** phrase. Answers to **Shall . . .?** questions in the first table in **18** above appear opposite. These phrases can also come before a very polite request for a service, with an imperative verb. The imperative phrase alone can be an order and is often less than polite.

20 Requests for information

a **Could/Can you** tell me the way to St Paul's, please?

b **Could/Can you** direct me to London Airport, please?

c **Could/Can** anyone show me how to use this machine?

d **Could/Can** you tell me the right time, please?

Requests for information begin with **Could** or **Can. Could** is more formal, and shows a little more respect for the person whose answer we want. **Can** is informal, but not disrespectful.

21 Persistence

a Jack is a very difficult person. He knows when he's wrong but **he 'will argue. He 'will have the last word,** about everything.

b Joe has to pay six different parking fines. As **he 'will leave his car** just anywhere and **'won't park it properly,** I'm not sorry for him.

c Ann feels sleepy. Well, **she 'will sit up half the night** with a book and **'won't wear reading glasses!**

Will + *base verbs:* **will** is for all persons, singular and plural, is often said with stress and does not become **'ll**. The negative **will not** can sometimes be **won't** in conversation, with stress. Generally, when people repeatedly do the same silly, wrong, unpleasant or harmful things, we say **they will not learn; they will not stop.** They persist, they are stubborn. They do not mean to change their ways. Notice that **will** here refers to the general present time; it is NOT an auxiliary in a future tense.

22 Personal habit in past time

a In those days, **we'd always take a walk** before lunch.

b **We would always have our dogs** with us, then.

c In summer, **Bill would go fishing** on fine days.

d He seldom caught fish but **he would always try.**

e **Grandma would often get up** to watch the sunrise.

f **She would sit** in her rocking chair, at the window.

g **There used to be** *a block of flats here.

h Our family **used to live** on the top floor.

i That factory **used to make** writing ink.

j People **used to need it** before ball-points were invented.

*a block of flats (Br) = an apartment block (Am)

Would: people did whatever they did in the past as a matter of personal habit. They repeatedly did the same thing, by intention. The activities were characteristic of the person. **Would** is for all persons, singular and plural, and sometimes in conversation becomes **'d.** **Would** and **used to** in **a-f** opposite can be used one for the other, but **would** (past of **will**) shows personal intention. **Used to** does not show this and **would** could not stand instead of **used to** in examples **g-j** (▶ **Chapter 21, B1-3** for **used to).**

23 Preference

I/We You/They He/She	would 'd	rather fly rather drive rather walk	than go by train. than travel by coach. than wait here.

You We He	had 'd	better	call a doctor at once. get in touch with the police. not move the body. do as I say — or else!

We use **would rather** for all persons. The subject expresses a preference for one or two or more possibilities. **Would** can be **'d** in conversation

Had better expresses the speaker's opinion and suggests that, if you prefer not to take his advice, the consequence may be serious or unpleasant.

24 Command and request

The police propose The council agrees Joe suggested We decided They will advise	that	drivers cyclists we everybody you	*should	not drink. co-operate. take a test. use seat-belts. wear a helmet.

***Should** usually appears in Br but often does not appear in Am; we can have (Am) *subject* + *base verb* in affirmative **that** clauses. eg The police propose **that drivers take a test.** but They propose that drivers **should not drink.** In very formal style, such as the law uses, we also have *subject* + *base verb* without **should** in Br.

We use **should** + *base verb* for all persons, singular and plural. The usual meanings of some verbs express a command, request, decision, a suggestion or a proposal:
eg **advise, agree, ask, authorise,** . **command, decide, demand, expect, forbid, intend, order, prefer, promise, propose, recommend, remind (someone), request, suggest, order.**
These are the most common of such verbs. Generally, these verbs have their own subjects; a **that** clause with its own subject can follow. The verb in the **that** clause can be **should** + *base verb* and refers to any time after the activity in the first clause.

25 Let: proposals and suggestions

a Now we're all here, **let's start dancing.**

b **Let's go** to the harbour and see the ships.

c **Let's not take the dog** this time, Tom.

d **Don't let's take the dog.** He goes into the water.

e **Let's walk** all the way **Let's not get** a bus.

Let us (Lets) + *base verb*: speakers make suggestions and proposals for doing something which the speakers and the others will do together, if they agree to the proposal.

Let us not or **Let's not** + base verb is the usual negative form. In familiar conversation we sometimes say, **Don't let's** quarrel. or **Don't let's** waste time. etc.

26 Obligation: need . . .? needn't

a 'Need I type the whole page again for one error?' '**No, you needn't.** Just correct the error, please.'

b 'Need the staff all start and finish work together?' '**No, they needn't,** but **everyone must start** before ten.'

c 'Need Tom drive so fast? Ninety miles an hour!' '**He has to hurry now.** We were in a jam for ages.'

Need Jane	**take** this medicine?	No, she **needn't.**
Need Ann	**take** the dog, too?'	She **doesn't have to.**
Need she	**work** such long **hours?**	Yes, she **must/has to.**
Need you	**tell** anyone about this?	No, we **don't have to.**
Need we	**mention** this to Tom?	Yes, we **must.**
Need you	**get** a licence?	Yes, we **have to.**

The speaker asks whether obligation, compulsion or necessity is the reason for an activity or not. **Need not** or **needn't** means that there is no obligation, no compulsion and no necessity; do this or don't do this, as you wish. As a result, you, or whoever the subject is, will probably decide not to do what isn't necessary. The answer to a **Need . . .?** question can be affirmative: **Yes, she must. I'm sorry, but you'll have to . . .** etc (▶ 7-8 above).

27 Have, get: causative

a '**I'll have the baker send** some extra bread.' 'Could you **get the baker to slice** the bread?'

b 'This phone isn't working. **Have someone fix it,** now.' '**I'll get the man** from the telephone company **to come.**'

c 'Joe got the other side's lawyers to agree at last.' '**They'll have him pay** their costs and losses, of course.'

d 'We'll have twenty men work overtime for a week.' '**You'll get them to do the job** in time, for more pay.'

Have and **get** both take all the usual tense forms and auxiliaries; in this way they act like ordinary finite verbs and differ from other modal auxiliaries. **NOTE** (*Subject* + **have**) + (*object* + *base verb*) and (*Subject* + **get**) + (*object* + **to** + *base verb*). The subjects of **have** and **get** cause the objects to perform the activity in the base verb. The objects are persons. In the personal causative, **have** often shows that the subject speaks with authority — he/she has the right, rank or power to **have people do things.** This is less so in Am; **have and get . . . to** are practically the same.

28a I'm short of money. **I'll get Ann to lend** me some until tomorrow.

b If they're in a hurry, **they'll get Tom to drive** them to the station.

c If he does that, **I'll get him to do** the shopping on his way back.

d **We must try to get** these youngsters to rise earlier in the mornings.

Get someone to do something does not necessarily mean use of authority; often diplomacy, tact, personal charm, skill, persuasion are what we use to get someone to do something.

29a This old clock is quite valuable. **Can you get it to work?**

b I can, but perhaps **I won't get it to tell** the right time.

c **You'll never get this dog to eat fish.**

d This wood is still green. Nobody can **get it to burn well.**

e Push the car **to get it to start.** It's cold.

Get can have an impersonal object that performs the action of **to** + *base verb.*

30a Bob **has** special shoes **made** for him. He **gets** them **made** by an expert shoemaker.

b '**I must have** my glasses and eyes **checked.**' '**You can get** that **done** at the local clinic.'

c '**Would you get** these letters **typed** today?' '**I'd like to have** them **posted** this evening.'

d **They're having** all policewomen **trained** in judo. **They get** them **taken** to a gymnasium, daily.

e '**You should get** yourself **interested** in your job.' '**My employer got** me **interested** in looking for another job.'

(Have/get) + *object* + *past participle*: the subjects of **have** and **get** cause something to happen to their objects.
  I shall have / get my teeth **examined.** = I shall have/get a dentist.
  The dentist will examine my teeth. = my teeth will be examined by the dentist.
That is to say, we use past participles of transitive verbs, and in a passive sense.

C Modal auxiliaries: progressive

You	may	be waiting.
They	might	be working overtime.
She	could	be living very quietly.
He	should	be saving money.
The men	must	be having difficulties.
The others	needn't	be feeling unhappy.
You all	can't	be telling the truth.

Modal + **be** + *-ing participle*: modal auxiliaries that can normally go with the base form of the verb (with or without **to**) can also appear in progressive constructions. In modal usages, **have** and **get** can have progressive forms of their own and do not follow this pattern. We mention activities that are in progress now during the present time, or at any period in future time that suits the general meaning of the whole sentence or dialogue.

Modal auxiliaries: perfect progressive

They	might	have been	making a fortune.
You	could	have been	saving money.
She	must	have been	earning a good salary.
People	ought to	have been	working very hard.
He	should	have been	feeling sorry.
We	couldn't	have been	hearing the truth.
Father	needn't	have been	waiting for a bus.
Who (?)	can't	have been	having trouble.

Modal auxiliaries: perfect

They	might have	gone out later.
You	could have	arrived in time.
She	wouldn't have	tried to ring up.
He	should have	come on the early train.
I	*needn't have	said such a thing.
Tom	couldn't have	bought a new car.
Ann	can't have	expected that.
Who (?)	must have	known about that.

*She needn't have said such a thing.
= It was unnecessary but it happened.
He needn't have bought a car. = He had two already. Then there were three!

Auxiliary verbs: other uses

1 a Harry said that he **might go** to town that day if I **would** (go) too, although he **didn't have to** (go) then but **must** (go) before the end of the week. I said that I **could manage** without him and I **did** (manage) just as I **used to** (manage) before and **will** (manage) again when Harry has gone.

 b John **could have worked** in the office as his father **had** (worked) and **might be managing** the firm now as Father **was** (managing) all those years.

2 a I 'do thank you for a very pleasant evening at your home and **my sister does** (thank you) too.

 b My brother **has never heard** of an Aunt Bertha. Perhaps **our parents have** (heard).

 c **Ann is sitting** in the garden where **Tom was** (sitting) earlier. **She's reading** the same story as Tom **read.**

Modal + **have been** + -ing participle: we mention activities and happenings that have been or were or had been in progress during any period of time before now. The meanings of the modal auxiliaries do not change. **Can't** is usual with time before now, ie present perfect, and **couldn't** refers to any time in the past (▶ 17 above for **must/can't**).

Modal + **have** + past participle: we mention activities and happenings that have taken place at any time before now. The time can be indefinite or definite, eg **I could have caught** the early train **that day** / **I could have** arrived there **at three o'clock.** The modals **should have** / **ought to have** suggest doubt or definite negation of what the subject actually did (▶ 17 above). **He could have caught** the train. = I wonder whether he did catch it or, I know that he didn't catch it (because he hasn't arrived yet).

A complex verb phrase is a phrase that has tense auxiliaries or modal auxiliaries or both kinds in it, with a part of a finite verb. There are many examples in **C, D, E** above.

When a complex verb phrase has already appeared once in a sentence or short dialogue, we can use the first auxiliary again to avoid repetition of the whole phrase, if the subject of the verb is the same, or if two different subjects can go with the same form of the auxiliary.

Do/does; have/has; parts of **be:** we can use these but must take care to choose the forms that go with each subject, when they are different.

3 a He **might have offered you money** and he **might have offered advice.** = He might have offered money and advice.

b He **could have been waiting** for a bus as **everyone else was** (waiting for a bus) or for a friend, as I often **am** (waiting for a friend) near a bus stop.

If the form of the finite verb changes, we must have a complete new verb phrase; compare Tom **has gone** into the army and Peter **will go.** with — Tom **has gone** and Bill **has** (gone) too. When the objects are different, we repeat the whole verb phrase, or join the objects with **and,** sometimes with **or.**

4

	'Yes, we are.'
'Are you going to the party?'	'No, **I'm not.**'
	'If **I can.**'
'Are you coming in Tom's car?'	'I wish **I could.**'
	'If he is, then **I will** too.'

Generally, when a verb phrase has already appeared in full in a dialogue, the same or another speaker can use an auxiliary to stand for a whole verb phrase, whenever meaning is clear.

5 Sentence tags

'Uncle Jack **is** Mother's brother, **isn't he?**' 'Yes. He **isn't** her eldest brother, **is he?**' 'He **was born** in 1945, **wasn't he?**' 'He **went** to Canada in 1970, **didn't he?**' 'Uncle Jack still **writes** to Mother, **doesn't he?**' 'He **never married, did he?**' 'We **haven't** any cousins in Canada, **have we?**'

Sentence tags are interrogative in form, but they are not questions generally. Speakers add them to statements that other people easily agree with; the speaker does not expect an answer to his statement, he expects agreement. So the voice rises towards the end of a sentence tag only on occasions when we are really asking for information, not giving it.

Sentence tags come at the ends of sentences. They repeat any auxiliary verb that has already appeared in a spoken affirmative or negative sentence.

Simple tenses do not have **do/does** and **did** in their affirmative forms; we supply them for the sentence tags. We use the first auxiliary when there are two or more.

6 a 'Hello, I'm Tom Brown. **You remember** me, **don't you?**'

b 'Of course. **We lived** next door to you, **didn't we?**'

c '**You were** still at school then, **weren't you?**'

d '**I'll make** tea, **shall I? You'd like** some, **wouldn't you?**'

e '**We can have it** in the kitchen, **can't we?**'

f '**We needn't lay** the dining-room table, **need we?**'

Sentence tags are always interrogative form. Negative sentences take a plain interrogative sentence tag of *auxiliary subject pronoun,* eg **does he? will you? can I?** etc. Affirmative sentences take interrogative-negative sentence tags, eg **can't she? won't you? doesn't it? don't we?** etc.

7
  a Let's send a birthday telegram, **shall we?**
  b Let's do it now, before we forget, **shall we?**
  c Let's not waste any more time, **shall we?**

After **Let's**, the question tag is **shall we?** in both affirmative and negative sentences.

8
  a Be quiet, will you! Stand still, will you! Come here, please, **will you?** Sit down, please, **will you?** = Will you sit down, please?
  b Goodbye, Bob. Mind the traffic, won't you? Look after yourself, won't you? Drive carefully, won't you? Come home safe, won't you? Don't forget to ring me up, **will you?** Don't be too busy to have lunch, will you?

After imperatives, the question tag is **will you?** when the speaker gives a command or expresses anger, impatience and similar attitudes; **will you?** (or **will you!**) goes with both affirmative and negative. When the imperative expresses kindness, advice, affection and similar attitudes we have **won't you?** after affirmatives, and **will you?** after negatives.

9
  a 'That old building **used to be** a prison, **didn't it?**' 'I don't know. It **might have been, mightn't it?**'
  b 'Tom's father **used to own** that farm, **didn't he?**' 'Yes. We **used to stay** there in summer, **didn't we?**'
  c 'Tom and I **used to go** to school here, **didn't we?**' '**You did**, but **I didn't, did I?**'

After **used to**, we use **did they? did she?** etc in negative sentences, and **didn't they? didn't you?** etc after affirmative sentences. Forms such as **used he? usedn't she?** are almost dead nowadays, as sentence tags.

Auxiliary verbs: participation

1 Affirmative

  a I'm against war. **So is everyone else.**
  b John plays the guitar. **So does Jane.**
  c 'I went to their concert.' '**So did we.**'
  d They're coming to dinner with us. **So are you, I hope.**
  e Yes, I've already told Mary. **So has Ann.** She said so.
  f We'll meet again this evening. **So will they,** at seven.
  g She promised to help and **so did I.**

Speakers make statements about their own or other people's activities, opinions, feelings and so on. The speakers then add a phrase to say that others also take part in the activities or have the same feelings and opinions.
  Participation in affirmative activities: **so** + *auxiliary* + *subject*.
  Participation in negative activities: **neither/nor** + *auxiliary* + *subject*.

2 Negative

  a Tom won't be here on Sunday. **Neither will Ann.**
  b They mightn't come before Tuesday. **Nor might I.**
  c I mustn't stay longer. **Neither must he.**
  d Joe's story can't be right but **neither can yours.**

A statement and participation phrase can make one sentence. We join them with **and** or **but** before **so** and **neither.** We do not use **nor** after conjunctions.

NOTE simple agreement with a previous affirmative statement does not follow these patterns,

e **He isn't telling** the whole truth. **Neither are you.**

f **She wouldn't listen** to me and **neither would he.**

g **I couldn't talk** to them but **neither could the doctor.**

3 **a** **Bob loves** sweet things. **So did his father.**

b **She can** always find work. **So could you,** if you tried.

c '**We do our best** for our girls.' 'So would **I** (if I had any).'

d **Tom doesn't want** to become a farmer. **Neither did Father.**

e In the end, **Father left** the land. **So should we,** too.

4 **a** 'You **didn't clean** your shoes today, Bob.' 'I **'did clean** them but I **'didn't press** my trousers.'

b 'When **will you finish** typing my letter?' 'But I **'have finished.** It's on your desk.'

c 'You **don't know** Mr Jones, our manager, **do you?**' 'We **'do know** each other very well. We're old friends.'

d 'You're **not taking** your sister Ann with you.' 'I 'am taking Ann with me. **Ann 'will be** there.'

e 'John has left the firm, I hear.' 'John **'hasn't left.** He **'wouldn't** (leave them).'

eg '**Tom might** be here on Tuesday.' '**So he might.**' '**Mary could do** this job easily.' '**So she could.**'

The auxiliaries need not match for timing or mode. The statement can be one tense form, and if the participation phrase refers to another time and person, it will be in the tense and form for them.

All auxiliary verbs can take stress in speech, for emphasis. The affirmative forms of simple present and past tenses have their auxiliary verbs **do/does** and **did** in emphatic statements. Generally we use the full form of auxiliaries, eg **shall/will** not **'ll; have/has,** not **'ve, 's** etc Emphasis often contradicts or protests against a previous statement; it can also contrast a negative action with another positive action.

25 The passive voice

The table below shows the forms of regular verbs. Irregular verbs require their own past participles which can be seen in **Chapter 17.**
*These forms are almost never used; we use the passive forms that appear immediately above them.

		Active voice	Passive voice
Infinitive:	plain	(to) advise	**(to) be advised**
	progressive	(to) be advising	**(to) be being advised**
	perfect	(to) have advised	**(to) have been advised**
Imperative:		advise	**be advised**
Present:	simple	advise/advises	**am/are/is advised**
	progressive	am/are/is advising	**am/are/is being advised**
	perfect	have/has advised	**have/has been advised**
	perfect progressive	have/has been advising	**have/has been being advised***
Past:	simple	advised	**was/were advised**
	progressive	was/were advising	**was/were being advised**
	perfect	had advised	**had been advised**
	perfect progressive	had been advising	**had been being advised***
Future:	simple	shall/will advise	**shall/will be advised**
	progressive	shall/will be advising	**shall/will be being advised**
	perfect	shall/will have advised	**shall/will have been advised**
	perfect progressive	shall/will have been advising	**shall/will have been being advised***
Future-in-the-past:	simple	should/would advise	**should/would be advised**
	progressive	should/would be advising	**should/would be being advised***
	perfect	should/would have advised	**should/would have been advised**
	perfect progressive	should/would have been advising	**should/would have been being advised***

1 Transitive verbs

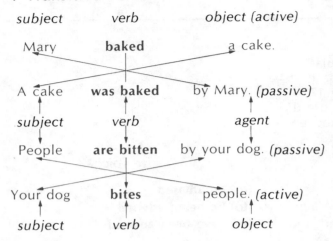

subject	verb	object (active)
Mary	**baked**	a cake.

A cake	**was baked**	by Mary. *(passive)*
subject	verb	agent

People	**are bitten**	by your dog. *(passive)*

Your dog	**bites**	people. *(active)*
subject	verb	object

Transitive verbs are verbs that have direct objects. In the order *subject + verb + object* (eg **Your dog bites people.**) we say that the verb is in the active voice — the subject and verb act and do something to the object or produce the object, eg **Mary baked a chocolate cake.** Only transitive verbs can be passive. Their objects can become subjects of the same verbs in their passive forms, as receivers of the actions of these passive verbs.

2 Passive agent

This play was written by Shakespeare.
= Shakespeare wrote this play.
A story was told by the teacher.
= The teacher told a story.

The passive agent (**by** Mary, **by** your dog etc) names the doer of the activity in a passive verb; the doer would be subject of an active verb (▶ also **8** below).

3 Passive verbs

She **is**	advised	by her doctor.
She **is being**	taken	by a friend.
She **has been**	told	by her husband.
She **will be**	seen	by her parents.
She **would be**	sent	by her employers.
She **had been**	brought	by a policeman.
She **was**	helped	by a neighbour.

The passive voice form of the base verb is **be** + *past participle:* **be added, be bought, be called** etc. We make tenses from all the parts of **be,** and **be** with other auxiliaries; the past participle stands without change as in the table opposite.

4 Uses of the passive voice

a They say that the summer will be very hot.
It **is said** that the summer will be very hot.
People tell me that I'm looking well again.
I **am told** that I'm looking well again.

b The postman delivers the mail about midday.
The mail **is delivered** about midday.
We shall serve lunch at one o'clock exactly.
Lunch **will be served** at one o'clock exactly.

c Ann Lee saw him running out of the bank.
He **was seen running** out of the bank.

A transitive verb can be in a passive form when we do not wish to name or identify the doer of an action because to do so would not add any information to the sentence, because the identity of the doer is already clear enough, in the overall meaning of the sentence, or because we have our own right or wrong reasons for not naming the doer — we, the speakers, are not giving full information. Often, there is no agent in a passive sentence.

5 Active verbs with two objects

	active	direct	indirect
	Someone sends	red roses	to Ann =
	Someone sends	Ann	red roses.

passive

Red roses **are sent** to Ann.

Ann **is sent** red roses.

a They offered us some lemonade.
Some lemonade **was offered** to us.
We **were offered** some lemonade.

b We'll buy a new bike for Flora.
A new bike **will be bought** for Flora.
Flora **will be bought** a new bike.

c Mr Cross is teaching them algebra.
Algebra **is being taught** to them by Mr Cross.
They **are being taught** algebra by Mr Cross.

Subject + active verb + indirect object (without preposition) + direct object

Verbs can have two objects — one direct object and one indirect object. Some but not all verbs with two objects can have the indirect object first without a preposition: **Someone sends Ann red roses.** Verbs that follow this pattern are:

> **ask, bring, buy, deny, give, grant, hand, leave** (as in **please leave a note for me), lend, offer, owe, promise, read, send, show, teach.**

In the passive voice, indirect objects keep their prepositions: **Roses were sent to Ann.**
The prepositions are generally **to** and **for** but ask a question **of** someone. Both objects can serve as passive subjects; the passive verb is singular or plural to go with the subject (**a-c**).
NOTE other verbs have indirect objects that must follow the prepositions; these indirect objects cannot be passive subjects.

6

> **Have** = own, possess, eg They have a large house/three children.
> **Have** (causative), eg We had the doctor come.
> **Lack,** eg The soup lacks salt. He lacks experience.
> **Hold** = accommodate, eg This hall holds six hundred people comfortably.
> **Become** = suit, eg Your new hair style becomes you.
> **Suit** = be convenient for, eg Does five o'clock on Tuesday suit you?
> **Fit,** eg None of those old clothes fit me nowadays; I'm too fat/thin.
> **Resemble** = look like, eg Ann resembles her mother.

Some transitive verbs do not take the passive voice in some of their meanings. The list opposite shows them. Some of them can be passive with a change of meaning, eg New locks **were fitted** to all the doors. The pattern *subject + verb + object + effect,* eg **The people made him President.** can have only the object to serve as a passive subject: **He was made President** by the people. The effect — **President** — cannot be a passive subject. Common verbs in this pattern are: **appoint, create, declare, elect, make, promote, vote.** Notice also that when the object of a verb is a reflexive pronoun (**-self/selves, each other/one another**) it cannot become the subject.

7 Passive voice of prepositional and phrasal verbs

a They **are looking for** the stolen banknotes.
The stolen banknotes **are being looked for*.**

A prepositional verb is one that needs a preposition after it to complete its meaning, and its direct object follows the preposition. For example, the verb

b Someone **will take care of** the children.
The children **will be taken care of***.

c People aren't perfect. We must **allow for** human error.
Human error must **be allowed for.** We aren't perfect.

d A traffic jam **held us up** for an hour.
We were held up for an hour in a traffic jam.

e You **can't put up with** such laziness.
Such laziness **can't be put up with***.

*In English sentences, very often and quite correctly, the last word is a preposition.

8 Passive agents

a The tree was cut down **with a saw.**
b It was cut into pieces **by two men.**
c The job was done **with heavy axes.**
d Most of my work is done **with a pen.**
e This cloth is made at home **by hand.**
f Farm work in the fields is done **with tractors.**

look for something/someone has a different meaning from **look after** something/someone. Prepositional verbs are all transitive; most of them can appear in passive forms. When they are passive, the preposition must be with them, to keep the meaning of the verb.

Some phrasal verbs can have direct objects and can become passive. Their adverbs/prepositions must appear with the passive forms, to keep the meaning right. If there are two particles they must both appear.

In **1-3** above we can see that people and living things can be doers of a passive action (they are passive agents)
I was bitten **by** your dog.
John was helped **by** a policeman.
When we mention tools or instruments as doers the preposition is usually **with.**

26 Conditional sentences

A Real conditions

Every conditional sentence contains two parts: one part is a conditional clause (with its own verb) and the other part is an outcome clause (with its own verb). Conditional clauses begin with **if;** the outcome can be affirmative or negative in real terms.

A real condition makes a clear, normal statement of fact; the outcome becomes fact when we perform the activity in the condition. Real conditional sentences are very often cause (conditional) and effect (outcome): If someone does this, something happens or something will happen, as in the examples at **1** and **2** opposite.

1

conditions	outcomes
If we hurry	we'll catch that train.
If we leave now	we'll be there in good time.
If we take a taxi	we shan't miss the train.

2

imperative cause	effect
Press this button	and the light comes on.
Turn the switch	and the door opens.
Pull the cord	and a bell will ring.

conditional clause	effect (outcome)
If you press the button	the light comes on.
If you turn the switch	the door opens.
If you pull the cord	a bell will ring.

3

present condition		present outcome
It we need	something	you provide it.
If she wants	help	I always give it.
If they ask for	food	he does what he can.

Real conditions all refer to present time or to future time; we use present tense forms only. Generally, **shall/will** future forms do NOT appear in conditions (▶ **8-9** below). Outcomes, when they refer to present time, can be in a present tense and, when they refer to future time they can be in a future tense. Sometimes we have an imperative outcome: **If this happens, do that.**

future condition	future outcome
If we need something	we'll buy it.
If she wants help	she'll ask for it.
If they ask for food	we'll make sandwiches.

future condition	imperative outcome
If anyone phones	please let me know.
If Tom comes in	ask him to call back.
If anyone asks for me	say I'm at a meeting.

4

outcomes	conditions
The light comes on	**if you press the button.**
We always give it	**if she asks for help.**
I'll buy more food	**if we need it.**
Ask Tom to call back	**if he phones me.**

Usually, conditional clauses come first, but outcome clauses can come first in the sentence, too. Speakers generally put the part that seems more important in first place.

123

5 Previous (perfect) present time

If she has read today's paper	she already knows.
If she has heard the radio news	she'll be worried.

present progressive	
If he isn't taking medicine	he won't get well.
If he isn't taking exercise	he'll be ill again.

future perfect	
If you haven't called before then	I won't wait.
If Tom hasn't arrived before seven	she'll be annoyed.

Any present tense can appear in a real condition and refer to either present or future time. The outcome can be either present or future with its own verb. Present tenses stand for future time, as well as for present time.

6

I'll speak to you	as soon as before once when after by the time	supper is served. everyone has arrived. Tom comes in. Ann goes out. they've gone to bed. the clock strikes ten.
He'll tell us		
We'll hear it all		

Time conditions: **after, as, before, once, till/until, when, whenever, while** and **as soon as, by the time.** These can all introduce a **temporal** or time conditional clause, in exactly the same way as **if. Shall/will** future tenses do not appear in temporal clauses; present tenses can refer to either present or future time. **NOTE when** can introduce non-conditional interrogative clauses
eg When shall we meet again?
   I don't know **when they will meet.**

7

If you don't	work	I won't pay.
If he doesn't	hurry	we shan't be in time.
If they haven't	**paid** me	I can't pay you.

- **a** **Unless you work** (I doubt whether you will work) I won't pay you.
- **b** **Unless he hurries** (and he isn't hurrying) we shan't be in time.
- **c** I can't pay you **unless they have paid me** (and they haven't/and I don't think they will).
- **d** **Unless they've had lunch** (improbable) they'll be hungry when they arrive.
- **e** I'll make some tea, **unless you don't want any** (very improbable that you don't).
- **f** Mother will answer the phone, **unless she isn't at home,** of course (improbable — Mother is nearly always at home on Sundays).

Unless can usually replace **if... not** in negative conditions. **If...** and **if...not** real conditions are open conditions — the speaker does not express feelings that the condition will become fact or that it will not become fact — one or the other is equally probable.

Unless conditions, whether negative or affirmative, refer to improbability in the speaker's mind. The terms of both affirmative and negative conditions with **unless** seem improbable.

8 **If it will help you,** mention my name. I can go to the conference **if the firm will pay.**
If you will marry me, I must buy two rings.

9 a 'Are you taking part in the march tomorrow?' 'I'll be there, **if you'll come too.'**

b 'Will Ann join the Nature Lovers' Society?' 'She will but only **if Tom will,** too.'

c Will you vote for the other party's candidate?' 'I certainly will not, even **if you will.'**

d 'Will you volunteer to give blood to the hospital?' **'If others will,** we will too.'

10 a **Whether** we travel by air **or** first class by train the cost will be the same.

b **Whether** he wants to **or** (doesn't want to)/not, he must pay his taxes.

c **Whether** the sun is shining **or** snow is falling, we have to go out to our jobs.

d You can borrow books from the town library **whether** you live here **or** in the country.

11

a Provided (that)	he drives carefully,	I'll lend them my car.
b As long as	they don't drink at all,	they may go to the party.
c On condition (that)	they return before midnight,	we'll go with them.

Unless	he drives carefully they don't drink they return by then	I won't lend my car. I won't let them go. we'll take a taxi.

B Unreal conditions

1 a If pigs **had** wings, they would fly. (they don't have them) (they don't fly)

b If I **were** king, you would be queen. (I am not king) (you cannot be queen)

c If wishes **were** horses, beggars would ride. (wishes aren't horses) (beggars don't ride horses)

When an **if** clause refers to a future happening which immediately affects present activity, **will** can appear. Notice that **will** is not always an auxiliary and can have other meanings more like **want, wish, agree.**

Conditional agreement: the speaker or subject is willing to take part in an activity, on condition that someone else also takes part in it. We use **will** in the condition and may also express non-participation (**c** opposite). Normal present tenses can appear in these conditions, instead of **will,** but with less emphasis on willingness to take part.

Whether. . .or: there are two conditions — **whether** we do this **or** we do that **the outcome will be the same.**
NOTE **whether** can also report non-conditional questions to which **yes/no** answers are usual:
She asks **whether you will be free tonight (or not).**

Other introductions to real conditions are: **provided** (or **providing) that, as long as/so long as, on condition that.** These all have the basic meaning of **if. Unless** is the direct opposite in meaning: it means **except if** or **if. . .not.**

For unreal conditions, we use the past tense forms of verbs only, and **should/would** auxiliary verbs (the past forms of **shall/will**) in outcome clauses, with the base verb. Although we use past tense forms of verbs we refer only to present and future time.

125

Were is for all persons, singular and plural, in unreal conditions. In familiar conversation, some people do sometimes use **was** with singular subjects, but **were** is always correct.

In these examples, the conditions state impossibilities and imaginary situations.

Unreal conditions have this name because the conditions do not mention real facts or probabilities. Affirmative unreal conditions can express impossibility, extreme improbability and the speaker does not expect that anyone will fulfil the condition; Someone might, if the terms of the condition allow a small degree of probability. When the conditions are impossible or doubtful, outcomes are equally impossible or doubtful.

We can use the past forms **could** and **might** in place of **would**, when the outcome is not absolutely improbable or impossible: somebody **could/might** fulfil the terms of the condition, and the outcome **could/might** follow.

The sentences in table **2** can have adverbs or phrases that refer to present time or to future time, but not past.

2			
If	I were younger, I	**would**	stay in London.
	he knew English, he	**could**	work abroad.
	she came with me, we	**might**	study there.
	everyone agreed, they		go into business.

> ...I would stay in London **now / for a few years.**
> ...he could work abroad **immediately / eventually.**
> ...we might study there **next year / sometime.**
> ...they'd go into business **now / later / next week.**

Negative unreal conditions generally state negative terms which are contrary to actual fact and have outcomes which are also contrary to the facts. Negative outcomes can be understood in affirmative terms; affirmative outcomes can be understood in negative terms.

3 **a** If I **didn't know** him I **wouldn't trust** him.
(But I do know him) (I do trust him)

  b If he **weren't** Ann's brother I **wouldn't believe** him.
(He is Ann's brother) (I do believe him)
If he **didn't tell** the truth I**'d refuse** to listen.
(He is a truthful man) (I don't refuse to listen)
If we **didn't recognise** him I**'d ask** his name.
(We do recognise him) (we needn't ask his name)

4

If		
	I made a fortune	**would** it matter?
	he **had** millions	it **would** make a difference.
	she **owned** a gold mine	it **wouldn't** be yours.
	they **built** a place	what **would** you say?
	this **ever** happened	what *****should** we do?

*****should** can also mean **ought to**; there can be confusion of meaning sometimes with formally correct **should** for first persons. Often we say **would,** equally correctly, to avoid confusion.

An unreal condition is often a statement of some imaginary happening in the present or future time: **If this happened, what would follow?** Generally, in unreal conditions, imagination (**Let's pretend** or **Let's suppose this happened** now or in the future) is a strong element.

5

If you	stopped smoking	you'd feel better.
	took more exercise	you'd lose weight.
	kept to a strict diet	you wouldn't get fat.

If		
	he didn't smoke,	his health would improve.
	she didn't use her car,	her weight would go down.
	they didn't over-eat,	their costs would be lower.

We can advise and recommend that others **should do this** or **should not do that,** and we can feel that we shall have no success at all; the others will act as they always have done before. More often, we do not wish to speak too strongly; we do not wish to seem to force advice and opinions on others. The unreal conditional expresses these feelings.

6 If + *subject* + (**were to** + *base verb);*
Were + *subject* (+ **to** + *base verb)*

a If she were to inherit a fortune, I'd be delighted.

b If you were to ask Jane, she mightn't agree.

c If he were to take more exercise, he'd feel better.

d Were I to lose my job, I might find a better one.

e If they were to economise, they wouldn't need a loan.

f Were I to tell you what he said you'd never believe it!

Unreal conditions of the kinds in **4** and **5** above can appear with **were to** + *base verb.* The negative form seldom appears in conditions. When **were not to** appears, it can be the past of **must not,** eg **If they were not to leave this room, why have they gone out?** (▶ **Chapter 24, B**). **Were I to . . .** is a stylish variation meaning the same as **If I were to . . .**

7 If I should/Should I + **base verb**

a I'll be home by seven. **If I should be late,** please start dinner without me.

b We don't expect visitors today, but **if anyone should call,** they'll be welcome.

c Should I be late, please start without me. **Should anyone call,** they'll be welcome.

If + *subject* (**should** + *base verb):* the speaker refers to a probability which is not at all a certainty; it might happen, more probably it might not happen. **Should** + *subject* + *base verb* is more formal; the meaning does not change (**C**).

8

Provided that	they paid in advance,	I would do business with them.
	they used their own transport.	we wouldn't lose anything.
As long as	we could insure the goods,	we could consider their offers.
	we had a firm contract,	they might serve our firm very well.
On condition that	they would order regularly	we could agree about special prices.

9 a If they didn't pay, I wouldn't do business.
(They do pay) (I do business with them)

b I couldn't pay, if I didn't have the money.
(I can pay) (I have the money)

c He wouldn't pay **unless he had the money.**
(He wouldn't pay) (except, if he had the money)

d He would pay **unless he hadn't any money.**
(He would pay) (except if he didn't have money)

We have seen in **3** and **4** above that the terms in unreal conditions are generally contrary to actual fact: unreal affirmative terms are in contrast with negative facts; unreal negative terms are in contrast with affirmative facts. The terms are not always in absolute opposition to the facts; they can express the speaker's feelings of doubt or improbability (**5** and **6** above). We can use the conditional expressions in **A11** above in unreal conditions too. These are open conditions and might or might not become fact.

Unless in unreal conditions has a strong sense of improbability; — the condition is an open one but the speaker feels or knows that fulfilment is highly improbable. So **unless** does not usually replace **if ... did not** which expresses negative conditions as contrasts with real facts. **Unless = except if.**

C Unreal past

1

If I had seen you, I would have spoken.
(I didn't see you) (I didn't speak)
If she hadn't been there, she wouldn't have seen him.
(She was there) (she did see him)
If the car hadn't broken down (it did), we'd have arrived there earlier (we arrived late).
If Ann and Tom had married each other (they didn't), they wouldn't have needed two houses (but they did need two, one each).

The unreal past takes the form of **If** + *past perfect tense* with an outcome in **should/would** + (**have** + *past participle*). In grammar, the unreal past is a conditional form. However, when we talk about happenings that took place at any time before now, we already know what actually happened then; it is too late now to make conditions about it. What we do in the unreal past is mention that **if that had happened otherwise (differently), the outcome would have happened otherwise, too.** The condition and the outcome are equally unreal.

2 a If you had saved your money, **you wouldn't need to borrow now.**

Because of what happened or did not happen in the past or at any time before

b She would need false teeth (now) if she hadn't taken good care of her own all the time.

c If Joe had continued his studies, **he'd be Dr Joe Ray today.**

d I'd still be standing at the bus stop, if Dick hadn't given me a lift.

now, there can be an unreal conditional outcome now.

3 **a** **Had you saved** your money, you would have it.

b **Had the car not broken down,** we'd have been early.

c I would have spoken, **had I seen you there.**

d She wouldn't have seen him, **had she not been there.**

Had + *subject* + *past participle:* this is the pattern for the unreal past in careful, more formal styles of speech and writing. There is no short negative form.

4 **a** Tom wouldn't have stayed in bed all day — **unless he felt ill.**

b He wouldn't have been at home on a Monday — **unless he'd asked for a day off.**

c He might have supposed it was Sunday. **Unless he'd gone mad,** he couldn't have thought it was Sunday.

Unless = except if . . . in unreal conditions generally: **unless** conditions usually mention some more or less probable exception that might explain the happenings in the outcomes.

5 **a** **Tom could have helped,** if you had asked him.

b If he had been here, **I might have asked him.**

c **I couldn't have done anything** if I hadn't borrowed some tools.

d If you hadn't met Professor Black before, **you must have heard of him,** surely.

Instead of **should/would have** in outcome clauses, we can have other auxiliaries with perfect forms (▶ **Chapter 24**) and with their own meanings. Again, the grammatically correct **should have** for first persons is more often **would have,** equally correctly, to avoid confusion with **should have = ought to have.**

27 Non-finite verbs

1 General description

These are forms of ordinary verbs but they cannot form tenses by themselves; they cannot show singular and plural number; they cannot appear with modal auxiliary verbs (**can, must, may** etc); and they do not have subjects of their own, in the ways that finite verbs do.

a I'd **prefer to wait.**
Ann **likes to dance/dancing** with Tom.

As these are verb forms, we can talk of non-finite verb clauses. The subject of a verb in the main clause of a sentence is also the subject of an infinitive or **-ing** participle in the same sentence.

b She wants to see **me** today.
We heard **a man shout for help.**
She spoke to **a girl sitting at a desk.**
Meeting old friends is a great pleasure.

Non-finite parts of transitive verbs can have objects of their own, and prepositional phrases.

c We heard **a man shout for help.** (A man shouted.)
She spoke to **a girl** (the girl was) **sitting at a desk.**

Infinitive and **-ing** participles often follow objects of other transitive verbs. These objects are then also subjects for the infinitive and participle. Compare: **She** called a taxi, **hoping to save time.** She called **a taxi passing the front door.** We need a comma after the object when it is not also the subject of the **-ing** participle or infinitive. **They** will blame **me, to keep** Jane out of trouble.

2 *Infinitive with to* (**to** + base verb)
She wants **to see you today.**
I'd prefer **to wait until tomorrow.**

3 *Infinitive without to* (base verb)
I saw someone **go into the house.**
We heard a man **shout for help.**

4 *-ing participle*
She called a taxi, **hoping to save time.**
Taking her handbag, she left the house.
She spoke to a girl **sitting at a desk.**

5 *-ing gerund*
Meeting old friends again is a great pleasure,
We don't like your **staying out** so late.

6 *Past participle*
Repaired and **painted,** the boat will look fine.

Past participles stand for a whole passive voice phrase, or a perfect verb

They bought the house for £50,000, **paid** in cash.
Returned to England, we started to look for a house.

tense: The price of the house **was paid** in cash. **When we have** repaired the boat it will look fine.

A The infinitive

1 Without to (base verb)

feel, hear, notice, observe, see, smell, watch; make = force, oblige, compel; let = allow, permit. **Help** can have a bare or a **to**-infinitive after it.

a **I felt** something **touch** my ear.

b **We heard** something **fly** against the window.

c Then **we saw** an insect **fall** onto the floor.

d Joe **was made to pick it up. I made** him **put** it out.

e I wouldn't **let** the poor thing **be killed.**

The infinitive without **to** is often called the bare infinitive; **not** comes before the bare infinitive to make it negative.

The particle **to** does not appear with infinitives after these verbs of perception, ie. verbs that express actions of the physical senses, and after **make** and **let**. When these verbs are in passive voice forms, the **to** infinitive form follows, NOT the bare infinitive. **Let** usually takes bare infinitives in the passive, too.

2

can, could; may, might; must, let, need; shall, will; should, would, have (have the doctor see her etc)

a Let's all meet tomorrow. We **could go** to the zoo.

b Tom **might lend** me his camera. We'll take pictures.

c 'Shall I buy a colour film?' 'No, you **needn't do** that.'

d Could we **have Tom develop** the film for us?

e I **must ask** him. It **should be** all right.

After most modal auxiliary verbs, we use the bare infinitive (base form) only. Exceptions are: **have (to), ought (to), be (to), used (to),** ▶ **Chapter 24.** Also, after expressions of preference, eg. **I'd rather . . ., I'd sooner . . .** and **You had better** we use bare infinitives only.

3

a We must try **not to spend** so much money.

b They decided **not to go away** on holiday.

c I shall advise them **not to buy** that house.

d Ask the boys **not to make** so much noise, please.

e We want to play football. He told us **not to play.**

Except for **1** and **2** above we always use **to** + *base verb* for the infinitive form. In the negative, **not** comes before **to**: **not to talk, not to go** etc.

4

		to see us. to help. to stay a few days. to look after Grandma. to talk to us. to tell us the news. to have tea with us.
Susan Tom Someone	**came** often **comes** **has come** **is coming** **will come** **had come** **was coming**	

The infinitive has neither tense nor person of its own (finite verbs have these). So the infinitive can refer to past, present or future; it refers to the same time as the verb in the main clause in the sentence.

5

It was kind	**of Susan**	to help us now.
It would be good	**of Tom**	to take care of Billy.
It is considerate	**of them**	to look after Grandma.

We can mention some personal manner in the subject: **It is/was** + *adjective* + **of** + *person*. We can also have the infinitive first: **To look after Grandma** was kind of **Susan**. **It** drops out of the sentence. The **of** phrase does not appear at the beginning of a sentence, as **for** phrases do (▶ **9** below).

6 Infinitive of purpose

We met He means She'll try They will come	**to discuss** business. **to catch** the bus. **to let** them know. **to help** the girls.

People do things for a purpose. The verb in a main clause can be any verb that makes sense with a following purpose clause or phrase. A **to** infinitive can express purpose. Verbs in main clauses can be intransitive or transitive.

They sent us a telegram	**to let** us know.
She wrote a letter	**to tell** me the news.
He phoned me at home	**to explain** the matter.

To **In order to** **So as to**	**save** time **speed** things up **avoid** delay	we sent a telex. I went, myself. she telephoned.

The infinitive purpose clause can be first in the sentence; also we can begin **In order to.** This is not necessary, but is a little more formal, with all infinitive purpose clauses. We can also use **So as to** when we offer a reason for unusual or extraordinary doings, eg **So as to . . . I went myself.**

She felt the sheets	**to make sure** they were dry.
I watched the man	**to see** what he'd do.
He smelt the milk	**to see** whether it was fresh.
I made a face	**to amuse** the baby.

In **A1** above, certain finite verbs appear with the bare infinitive. When these verbs express the means towards a purpose, the full infinitive is necessary.

7

Someone brought a cake	for the girls	to eat.
I'll make sandwiches	for them	to take.
We'll get some apples	for you	to nibble.
I've got some chocolate	for us	to share.

8 It is . . . + infinitive

It is a pleasure	to meet you again.
It was pleasant	to see old friends.
To meet you again = **This**	is a pleasure.
To see old friends = **That**	was a pleasure.

The main clause and the infinitive purpose clause can have different subjects. The subject phrase before an infinitive is: **for** + *noun or object pronoun.*

It + *state verb* (**appear, be, become, feel, look, seem, sound**) can be the first clause in a sentence: **It** + *state verb* + *adjective or noun; + infinitive clause.* If we put the infinitive clause first, **it** drops out of the sentence: a pronoun, usually **this** or **that** can stand for the whole infinitive clause. The pronouns in the examples opposite are subjects in their sentences; so, the infinitive clauses are also subjects. **It** stands for the infinitive subject that follows the **it** clause.

9

It seemed	unwise	to borrow so much money.
It appears	easy	to treat people like that.
It was	normal	to question the president.
It would be	unusual	to speak so frankly.
It may be	right	to remain silent.

a It would be unwise **for Joe to borrow** so much.

b **For him to borrow** so much would be unwise.

c **For Mary to speak** so frankly was unusual.

d **(For anyone) To remain** silent seems easy.

e **(For everyone) To question** is normal and right.

The infinitive clause can have its own subject (▶ 7 above). **For** + *noun or object pronoun* + *infinitive* can come first in the sentence. When there is no other subject and no **for** phrase, the speaker refers to everybody and anybody, including himself, in general terms.

10a It is **silly of you** to waste time like this. = **You are silly** to waste time like this.

b It is **silly for you** to waste time like this. = **The situation is silly**; it wastes your time.

c It is **helpful of Ann** to visit us so often. **Ann is helpful. = She gives help . . .**

d It is **helpful for Ann.** to visit us so often. = To visit us is helpful **for Ann. = Ann receives help.**

e It is **good for you** to eat fresh fruit. It was **good of you** to get some for me.

It + *state verb* + *adjective* + **of him** + *infinitive*: we mention some quality or value in a person eg **It** was **rude of me.** = I was rude.

Adjective + **for** refers to a state of affairs, a situation and its effect on someone or something: **It** was **impossible for Jane** to keep silent. = The situation made her silence impossible; she had to speak.

The infinitive clause can come first in the sentence but these prepositional phrases stay in place; they do not belong to the infinitive. **It** drops out of the sentence. The verbs are usually **be, appear, seem** and other state verbs.

11

I	would be	**unable**	to help them.
Mary	will be	**ready**	to give advice.
Everyone	became	**willing**	to offer an opinion.
Tom	appears	**quick**	to agree with them.
She	sounded	**anxious**	to discuss the matter.

He is	a hard man	to work **with**.
She seems	a pleasant person	to talk **to**.
He looks	a capable fellow	to deal **with**.

| They are | charming people | to go out **with**. |
| They can be | difficult men | to do business **with**. |

Personal subject + adjective + infinitive: the adjectives refer to the subject's feelings and attitudes towards the activity in the infinitive. The verbs in the main clause are state verbs (be, seem, appear; become, feel, look, sound). We do not change the order of these clauses.

NOTE the end prepositions after the infinitives; we would almost never use the relative clause Xwith whom to workX etc. For end prepositions in relative clauses, ▶ **Chapter 14, B8-9.**

12 'Too' and 'enough' + infinitive

cause	*consequence*
The tea is **too hot**	(for me) **to drink.**
The tea isn't **cool enough**	(for anyone) **to drink.**
The top shelf was **too high.**	(I couldn't reach it)
The top shelf wasn't **too high.**	(I could reach it)
The ladder was **long enough.**	(it reached the roof)
The ladder wasn't **long enough.**	(it didn't reach the roof)
Ann is **too young**	**to marry** yet.
Ann isn't **old enough**	**to marry** yet.

The infinitive expresses a result or consequence of the cause in the main clause.

Too: an affirmative cause has a negative result or consequence; a negative cause has an affirmative result. The infinitive remains in the same form after both kinds of cause.

Enough: affirmative causes have affirmative results and consequences: negative causes have negative results and consequences; the infinitive is the same after both kinds of cause. **Enough** goes before nouns and after adjectives and adverbs.

13 Verb + how + infinitive

You	should advise	us		put a tent up.
Someone	will inform	them		live in camp.
	must instruct			use ropes.
The	might remind	her	**how to**	wear a pack.
	can show			read a map.
leader	could teach	him		light a fire.
	had to tell			find food.

How + *(full infinitive + object)* = the way to do something; **how to** clauses are usually objects of other verbs whose general meanings refer to **teaching, learning, knowing** or **not knowing** how to do something. The verbs **advise, inform, instruct, remind, show*, teach*, tell*** can all have a direct personal object (sometimes the object is an animal). ***Show, teach, tell** never take prepositions before **how to.** The other verbs can, but the prepositions are not always necessary. Prepositions (when we use them with some of these verbs) are usually **about, on, concerning,** or **with regard to + how to;** they all mean the same, and **remind** can also have **of + how to. They informed us (about) how to** find drinking water (etc).

I We You They She	didn't know had forgotten remember explained demonstrated understood	how to	cook macaroni. make ice-cream. draw a diagram. read Sanskrit. play chess. do the job.

Forget, know, learn, remember, understand cannot have objects except for the **how to** clause itself; **demonstrate** and **explain** sometimes have an indirect prepositional object: **They explained** (to me) how to read a map (to me). The **how to** infinitive clause is the object of the verb in the first clause.

eg 'We've forgotten **something.**' 'What have you forgotten?' '(We've forgotten) **How to make ice-cream.** We've forgotten **that/this/it.**'

14 Infinitives as nouns

Subjects	*Objects*
I would like	**to have a larger house.**
She didn't want	**to move into the country.**
We shan't need	**to live here** all the time.
Do you intend (?)	**to sell this property.**

a **To travel** well is often better than **to arrive.**

b **To know** means **to understand.**

c **Not to understand** means **not to know.**

d **To have two cars costs** too much money.

e **To ride horses** in busy streets **seems** foolish.

f **To break the law** would put you in prison.

A noun is a word, phrase or clause that can be subject of a verb or object of a verb or complement of a preposition. We have already seen in **8-10** above that infinitive clauses can be subjects and, in **13** above, objects. Infinitives cannot be complements of prepositions at any time. The infinitive, with or without object, is always third person singular, **it, this, that,** when it is subject or object of a sentence (▶ examples **d-e** opposite).

15	To take a bus To go on foot To have dinner here To share Tom's taxi	would might will could	be better. make us late. not be convenient. save some money.

Subject infinitives can go with verbs in any tense and with verbs that have modal auxiliaries. The clauses can change places with **It** before the finite clause:

It might be better **to take a bus.**
It would save money to share Tom's taxi etc.

There can be a **for** + *noun or object pronoun* with a subject infinitive. ▶ also **17** below.

135

16

He wants to move	but I **don't want to**.
You must buy a car	but I **can't afford to**.
You could take a holiday	but I **don't have to**.
*They're giving a party.	We**'re going to**, soon.
*Ann's going to London.	We **intend to**, next year.

***to** stands for any infinitive that we would normally use; we need not have an infinitive in the first speech.

The infinitive particle **to** can stand for a whole infinitive clause. In this way we can avoid repeating words that the speaker or someone has already said.

17
Taking a bus would be better.
Having two cars costs too much.
Sharing a taxi will save some money.
Breaking the law would put you in prison.

When an infinitive is subject of a verb, as in **14-15** above, a gerund can usually stand instead, without change of meaning. For gerund as noun ▶ **D1-6** below.

18 Certain verbs are followed by infinitives or by infinitive clauses. They are listed below and in **19** and **20**.

ache	plan †
afford	prefer
agree* †	prepare*
aim (intend, propose)	presume (take the liberty)
arrange* †	pretend
ask* †	proceed
attempt	profess
bother*	promise
claim	propose (state one's
choose*	intentions)
consent †	prove (turn out to be)
contrive	reckon (calculate, assess)
decide †	refuse
decline (refuse)	request*
demand	resolve
determine	seek*
endeavour	swear (take an oath)
expect*	trouble*
fail	tend (have a tendency)
guarantee*	threaten
help*	try (attempt, endeavour)
hesitate	undertake
hope	volunteer
long	vow
manage	want*
mean* (intend)	wish* (request, want)
offer	yearn
omit	

All the verbs above can have an infinitive immediately following:
I can afford **to buy a better car.**
He failed **to pass the test.**
They threatened **to cause trouble.**
You undertook **to represent us.**

Verbs with a dagger (†) can also be followed by a preposition and its noun or pronoun complement:

We decided **on a Bentley** to replace our old car.
They have planned **for Mary** to spend a month in Greece.
He consented **to their request** to pay in four instalments.

The verbs marked * may also have a noun or object pronoun, as object:

She helps to look after the dogs.
She helps me to look after the dogs.
We agreed **with a decision** to encourage independent craftsmen.
Mary arranged **for the doctor** to come in once a week.
We shall prepare **for fifty people** to sit down to lunch.

The prepositions are the ones we normally find in association with these verbs.

19 **The verbs listed below can all take the infinitive immediately after them. Alternatively, they take that ... should ... clauses as direct objects; I prefer that I (should) go/that you (should) stay. (▶ also Chapter 24, B24).**

agree	hope †
arrange	plan †
ask* †	prefer
claim	presume* (suppose, assume,
choose*	take it)
consent †	pretend
contrive	promise
decide †	propose (suggest, put
decline*	forward)
demand	prove* (show evidence)
determine	reckon
expect*	request*
guarantee*	resolve
	swear (take an oath)
	threaten
	undertake
	vow

The verbs marked * can have an object and the infinitive follows it:

She asked **someone** to show her the way.
I expect **him** to arrive tomorrow.
They will prove **the witness** to be a liar.
We presume **him** to be an honest man.

The verbs marked (†) can have a preposition, with its complement, as object, and the infinitive following them:
She asked **for a specialist to give** an opinion.

In the list at **19**, as we have seen, all the verbs can take infinitives after them; alternatively, they can all have **that ...** clauses.

| She expects | **him to arrive** tomorrow. |
| | **that he will arrive** tomorrow. |

| They have planned | **for Mary to spend** a month in Greece. |
| | **that Mary will spend** a month in Greece. |

| They hope | **to hear** from him soon. |
| | **that they will hear** from him soon. |

These infinitive and **that** clauses are direct objects of the verb in the main clause:

She expects	
We have decided (on)	something.
They hope (for)	

As neither infinitive nor **that** clauses can be complements of prepositions at any time, the verbs marked † drop their prepositions before **that** clauses and infinitives.

20 Causative verbs and infinitives

The subject of a causative verb exerts greater or lesser degrees of authority, influence, persuasion, help, recommendation, directly upon the object of the same verb, to bring about the activity which we mention in a following infinitive clause. The infinitive follows the object of a causative verb (▶ also **have** and **get**). For example,

The cold weather forced us to stay indoors.
A nurse assisted the injured man to remove his boots.

aid †
advise*
allow* (let, permit) †
ask* †
appoint †
assist †
authorise †
beg* (implore, entreat)
cause
caution* (warn)
challenge
coax
command*
commission
compel †
counsel*
dare
demand*
defy
direct* (order, demand)
drive (someone to . . .) †
empower

incite †
induce
influence
inspire †
instruct* (order, request)
intend*
invite †
lead (one to believe etc)
leave (allow, let)
mean* (intend) †
motivate †
oblige †
order* (command)
persuade* †
press †
prompt
provoke
recommend*
remind*
request*
require*
rouse †

enable †	stimulate †
encourage †	summon
entice	tell* (order, instruct) †
entitle	tempt †
entreat	train †
exhort †	trust* †
expect* (require) †	warn*
force †	
impel	
implore*	

NOTES

1 Verbs marked * can also take **that** clauses,
   eg **I recommend that he should not go to school today.**
   with **should** + *bare infinitive* (base verb) or other modal
   auxiliary where sense permits.

2 In the causative sense, **demand** does not have a noun or pronoun
   object:
   I demand to see the prisoner.
   I demand that I (should) see the prisoner.

3 **Persuade, remind** and **tell** retain their objects before a **that** clause;
   eg She told him to go/She told him **that he should go.**

4 **Caution, instruct** and **warn** can either keep their objects or be
   without them before **that** clauses,
   eg He warned (us) **that we should travel only at night.**

5 **Trust:**
   I trust **him to act** honestly. (I place confidence in him). I trust
   that he will act honestly. (I hope that he will . . .)

6 **Make** and **let** take the bare infinitive, when they are causative
   verbs, in the active voice.
   Otherwise, the causative verbs drop their objective nouns and
   pronouns before **that** clauses; these items then appear as subjects
   in the **that** clause:
   I advise you to arrive early/**I advise that you should arrive
   early.**
   We intend her to study music./**We intend that she should study
   music.**

B Participles

1 The past participle

a Someone has **made** a pot of tea.
(perfect)
A pot of tea has **been made.** (passive)

b We had **written** a full report. (perfect)
A full report had **been written.** (passive)

All past participles serve with the
auxiliary verb **have** to form perfect
tenses. Past participles of transitive
verbs only, with auxiliary verb **be,** serve
to make the passive voice of verbs.

2 Past participles in relative clauses

a An engineer (who was) **employed** at the factory gave us an interesting talk.

b A ship (which was) **built** for service in the Antarctic left Britain yesterday.

c The doctors (who had been) **engaged** in the research made important discoveries.

d The report (that was) **published** in the newspapers said nothing about alcohol.

e I shall try to get the job (that is) **advertised** in today's *Morning News*.

f The manager himself must sign letters (that are) **addressed** to government offices.

g The museum was crowded with visitors (who had been) **brought** by tourist agencies.

h We deal promptly with any complaints (that are) **made** by our customers.

Defining relative clause: transitive verbs in relative clauses can be in the passive voice. The relative pronoun can be the subject of the passive verb in the relative clause. Often, especially in print, the past participle stands alone, without relative pronoun, and represents the whole passive verb. In the examples **a-d** opposite, the antecedent nouns are all subjects in their clauses. The antecedents can be objects (**e-f**), or complements of prepositions (**g-h**), but the relative pronoun must be subject of its own passive relative clause and define the antecedent.

3

a Billy, (who had been) **given** a book, really wanted a football.

b Little Jenny, (who was) **dressed** all in white by her mother, looked very sweet.

c Good dogs, (which are) properly **trained,** can be very useful to the police.

Non-defining relative clause: passive participles can stand alone for non-defining relative clauses. Commas are necessary to separate antecedents from the passive participle and the rest of the main clause.

4 Conditional

a **Susan,** (if she were) **given the opportunity,** could become a first-class mathematician.

b **Dogs,** (when they are) **well-trained,** would be more useful than horses in the Arctic.

c (When it is/If it were) **Explained** in plain English, **technology** might not seem so mysterious.

A modal auxiliary in its past tense form can appear in the main clause; the past participle can refer to an unreal condition with **if** or **when.** A non-defining passive participle can stand at the beginning of a sentence. It may or may not have a prepositional phrase after it.

5 Past participle as adjective

> a **broken** plate, a **boiled** egg, a **frightened** child, a **hired** car, **paid** bills, a **rented** house, **stolen** goods, a **tested** formula, **wrinkled** stockings, a **worn** old coat
>
> the **Unknown** Soldier, **unpaid** debts, **unspoken** thoughts, **unwritten** law, **unwanted** advice, **unspoilt** country, **unsalted** butter

Past participles of transitive verbs can be adjectives and stand with nouns, usually before them. The general meaning is that something has happened and a noun is in a state that results from that happening.

Some past participles appear in negative forms as adjectives, usually with the prefix **un-.**

6

> deceased = who has died, diseased, gifted, talented, able-bodied, broad-minded, downhearted, harebrained, high-minded, light-headed, light-hearted, low-minded, narrow-minded

Some adjectives end in **-ed;** they look like past participles but they have no verb at all,
eg **diseased:** there is no verb Xto diseaseX.
Red-haired exists but there is no verb Xto hairX.
Adjectives of this kind usually mean **having a disease, who has red hair** etc (▶ **Chapter 33**).

7

> well-mannered/ill-mannered; well-bred/ill-bred; well-informed/ill-informed (badly informed); well-educated/ill-educated

Some adjectives from passive participles take the prefix **ill-** (= **badly**); **well-** gives the opposite meaning. Often, in less formal styles, we prefer **badly** in place of **ill-**. The examples opposite generally have **ill-**.

8

> full-grown, fully-finished, half-baked, half-hearted, heart-broken, hard-boiled, semi-detached, overcooked, overdone, under-cooked, under-valued

Compound adjectives with past participles are quite common. The hyphen (-) between the two parts does not always appear eg we can have **heart-broken** or **heartbroken**.

9 a Dr Jones is **a person well-known for his work** on children's diseases.
  b We like **bread covered with honey.**
  c **A house built on sand** will not stand long.

Past participles as adjectives after nouns generally have prepositional phrases after them and are generally of the reduced relative clause type which you can see in **B2** above.

10a We stepped carefully over the **broken** glass.
  b Tom tried to open the **locked** door but couldn't.
  c They always put **whipped** cream on their cakes.

Sentence positions for past participles as adjectives can be before their nouns or after **be, seem, become** and other state verbs as complements.

Tom	is	more	**upset**	than John.
Ann	sounds	less	**annoyed**	than Jane.
You	look	the most	**excited**	of all
The girls	seem	the least	**worried**	of us.

More, most, less, least are used for comparative and superlative degrees of participial adjectives. They do not take the endings **-er** and **-est.**

11

> aged, beloved, blessed, crooked, learned, ragged, wretched; a three-legged table, a four-legged animal
>
> drunken = habitually drunk (a drunken man); shaven, well-shaven; shrunken; cloven (a cloven hoof); ill-gotten gains/profits

Some past participles have an extra syllable when we use them as adjectives; as parts of verb tenses they have only one syllable. In these adjectives, **-ed** is a syllable, but not stressed. Extra participles appear with some irregular verbs; they are more often used as adjectives.

C -ing as participle

1
a A 'barking 'dog kept me awake half the night.
b Get the right time on the phone, from the 'talking 'clock.
c Tell your troubles to Jane. She's an under'standing 'person.
d 'Growing 'children need good food and exercise.
e Do you know a song called 'The 'Laughing 'Boy?'
f There are three large 'frying pans in the kitchen.
g Put them on the 'cooking stove, with very little oil.
h Then put twelve eggs into the 'mixing machine.
i Beat the eggs, then pour them into a 'measuring jug.
j Make coffee and take it into the 'dining-room.

2
a **A man** (who was) **wearing a top hat** spoke to me.
b I didn't recognise **the man** (who was) **speaking to you.**
c Tom didn't see **a cat** (that was) **running across the road.**
d Joe has connections with **someone** (who is) **working there.**
e **Policemen** (who are) **sorting out** this traffic jam will need great patience.
f **Anyone** (who has been) **working hard** in extreme heat or cold, needs extra sleep.

3
a **Wearing her new hat,** she looked very pretty.
b I hear some funny mistakes, **listening to the radio.**
c **Working with dogs,** Tom tries to be kind but firm.

Participles: we stress participle and noun; **'growing 'children** = children who are growing.

The **-ing** participles, with parts of auxiliary **be,** form progressive tenses. As non-finite verbs, they have other uses. Adjectives generally keep the sense of progression, eg. **boiled water** is water that **was boiled;** it might be quite cold now.

Boiling water is water that **is/will be/was boiling** (at 100°C at a particular time; we make tea with **boiling water** and, if necessary, we drink **boiled water,** when it is cool enough.

Gerunds: the noun after a gerund is not stressed; the **'dining-room** is a room for dining in.

Adjectives in **-ing** often name the purpose of the nouns they go with: eg **cooking oil** is **oil for cooking** food in; it isn't **heating oil** or **lubricating oil** or **lamp oil.**

Purpose adjectives in **-ing** are not participles; they are gerunds (after **for**) — oil **for cooking,** a machine **for mixing** etc.

-ing *participle in reduced relative clauses:* the relative pronoun is subject in its own clause and refers directly to its antecedent noun. The antecedent need not be subject in its own clause; it can be subject or object or complement of a preposition. The participle takes its timing from the verb in the main clause.

-ing *and periods of time:* a clause which mentions an activity that takes place during a length of time is a duration (of time) clause and can begin with **as/while/when** + *subject and progressive verb* eg I'll read the newspaper, (**while I'm**)

d **Going through the newspaper,** she found twenty misprints.

e Tom felt lonely, **coming home to an empty house.**

f **Sitting at the table for two,** we ordered lunch.

g **Being the only doctor here,** Peter has a busy life.

h **Having an early breakfast,** she turned the radio on.

i **While working with dogs,** Tom has to be firm.

j I hear funny mistakes, **while listening to the radio.**

k **While having breakfast,** she turned the radio on.

l You'll need an umbrella, **while visiting Manchester.**

NOTE the **-ing** clause can come first in the sentence; the comma is still necessary.

4 **a** **Putting his hand into his pocket,** Joe found a bunch of keys.

b **Keeping his eyes on the target,** Tom threw a stone.

c **Covering them with his gun,** Bull made the bandits lie down.

d **Taking out his note book,** the policeman asked my name.

e **Giving him my name,** I asked why he wanted to know.

f **Answering with a smile,** he said it was just police routine.

g Ann, **running for a bus,** lost a shoe.

h Tom, **picking up the shoe,** dropped his umbrella.

i The bus driver, **watching the scene,** waited for them.

j Tom, **taking a seat beside Ann,** thanked the driver.

5 **a** **We heard** someone **cough** in the next room. Then **we heard** him **sneezing.**

b **We watched** the police car **stop** outside number 12. **A policeman observed us standing** outside number 14.

sitting in the train., with a comma to separate the clauses.

The same subject appears in each clause; we can drop **as/when/while** from the duration clause together with the subject and auxiliary verb(s): I'll read the newspaper, **sitting in the train.**

The comma is necessary: non-finite verbs often take the nearest noun as subject; **I saw two dinosaurs (while I was) walking round the museum.** can also be **I saw two dinosaurs (that were) walking round the museum (▶ 2** above). So we must take care to avoid absurd meanings; sometimes, the full duration or relative clause is necessary for clear meaning. We can see a comma in print (if the writer is careful); we don't always hear it in speech. In duration clauses we can keep **while + -ing** to avoid mis-understandings, except when the participle is **being,** and only when we make good sense (▶ examples **i-l** opposite).

-ing *clause + main clause:* the actions in the two clauses take place at exactly the same time, or almost so. The **-ing** clause is progressive, and can show a very short space of time; within that short duration, the second action happens. The same subject belongs to each clause. The subject, marked off by a comma, can come before the **-ing** participle; there is a second comma at the end of the **-ing** clause.

-ing *participle or bare infinitive:* after the verbs **feel, hear, notice, observe, perceive, sense, smell, watch** we can have the bare infinitive (**A1** above) when they are in active voice forms. We can

143

c **I noticed him signal** to his colleague in the car. **I felt my knees knocking,** although I'd done no wrong.

D Gerunds

1

> The names of professions, sports, hobbies, habits and other occupations are often gerunds:
> acting, brewing (beer), cycling, engineering, marketing, playing (games, musical instruments), singing, skating, ski-ing, smoking, swimming, teaching, training, writing, wrestling; collecting, coin-collecting, art-collecting.
> Other compounds are: paper-making, steel-making, house-building, shipbuilding, wood carving, metal-working

2 **Meeting** you again was a pleasant surprise.

Eating sweets spoilt their teeth.

Your **doings** begin to annoy me, Jim.

I dislike these **comings and goings** at all hours.

Telephoning after midnight seems ill-mannered.

Have you ever thought of **going** to Australia?

3

> bearing(s) — ball-bearing, compass bearing; clipping(s) — press clippings; coating(s) — chocolate/plastic/glass coating; dressing(s) — salad dressing(s), dressings on cuts and injuries; feeling(s) — of respect, admiration; fitting(s) — electrical fittings, bathroom fittings; wrappings (for parcels, boxes)

4 There is too much **advertising** on some TV channels.

British **shipbuilding** has become profitable again.

Careful **pruning** helps fruit trees to grow well.

Campers use bottled gas for **cooking,** usually.

also have **-ing** participles; the bare infinitive can refer to a single or general activity (simple) and the **-ing** participle to an on-going activity (progressive). NOTE that **make** and **let** are not in the list.

Gerunds are **-ing** forms that look exactly like **-ing** participles (▶ **C1** above), but their uses are quite different. A gerund is a noun and can do all the work of a noun; it can be subject or object of a verb and complement of a preposition. (An infinitive can be a noun but not complement of a preposition) ▶ **A14-15** above. Verbal noun is the name we sometimes give to the gerund because it names an activity and the doing of the activity.

Sometimes compounds have a hyphen between the parts, sometimes they are one word.

A gerund is usually a mass noun and not countable. It is singular, third person, and the pronouns **it/this/that** can stand instead of a gerund phrase, eg **Eating sweets/This** spoilt their teeth. to avoid repetition. **Doings, coming and goings** and **goings-on** are usually plural and, as subjects, have a plural verb: the pronouns that stand for them are also plural.

Some gerunds are count nouns and can be either singular or plural to suit the speaker's meaning.

As nouns, gerunds can have articles, adjectives, possessive adjectives, and all the other items that normally go with nouns.

5   **The writing of books** takes a good deal longer than **the reading of them.**

The playing of a piece of music is more than just sounding the notes one after the other.

The breaking of a promise is a serious matter.

In formal style we have **the** + *gerund* + **of** and *complement*. Generally, we say and write:

writing books,
reading books,
playing a piece of music,
breaking a promise.

6

> 'air-conditioning, 'brain-washing, 'book-keeping, 'dressmaking, 'housekeeping, 'sight-seeing, 'stocktaking, 'coal-mining, 'metal-working, 'shipbuilding, 'steelmaking.

The gerund, or verbal noun, as we often call it, often has a strong sense of the action of a verb in it, and particularly in compound forms *noun* + *gerund;*
eg **the keeping of books**
    the making of dresses etc.

7

> 'cooking apples, 'drinking water, 'knitting wool, 'playing cards, 'racing cars, 'spending money, 'spinning top, 'writing materials
> 'Racing cars are **cars for racing** but 'racing 'cars cause accidents on the public highway — ordinary cars should not be racing.

Gerund + *noun:* the gerund states the purpose **for** the noun,
eg **drinking water = water for drinking.**

Stress on gerund only: in **6-7** opposite, stress comes on the gerund only:
'**playing cards** (gerund) are **cards for playing games** such as bridge, poker and so on, but '**playing 'cards** (participle) is an activity, such as playing bridge, poker, *patience.
*patience (Br) = solitaire (Am)

8

> avoid, celebrate, consider (= think about), complete, endanger, enjoy, entail, escape, excuse, favour, finish, forbid, persist (in), mind (don't mind, do you mind?), miss, necessitate, pardon, postpone, practise, prevent, prohibit, repent, resent, resist, resume, risk, suffer (= tolerate, put up with)
> can't bear . . .; can't endure . . .; can't stand . . .; it's no good . . .; it's no use . . .; it's not worth . . .;

Some transitive verbs take the usual noun objects or gerunds as verb forms; the verbs in the list opposite do not take infinitives as objects; they take gerunds as direct objects,
eg We also enjoy **being here** with you.
    Would you mind **living all alone?**
Generally, there is only one subject in the sentence and the gerund shares it with the verb in the main clause —
Would **you** mind that **you** were alone?

9 a Nobody will mind **John's arriving** a little later.

  b **His agreeing** to take part in our work pleased us all.

Gerund with its own subject: when a gerund does not share the subject of another verb, or to show that it refers to a particular person or any other thing,

c **Ann's suggesting** that he could record his speech was silly.

d **Our seeing** as well as **hearing** him is important.

e Please excuse **my criticising** Ann so sharply.

f I do appreciate **her being** so helpful in every way.

g Let's hope that John's speech is worth waiting for. I can't stand **his repeating** himself over and over.

we use a possessive noun or possessive adjective before the gerund. We cannot do this with **-ing** participles. They won't mind **starting a little later.** can mean **They won't mind that they start a little later.** The gerund can also be quite indefinite about who starts a little later; the unspoken, unwritten subject of a gerund can mean anybody/everybody in general.

E Gerund or infinitive

1

> advise, allow, authorise, forbid, permit, recommend, require, urge

a The doctor advised **Tom's going** into hospital. The doctor advised **Tom to go** into hospital.

b Father allowed **Peter's using** the family car.
Father allowed **Peter to use** the family car.

These verbs can have a noun or pronoun object. A gerund, marked as subject with a possessive noun or pronoun can follow that object. An infinitive can also follow (▶ **A1** and **7** above).

2

> attempt, begin, cease, continue, decline (= politely refuse); deserve, dread, fear, forbear, neglect, omit, plan, start, try (= endeavour), attempt, venture.

a We began **walking / to walk** towards the bus stop.

b Ann continued **talking / to talk** about her brother.

c I tried **changing / to change** the subject.

d Her brother didn't deserve **being blamed / to be blamed.**

e He had neglected **posting / to post** a card for her birthday.

f He had started **writing / to write** it. He didn't finish.

g He ventured **making / to make** an apology. She smiled.

h She omitted **mentioning / to mention** that I had forgotten, too.

These can have gerunds or infinitives immediately after them. We choose, if we choose, because of other words in the sentence, and for no grammatical reason: He is continu**ing** study**ing** engineer**ing next month.** is a grammatically correct sentence but the sound of **-ing -ing** is not pleasing. **He is continuing to study.** is easier on the ear.

3

> dread, fear, hate, like, loathe, love, prefer, regret, can't bear, detest, dislike

a We **regret to inform** you of the results of your tests.

b I always **regret informing** people of bad news.

c Jane **loves to have** people around. You're welcome.

d Jane **loves having** people around. Come again, soon.

e I **prefer flying.** We **dislike spending** weeks on ships.

These verbs express personal feelings. All of them can have gerunds or infinitives after them, except the last two, **detest** and **dislike,** which take gerunds only. The infinitive can have a sense of particular occasion — **I hate to disturb her.** (I am disturbing her but I hate to do it) but we say **I hate disturbing her.** (as a general rule), when she's busy.

4 Changes in meaning

Joe Tom Ann	remembers has forgotten regrets	**writing** that letter. **saying** how silly she was. **annoying** Peter that day.
I'll **remember** You might **forget**		**to post** the letters. **to put** the stamps on them.

a If noise disturbs you, **try wearing ear-plugs.**

b If they don't help, **try to get used to the noise.**

c Your hair **needs cutting / to be cut.**

d That fellow **deserves punishing / to be punished.**

e The roses **need watering / to be watered.**

f The workman **stopped to have lunch.**

g Uncle Tom has **stopped smoking in bed.**

Gerund objects after **forget, regret, remember** usually refer to actual happenings in the past or in previous time. Infinitives point forward to actions at the same or later time.

Try + *gerund* usually means **experiment, make a test (a)**

Try + *infinitive* = **attempt, endeavour, make an effort (b)**

After **stop** we can have an infinitive of purpose; stop + *gerund* as object: **cease, end, finish.**

Gerunds after **deserve, need, want** can have a passive sense (**c-e**).

F Gerunds and prepositions

1

I'm **tired of**	doing the same job every day.
There's no **need for**	organising our work so badly.
You don't **care about**	making things that nobody wants.
We **object to**	wasting our time like this.

Complement = **it/this/that.** The only verb form that can serve as complement of a preposition is the gerund, the verbal noun. After prepositions, prepositional verbs and phrasal verbs, if we need a verb form it must be **-ing** gerund.

2

The picture was sent for	**to show** to the man.
Please pass this picture round	**to help** the jury.
She put her diamond ring on	**to please** me.
She wouldn't take it off	**to please** anyone.

Infinitive clauses of purpose are not and cannot be complements of prepositions. They sometimes do appear after phrasal and prepositional verbs, as parts of sentences.

3

> adjust to, admit to, amount to, attend to, confess to, face up to, look forward to, object to, refer to, take to, be averse to, be committed to, be used to

a The man **confessed to stealing** the car.
The crime was **confessed to** (in order) **to avoid a long trial.**

b He is **committed to serving** the nation in politics.
What **I referred to** (in order) **to help him** was money.

4 a A knife is a tool **for cutting things with.**

b A thermometer is **for measuring temperature with.**

c A wardrobe is a *cupboard **for keeping clothes in.**

d A pot is **for cooking food in.**

e A stove is **for cooking food on.**
*cupboard (Br) = closet (Am)

5 a I use soft pencils **for drawing with.**

b She needs glasses **for reading with.**

c They had a garden **for growing flowers in.**

d A cement floor isn't ideal **for dancing on.**

e Don't use the bottle **for drinking out of.**

f There are glasses **for pouring beer into.**

g We have dictionaries **for looking words up in.**

h There's a platform **for loading *lorries up from.**
*lorry (Br) = truck (Am)

b She needs glasses **to read with.**

e Don't use the bottle **to drink out of.**

g We have dictionaries **to look words up in.**

6 Passive sense of 'for' + gerund

a These letters are ready **for posting / to be posted.**

b I must send the film away **for printing / to be printed.**

c Is this water fit **for drinking / to be drunk?**

d Send these clothes away **for cleaning / to be cleaned.**

To in these is a preposition, NOT the beginning of an infinitive. The complement of a preposition is a noun or pronoun or a gerund (a verbal noun). When an infinitive of purpose follows these, we often have **in order to** or **so as to** for the infinitive, in order to avoid **to to** (▶ **A6** above) or, if we like, to move the infinitive further from the preposition, but this is not necessary.

Purpose and use: **for** + *gerund* eg **What is this for? What do you use it for?** The answers to these questions explain the use and purpose for whatever we mention: eg Any sort of pot will do **for making coffee in** if you don't have a coffee pot **for making it in.**

We use tools, instruments, buildings, machines and everything else; we say what we use them **for,** or what we can do **in** them, **on** them, **with** them, **through** them, and so on. The prepositions come at the end of the **for** + *gerund* clause, after the gerund, and when the gerund has an object, after that.
Gerunds of prepositional and phrasal verbs keep their own prepositions; the purpose and use prepositions can follow them (**g-h** opposite).

The examples here in **5** could have infinitive clauses, to mention definite intention by the subject.

The **for** + *gerund* clause or phrase can have a passive sense. If we choose the passive infinitive instead of the gerund, **for** drops out.

7 Reason, cause, consequence

a Jenny got a prize **for winning the marathon.**

b You'll go to prison **for stealing people's money.**

c The police will arrest you **for breaking the law.**

d **For being so patient with him,** she deserves a medal.

e **For cleaning the car,** we give Joe extra pocket money.

f **For working all day,** he'll pay me £20.

g Tom made an apology **for being so late.**

The happenings in the gerund clause are reasons and causes of a consequence that happens afterwards; the main clause expresses the consequence. When the **for** + *gerund* comes first in the sentence, use a comma to separate the clauses. Infinitives cannot replace gerunds here. Infinitive happenings come after the cause or reason; they state purpose: **You'll go to prison (in order) to steal.**\ (**b**) seems a highly improbable purpose.

G Other forms of non-finite verbs

1 The progressive infinitive

a We hope **to be seeing** you often, in future.

b We ought **to be passing** this way quite soon again.

c I seem **to be taking** the wrong road to Barlow.

d I planned **to be arriving** there about now.

The infinitive can have a progressive form:

(to) be + **-ing**
(to) be living
(to) be working etc.

We use it in the same ways as the simple infinitive but mention an on-going activity during a period of time.

2 The perfect infinitive

a We intend **to have finished** the job by Saturday.

b I meant **to have seen** Peter again before he left.

c Ann was sorry **to have missed** your lecture.

d He couldn't **have been living** in Victorian times.

e Something seemed **to have been happening** in my absence.

The infinitive can have a perfect form, **(to) have** + *past participle*:

(to) have lived
(to) have worked
(to) have known etc.

We use this particularly to show a happening or an action before or at a previous time. Often the plain infinitive will do just as well. We can have a perfect progressive form, mentioning activities during a long period of previous time (**d-e** opposite).

3 -ing participle

a **Having slept** well for ten hours, Ann felt better.

b John is short of cash, **having forgotten** to go to the bank.

c I shall give my opinion tomorrow, **having read** your report.

d You **can be thinking** of what comes next, meantime.

The **-ing** participle can have a perfect form, **having** + *past participle*:

having walked
having slept etc.

We refer to previous happenings. In a progressive sense we have **be** + **-ing** after modal auxiliaries (**d-e** opposite). There is also a passive form: **having**

e They **must be expecting** us to solve the problem.

f We stood up to go, **business having been completed.**

4 -ing gerunds

a I regret **your having lost** so much money.

b **My having become poor** has shown me my true friends.

c I know all about **their having tried** to help me up.

d **Your having stood by me** has encouraged me.

5 a **My being hurt** at Tom's remark only made him laugh.

b **My dog's being fed** by strangers didn't please me.

c Father was amused at **your being mistaken** for him.

d We prefer **Tom's being given** a private room at college.

e **His having been allowed** a typewriter will be an advantage.

f We appreciate **our having been granted** an interview with the prime minister.

been + *past participle* (**f** opposite) in perfect form.

The perfect gerund refers to happenings at any time before the happenings in the main clauses; this is true of all non-finites in perfect forms. Perfect gerunds are nouns: subjects, objects of verbs and complements of prepositions.

The progressive gerund — **being** + *past participle* — can be passive when we have a transitive past participle. The perfect passive form is **having been** + *past participle of a transitive verb.*

28 The verb in reported or indirect speech

A Reporting verbs: present tenses

1 simple present   2 present progressive   3 present perfect   4 perfect progressive present

Liz says that	1	Dick goes back to work on Monday.
Tom is saying that	2	Mary's leaving her job next week.
You've told me that	3	she has worked there for over five years.
Joe's been asking whether	4	Mary's been earning a very good salary.

B Reporting verbs: past

1 simple past   2 past progressive   3 past perfect   4 perfect progressive past

Liz said that	1	Dick goes back to work on Monday (next).
Tom was saying that	2	Mary is leaving her job next week.
You had told me that	3	she has worked there for over five years.
Joe had been asking whether	4	Mary has been earning a very good salary.

C Reporting verbs: present or future

1 simple future   2 future progressive   3 future perfect   4 perfect progressive future

Ann will tell everyone that	1	our guests will arrive about seven.
John says that	2	they'll be ringing the doorbell quite soon.
I have confirmed that	3	I'll have spoken to Dick before dinner.
Jane wants to know whether	4	we'll have been discussing Dick's proposal.

D Verbs in the report: past

1 simple   2 progressive   3 perfect   4 perfect progressive
future-in-the-past   future-in-the-past   future-in-the-past   future-in-the-past

Ann told everyone that	1	our guests would arrive about seven.
John said that	2	they would be ringing the doorbell quite soon.
I had confirmed that	3	I would have spoken to Dick before dinner.
Jane wanted to know whether	4	we'd have been discussing Dick's proposal.

The whole situation in each reported question has already gone into the past as a matter of family history or memory. It was future once, then, in the past.

NOTE In familiar conversation and informal writing the linking word **that** often drops out of the sentence eg **He told me (that) she was going to Brazil.**

1

a 'I go back to work on Monday,' Dick said.

b 'Mary's leaving her job next week,' Liz said.

c 'She has worked there for over five years,' I remarked.

d 'She's been earning a very good salary,' I added.

2

The most common reporting verbs are: **inform, remark, say, suggest, tell, believe, suppose, think** (= have the opinion), **understand.** Reported questions usually have: **ask, doubt, enquire, wonder, want to know,** when the report refers to doubt or question.

Liz said that	Tom went back last Monday. Mary was leaving the following week. you had worked there for five years.
Ann asked whether	I had been earning a good salary.

a 'Our guests will arrive about seven,' she said.

b 'They'll be ringing the doorbell quite soon,' he replied.

c 'You'll have spoken to Dick before dinner,' she added.

d 'We'll have been discussing his proposal,' I said.

3

I **shall tell** her that	Socrates **is** right.
I always **tell** him that	Socrates **says** this.
I **told** them that	Socrates **will be forgotten.**
I **would tell** them that	Socrates also **made** mistakes.
I **wonder** whether	Socrates **would agree.**

The actual words that a person says are direct speech: **'I'm very hungry,'** Tom said. Tom or someone else can repeat these words in the form of reported (or indirect) speech:
I said that I was very hungry.
Tom said that he was very hungry.
You said that you were very hungry.
He told them that he was very hungry.
▶ **A** and **B** above.

If direct speech in **1** above refers to what people said in the past about happenings that took place in the past, both reporting verb and report must be in past time: the reports in **B** above refer to activities that are still in present or future time (▶ **3** below). For the past, we change time adverbs so that they refer to past time. Reporting verbs can be in any tense that suits the reporter's meaning.

Reports do NOT take interrogative forms of verbs; they are affirmative or negative, to accord with the speaker's words.
Subject + reporting verb + **that** introduces the original speaker's statements, affirmative and negative.
Subject + reporting verb + **whether** introduces the original speaker's doubts and questions. In spoken English, non-conditional **if** can mean **whether.**

In direct speech, the future uses **shall/will.** ▶ **C** and **D** above for the reports of **a-d.**

A reporting verb can be in any present tense and, if we wish to mention future time reports, the reporting verb can be in a future tense. We do not change the tenses of verbs that appear in direct speech when activities still refer to present or future time.

4 I told **her** that **the boys** are going out. **She** told **him** that **you** are going out. **We** told **you** that **we** are going out; **you** told **her, she** told **him,** and **he** told **everybody.**

We often find it necessary to change pronouns from first to second or third person: a person's words go from mouth to mouth and back to the original speaker, sometimes.

5 'We had even eaten the dogs,' he wrote. 'The men had been starving for weeks,' he reported.
= He wrote that they **had** even **eaten** the dogs and reported that the men **had been starving** for weeks.

Back-shift = moving the tenses of verbs one step backwards to their past tense forms. We do this with all verb tenses, when the reporting verb is in a past tense. Past perfect tenses cannot have back-shift; they refer to the past of the past, and the English verb cannot go farther.

6 Modal auxiliaries

a 'She can still swim quite fast,' he told me.
He told me that she **could** still swim quite fast.

b 'I may be able to see you tomorrow,' she said.
She said that she **might** be able to see me next day.

c 'You must start at nine and must not go out.'
The manager said I **was to** start at nine and **wasn't to** go out.

d 'Would you mind if I closed the window?'
She asked whether I **would** mind if she closed the window.

e 'Shall I help you with that bag?'
He asked whether he *should/could help with that bag.

f 'Peter **ought to/should** wear warmer socks,' she said.
She told me that Peter **ought to/should** wear warmer socks.

*Avoid **should** when other auxiliaries are possible.

The simple present becomes the simple past, the present progressive becomes the past progressive, the present perfect becomes the past perfect. Future tenses take their future-in-the-past forms and so on. Auxiliary verbs take their past forms; **can = could, may = might** etc. **Must** has no past form of its own so we use **had to/didn't have to** or **was to/were to**. She asked whether **I would/could** help her. **'Would/Could you** help me, please?' is without tense in offers and requests; we report without change (▶ **Chapter 24, B18-20**). **Ought to/should** are reported as they stand, without change.

7 Past tenses: simple and progressive

a 'My father worked there when I was little.'
Liz said that **her father (had) worked there when she was little.**

When the direct speech gives a clear indication of a definite time or period in the past, we need not use back-shift. Past time adverbs, prepositional time

b 'He graduated in physics in 1983,' Jane told me.

Jane told me that **Bob (had) graduated in physics in 1983.**

c 'I was serving in the navy in 1983,' Joe said.

Joe said that **he was serving in the navy in 1983.**

d 'I was studying aboard ship and graduated in 1985.'

He said **he'd been studying** and **(had) graduated in 1985.**

e 'Joe didn't waste his time while he was at sea.'

I remarked that **Joe hadn't wasted his time while he was at sea.**

f 'We spent six weeks in Spain. We were staying with friends.'

Liz told us **they had spent six weeks in Spain** and **that they'd been staying with friends.**

phrases, or mention of these by the same or other speaker in a previous sentence, can define past time. Without back-shift we avoid confusion between past events as they happened then and events that happened already, before then, with later outcomes. Perfect and perfect progressive past tenses are necessary when the report mentions activities and happenings that had already taken place, before then in the past. These cannot backshift (▶ 5 above).

8 Imperative in reported speech

a He asked Tom **to come here.** ('Come here, Tom').

b I told the silly dog **to get down.** ('Get down, silly dog').

c She invited Mrs Brown **to sit down.** ('Sit down, please').

d I've asked Peter **to wait a few minutes.** ('Wait a few minutes').

e She'll advise him **not to drink.** ('Don't drink, will you?').

f The policeman ordered the thief **to stop.** ('Stop thief!').

We can address a person or animal eg **Come here, Tom.** The **to** infinitive is the reported form for the imperative verb. The reporting verbs can be in any tense to suit the speaker's meaning. Also, we choose a verb whose meaning shows how the imperative was said — **order, request, advise, invite** etc. NOTE we report infinitives in direct speech without change.

9

Ann proposes			**should go** to the cinema.
We suggested		we	**should organise** a rally.
I'll recommend	that	they	**should** all **wear** white.
Tom put forward		you	**should invite** the boss.
Jane says			**shouldn't eat** sweets.

Let as in **'Let's go to the cinema.'** mentions a suggestion, proposal and the like (▶ **Chapter 24, B25**). The reported form for **let's** is **should** + *base verb (bare infinitive)*. **Should** in Am is very often absent from sentences, and sometimes in Br, too (▶ also **Chapter 25, B24-25**).

10	
The critics said	how beautifully the choir sang. how well the musicians played. that the choir sang so beautifully. that the orchestra played so well. they had heard such beautiful music.
He mentioned	
We remarked	
They told us	
She wanted to know	how ever I had got so dirty.

What splendid singing! How well they sang! It was such beautiful music! They played so beautifully! (▶ Chapter 13, A-B) Exclamations must be in normal word order for an affirmative clause in reported speech. **'How ever did you get so dirty!'** becomes affirmative.

11 Sentence tags

a 'I can do anything better than you, can't I?'
He **boasts** that he can do anything better than me.

b 'You don't want a 'third pot of tea, do you?'
She **prompted** him to say that he didn't want it.

c 'You will remember to come straight home, won't you?'
She **reminded** him to come straight home.

d 'A man like you could use £50,000, couldn't he?'
He **practically offered** Tom **a bribe** of £50,000.

We do not report these at all, generally speaking. We take the meaning and tone of the whole sentence into account and choose a suitable reporting verb — usually a verb whose basic meaning is **speak;** or we can re-make the sentence altogether, (**d** opposite).

12 Conditional sentences: real

a 'If you come here on Friday we'll go out to lunch.'
I said that if he **comes** here on Friday, we'll go out to lunch.

b 'We'll go to the Savoy if you have time.'
He says that we'll go to the Savoy, if I **have** time.

c 'If you can spare an hour I shall be very pleased.'
He added that if I **can spare** an hour, he'll be very pleased.

Formally:

a I said that if he **came** here on Friday we'd go out to lunch.

b He said that we'd go to the Savoy if I **had** time.

c He added that if I **could** spare an hour he'd be very pleased.

Real conditions and their outcomes refer to present and future time (▶ **Chapter 26, A1-7**). The reporting verb can be in a present or past tense; if the condition still refers to the present or future, we need not change the tenses, and in order to avoid confusion between real and unreal conditions (which also refer to present and future time) we should supply future time adverbs (**next Monday, tomorrow**), prepositional phrases of time etc (▶ also **9** above for **should** with **propose, suggest** etc which can be reporting verbs, for conditionals.)

13 Unreal conditions

a 'If you left now you would catch the express train.'
She said that **if I left then I would catch the express train.**

b 'If Bill had ready money he would buy a new car.'
She says that **if Bill had ready money he'd buy a new car.**

c 'If you spoke in English we could understand you.'
She told me that **if I spoke in English they'd understand me.**

d 'If we took a taxi would it cost much more?'
He asked **whether it would cost much more if we took a taxi.**

Unreal conditions referring to present and future time stand as they are in reported speech, without back-shift. Pronouns, time adverbs and phrases usually need some changes. Reported questions in the outcome clause come first, with **whether, when, where, what, how, why** before the condition.

14 Unreal past conditions

a 'If I hadn't seen it, I wouldn't have believed it.'
He said that **if he hadn't seen it, he wouldn't have believed it.**

b 'If Tom had been here, I'd have felt safe.'
She says that **if you'd been there, she'd have felt safe.**

c 'We'd have helped you, if you had asked.'
They told us that **they'd have helped us if we'd asked.**

d 'If she hadn't told you, how would you have known?'
He asked us **how we'd have known, if you hadn't told us.**

Unreal past conditions cannot back-shift. Again, we usually have to adjust time adverbs and phrases, and pronouns.

29 Prepositions

A Kinds of prepositions

1 The most common *simple prepositions* appear in this list:

> about, above, across, after, against, along, alongside, among(st), around, as, at, before, behind, below, beneath, beside, besides, between, beyond, but, by, despite, down, during, except, for, from, in, inside, into, like, minus, near, of, off, on, onto, opposite, out, outside, over, past, per, plus, round, since, than, through, throughout, till, to, towards, under, underneath, unlike, until, up, via, with, within, without
>
> Certain **-ing** forms are also used as prepositions: barring, concerning, considering, excepting, pending, regarding, respecting

Some of the most common *compound prepositions* are shown below. There are a great many of this type in English.

> according to, in addition to, along with, apart from, as for, as from, as to, away from, because of, in case of, due to, except for, in favour of, in front of, instead of, on the left of, on the right of, by means of, near to, in need of, next to, on to, out of, owing to, in place of, with regard to, for the sake of, by the side of, in spite of, together with, on top of, in touch with, in view of, up to

There are two kinds of preposition: simple prepositions of one word only eg **in, on, about,** and compound prepositions which we make with more than one word eg **according to, because of, in front of, on top of** and very many more. Some of them appear in the lists opposite.

Prepositions appear with nouns of any kind, pronouns in their object forms and with gerunds. These take their position after prepositions as complements. We say that a preposition governs its complement; a preposition and its complement make a prepositional phrase eg **in a box, on a table, at two o'clock, in front of the house.** The gerund (**-ing**) is the only form of verb that can be complement of a preposition; the gerund is the verbal noun (**Chapter 27, 5 and D, E, F**).

2

place	*time*
at home	at one o'clock
in the kitchen	on Monday
behind the house	in July
in front of the car	before Friday
towards London	during the winter
from Cairo	about the tenth of June

Generally speaking, most prepositions connect their complements with place and time; prepositional phrases of place and time eg **at school, after the lesson** answer the questions **Where . . .?** and **When . . .?** and such phrases are, for practical purposes, adverbs of place and time.

With gerunds

a He's not very good **at doing things at home.**

b I don't complain **about washing up dishes.**

c She gets headaches **from sitting in the sun.**

d She could avoid them **by wearing a sun-hat.**

e The men took off their caps **on entering the house.**

3 Place prepositions: meanings and uses

a The train is standing **at platform ten.**

b It will start **from there** in seven minutes.

c You should get **onto the train** now, madam.

d I'll put your luggage **into a first-class coach.**

e The seat number is 42, **on the left hand side.**

Very often, place and time prepositions appear in phrases that seem to have little or no connection with place or time,

eg I'm **in** good health;
a book **on** Mongolia;
the matters **under** discussion;
good **at** games;
good **in** lessons

and many more idiomatic phrases. Learners become familiar with prepositional idioms when they already know the usual meanings and uses of prepositions.

There are two groups of place prepositions. In one group, the prepositions connect something with a point or space which is the complement — they say where it stands. We call them location prepositions. The other group mentions direction; they connect verbs of movement and places, or vehicles and places

eg the train **to** London
the plane **from** Lisbon etc.

We call them direction prepositions.

B Place prepositions: location

a tree at this end   a tree **at** the other end
a house **in** the middle

a tree **on** the left
a house **between** them

chairs **round** a table

a plant **in** a pot **on** a table

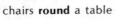

a man **at the top of** the ladder

a man **in the middle of** the ladder

a boy **at the bottom of** the ladder

a cat **on** a chair

a mouse **under** the chair

INFORMATION

a man **at** the desk

two boys **beside** a woman

two girls **in front of** their father, father **behind** his two girls

	+ 30
above zero	+ 20
	+ 10
0°C = zero	
	− 10
below zero	− 20

an open gate **in** the wall

a notice **on** the wall, **above** the picture

a picture **on** the wall, **below** the notice

ice-cream **in** a bowl,

cherries **on top of** the ice-cream

the roof **on top of** the building

the flat **above** mine

my flat here **in the middle**

the flat **below** mine

a man **in** a big car

people **on/in** a bus

somebody **in** jail

something **underneath** the tablecloth

a cloth **over** the table

a man **among** boys

a border **round** a plate

a bracelet **round** her wrist

a footbridge **over/across** a road

notices **all over** the wall
rubbish **all over** the floor

the school **opposite** the church
the church **opposite** the school

milk bottles **on** the doorstep,
outside number ten

bicycles leaning **against** a
fence

nobody **outside** the tent. Is
anybody **inside** the tent?

aeroplanes **in** the sky

a ship **on** the sea

traffic **on** the road

people **in** the street

and trains **on** the *lines
*line (Br) = track (Am)

1 In, on, at

a We live **in a small flat on the second floor.**

b It's **in Upping Street, at number 110.**

c You'll find milk **in a carton in the *fridge.**
*fridge = refrigerator (Br) = ice-box (Am)

d We've always spoken to our own girls **in English.**

e I'll meet you **at the corner** of First and Fifth Road.

f I've often been **in difficulties** but never **in debt.**

In an enclosed space: **in** a room, **in** a house, **in** a box, **in** a bottle etc.

In a state or condition: **in** good health, **in** comfort, **in** peace, **in** debt, **in** youth, **in** old age etc.

In a form of speech or writing: **in** English, **in** a whisper, **in** plain words, **in** print, **in** morse, **in** Braille, **in** ink, **in** pencil.

On a surface: **on** a wall, **on** a floor, **on** a ceiling, **on** a football pitch, tennis court, golf course etc.

At a point or certain spot: **at** home, **at**

g Whose picture is **in the frame on the little table in the corner?**

h Ann was **at home,** cooking something **on the stove in the kitchen.**

i Tom was **in the garden at the back** of the house, spraying water **on the plants.**

this/that address, **at** the corner (not \in the corner\), **at** number 10, Cable Street etc. **NOTE at Bromley** (a point on a map) or **in Bromley** (an area, a district or region in England).

2 Under, underneath

a In winter we wear woollen vests **under our shirts.**

b Divers work **under water** and miners work **under the ground.**

c The silly old fellow used to hide things **underneath his mattress.**

d There are mice **underneath the floor-boards.**

e I can hear them, **underneath the sofa.**

Under, underneath = in a lower place than the complement: There's a store room **under the kitchen** in the basement. **Underneath** has an extra meaning: **lower and covered by** + *complement:* eg He keeps **a pistol underneath the papers on his desk. Below and beneath:** are not synonyms. **Beneath** can mean **underneath** or we use it figuratively: She feels that she married **beneath her.**

3 Among/amongst; between

a I saw Bob **among the crowd outside the Houses of Parliament.**

b Next time we met he was **between two policemen.**

c The original sandwich was beef **between two slices of bread.**

d There's nearly always one black sheep **among the others.**

e Liz and Jane sat at the back with Billy **between them.**

We can use **among** or **amongst** with three or more persons or other things in the complement, eg The teacher stood **among the students,** they were **all round him.** We use **between** when we mention only two, eg Ann sat **between her parents.**

4 Beside

a Who are the girls sitting **beside you in this photograph?**

b They're my sisters, Mary **on the left,** Jane **on the right.**

c Our house is **right beside the Browns', on the right.**

d Mr Brown works **beside my brother, in the same office.**

Beside = on one or other side, on the left or on the right of the complement, NOT in front of or behind the complement. **NOTE right** + *preposition,* **right** means exactly, directly, all the way.

5 Opposite, against

a Dover, **on the English side** of the Channel, is **opposite Calais.**

b Grandpa is **against our playing cards on Sundays.**

c Don't lean **against that wall.** I've just painted it.

Opposite, against are not synonyms in any way as location prepositions; **opposite** means facing towards the complement, eg Jane's house is **opposite Ann's,** just across the street.

161

d She and I usually sit **opposite each other at meals.**

e **Facing each other/Opposite each other** we can talk more easily.

6 Round, about

a He wears a turban **round/about his head.**

b There are benches to sit on, **round the square.**

c You must have clear white lines **round a football pitch.**

d The dentist's is just **round the corner.**

7 Beyond, past

a The Lion Hotel is just **beyond/past the post office.**

b It's about a kilometre from here, **past the bridge.**

c We'll put up our tent there, **beyond those trees.**

d If the crocodiles in the river **beyond them** don't mind.

8 By, near

a The teacher's house is **by the village school.**

b The village is **near my mother's old home.**

c It still stands, **by their old watermill,** there.

9 Before, in front of

a There are two marble statues **before the palace gate.**

b A giant of a man sat **in front of me** so I didn't see much of the film.

You can leave your bike **opposite the front door** but **not against it,** please.

Round is the more common of these two. The complement of **round** can be round in shape, but need not be; as a location preposition **about** takes only complements that are round, or almost round, in shape.

As location prepositions, these mean the same; **past** is the more usual of the two. **Beyond** can have the additional meaning **out of sight and on the other side** as in **beyond the mountain, beyond the horizon;** we could not use **past** in these.

These are not quite the same in meaning:
    by = **beside** or **a little way beyond;**
    near = **not far from** the complement, **close to** the complement.

In spoken English, we seldom use **before** meaning **in front of;** it can appear in written English.

C Place prepositions: direction

Buses come **to** Oxford **from** London

and **from** Oxford **to** London.

Boys are throwing a ball **to** each other.

He aimed **at** the target.

Go **towards** Toledo.

Drive **along** this road.

Turn **off** to the right.

He's running **after** a butterfly.
It's flying **away from** him.

She's coming **out of** the Town Hall. She's coming **down** the steps.

He is going up the steps. He's going **into** the Town Hall.

Apples fall **off** the tree **onto** the ground.

The ball bounced **off** the floor **onto** Billy's head and **through** the open window.

People walking **across/over** the bridge to get **to** the other side.

Walking **against** the wind.

Going **with** the current.

Don't go **beyond** that notice.

He's going to jump **over** the bar.

She's going to jump **across** the stream.

They're going **by/past** the cinema.
They aren't going **into** the Rex.

A train is passing **through** a tunnel.

1 At, towards, for

a Suddenly, the cat sprang **at a bird** and almost caught it.

b The bird then flew **at the cat**, making **for its eyes.**

c The cat ran **for shelter** into the house.

d Is this the right train **for Scotland**, please?

e Scotland is a big place. **Where** are you making **for**, exactly?

f We want the express **for Edinburgh**, at ten o'clock.

g Go **towards the front** of the train. This part is **for Glasgow.**

h A porter came **towards us** and I asked him to carry our bags.

Prepositions of direction connect the complement with a verb whose activity refers to movement, physical or mechanical, intentional or accidental, in one or other direction.

To **aim, fly, shoot, spring, run, rush, + at/towards** someone or something does not necessarily mean that anyone reached the complement; eg He shot **at** the wolf and it ran away. **At** is the preposition we use when the verb implies attack, aggression and similar activity against the complement. **For** can connect a means of transport to a destination.

2 Into, onto

a Liz and Ann got **into the back** of my car. I had tied their luggage **onto the roof** and put my own **into the boot.**

b We went **into the waiting-room** at the airport, then stepped **into/onto** an airline bus that took us **to the aircraft.** Everyone walked **up the gangway onto the aeroplane.**

Generally, we can move **into** an enclosed place — a house, a room, a building of any kind, a car etc. We can move **onto** a surface: a platform, a dance-floor, a lawn, a football pitch etc. So, we get **into** or **onto** a bus or a train; **onto** a ship but **into** a boat, a car, a taxi. Movement upwards **onto** a raised surface and **into** an enclosed space are the usual ways.

3 Into, out of, onto, off

a Father went **into the public library** and didn't come **out of it** for ages.

b He'd taken some notes **out of several books**, to put **into his next lecture.**

c The committee came **onto the platform**, people moved **into their places**, and the meeting began.

d The soloist had gone **off the stage** but came back **onto it** to play an encore.

Into and **out of** are opposites. Whoever **goes into a place** will **come out of it,** sometime. **Onto** and **off**: these are direct opposites. We get **onto** (or **into**) a bus or train and at the end of the journey we get **off** (or **out of**) the bus or train. We move **off a platform** or any other surface. We get **out of** a car not **off.**

4 Above, over

a A black cloud is growing, just **above the hill.**

b Is it coming **over, from the sea?**

c Let's hope it will blow **over the town.**

d Do you ever go **over that hill**, Joe?

e Often. There are some lovely little villages **over there.** (= on the other side of the hill)

These both mean **in a higher position.** As direction prepositions they are not synonyms. If necessary, a person might go **over a mountain** on a mule, in a plane or on foot: **over** = across, from one side to the other. Men may fly to outer space but they cannot walk **above** a mountain.

5 Under, below, beneath

a You could make an extra room, **under the roof in the attic.**

b They live **in a village** called Middle Diddle on the side of a mountain. The village **above theirs** is Upper Diddle and Lower Diddle is the one **below their village.**

c They sink new oil wells as far as 500 metres **beneath/below** the sea-bed.

As direction prepositions, these all mean **in a lower position** than the complement. The complement of **under** usually names a surface:

under the ground
under the sea
under the roof;

in this way **under** and **above** are usually opposite positions.

Below often means the same as **under** but need not mention a surface: The village **below/above Linton** is called **Hillton Beneath. (beneath = under and covered by** the complement so that we cannot see it)

egThe tunnel runs **beneath the mountain.**

6 About, around

a We don't really need a car to go **about the town.**

b I travel **around London** on the Underground or by bus.

c Ann likes to walk **around the larger department stores.**

d Tom's working **about the garden.** He might be in the greenhouse or **around the apple trees.**

e He's somewhere **around/about the house,** for sure.

With verbs expressing movement, **about = from place to place, here, there and anywhere; around** can mean the same, or sometimes **round. All (a)round, all over the town** can mean **to** or **from** or **in** many different parts of the town/ country.

7 Along, across, over

Walk **along Main Street to the corner** of Sharp Road, then go **across Main Street,** take the first turning on your right **into Clare Place.** Go on **along that** for a hundred yards and you'll see the theatre opposite you (on the other side). You won't have to cross **over the road.** There's a subway passage **under the street.**

We go **along** any more or less horizontal line — a street, a *railway line, a canal etc — as far as we want to go. We go **across** a street, the Atlantic (etc), in order to get to the other side.

*railway line (Br) = railroad track (Am)

8 To, from, for

a If you take a bus **to the market square** and walk **from there to the bookshop** in Crown Street to buy some books **for Billy** to read, you can come home **for lunch,** in good time.

The complement of **to** mentions a place or a person as a destination (end of a journey or short walk, drive etc) or as a receiver

egI sent a letter **to Tom.**

b Grandma has sent a parcel **from her and Grandpa, for Billy and Jenny.** She has knitted woollen socks **for Bob,** and she'll give them **to him** when she comes to **our home,** or when we go **to hers.**

Activity does not always mean movement from place to place:
eg Ann made a sandwich **for Tom** (Tom was the receiver) (▶ also **1** above.)
The complement of **from** names a place or person as the point of departure, or as the sender
eg I had a letter **from Mexico/from Ann.**

9 Through, throughout

We had to bore four holes **through the front door** to put on a new lock. Police officers had visited houses **throughout the city.** They showed how a burglar could come in **through a door** with an old lock, without noise. Crimes of that sort had become more common **throughout the whole country,** especially where thieves had no need to enter **through a window.**

As direction prepositions, these have very little in common.
Through = from one end to the other
eg Ships pass **through the Suez Canal.**
You can't drive **through this village** — you must go round it.
Throughout = to / in every part of the complement eg
He has travelled **throughout Africa.**

10 Before, behind

a 'You must come **before a judge,**' the police officer said.
b 'Our car was **behind yours;** we saw how you were driving.'
c I didn't know the police were **behind me.** I don't like driving just **before a police car.** It makes me nervous.

Before = in front of and **behind** = at the rear of, as both location and direction prepositions.

11 By, past

'Was that Joe's motorbike that just went **by the house?**' 'Yes, he rode **past/by** the traffic lights and turned left.'

As direction prepositions, these mean the same thing: **to go past/by a place** = to pass it on the outside — we don't stop or go in.

12 In, within, inside, outside

a Prisoners were free to walk **about** and talk **within the prison walls.**
b They must stay **inside the building** during the hours of darkness, but can be **outside their cells** until bed-time.
c We'd like to build our house near Cambridge — **within a radius of twenty miles** or so.

Inside and **outside** as direction and location prepositions are opposites.
Inside refers to the interior and **outside** to the exterior of the complement.
Within usually means that there are limits and boundaries
eg Drivers must not go over thirty miles an hour **within the town.**

13 Towards, away from, off

a Are you going **towards Liverpool?** Could you give me a lift, please?

Movement **towards** a place or person in the complement, or **away from** them,

b I am, but only as far as Bolton. You can get **away from Bolton** easily enough. Jump in.

c They're repairing the road further ahead, so I'll have to turn **off it** near Shipley and come onto it further along.

D Time prepositions

does not always mean that we go all the way; movement is often for only part of the way (▶ **1** above). Especially on roads, we can start by going **towards Oxford** or **away from Oxford,** for example, and change direction later, by turning **off** that road **onto** another road that leads **to** our destination.

We have two kinds of time in connection with prepositions. There is time as we see it on a clock or calendar and there is time as it refers to lengths or periods of time, and we call these durations of time

1 Clock time

a As you intend to serve dinner **at eight o'clock** did you ask people to come **about half past seven** so that they'll all be here **by quarter to eight or so?**

b I'll be busy in the kitchen **between seven and eight** so I'll leave you to look after our guests **until eight o'clock.**

c If Ann and Bob haven't come home **by eight** they'll have to eat in the kitchen. Bob might come **after nine** but Ann should be home **before seven.**

d Can I do anything to help? Will everything be ready **by dinner time?** Perhaps I could peel potatoes, **until the first guests arrive.**

e No, thank you, John. Please keep out of the kitchen **until I call you.** I'll manage by myself **between now and then.**

f The office will be closed **(from)** 21st **through Saturday 29th July** (Am).

At: any definite time as it would appear on a clock.

About: a little earlier or later than the time in the complement; **about** = approximately.

By: possibly before, but not later than the time in the complement.

Until (till): an activity is already in progress and will go on **until** it stops at the time in the complement; **by** and **until** are opposites. ▶ also **11** below.

Between: an activity begins at the first time and ends at the second time in the complement; **through** often appears instead of **between** in Am.

Before and **after** as time prepositions mean **earlier than** and **later than** the time in their complements.

2 Calendar time

a They first met **at Christmas, on Christmas Eve,** actually, **in 1983.**

b **In the following spring,** they became engaged, and we were at their wedding **on the twenty-third of June.** It took place **at three in the afternoon.** We got home quite late **at night,** I remember.

c **The day before yesterday, on Tuesday,** Ann phoned to say they were coming **on Saturday,** which is **the day after tomorrow, in the afternoon.**

At: the complements of **at** can only be special times such as Christmas, Easter, Halloween; and **at** night, **at** the weekend.
On: any day or any date. We do not use **on** with **yesterday, tomorrow, next Friday, last** Friday (etc). eg They met last Tuesday. We also say **on the morning of the tenth of July,** for parts of a particular date. **In** any part of a day, except night (**at night**).

3 Time duration

> between, during, for, in, over, through, throughout, until (till), up to, within

4 Between

I wrote to Peter occasionally **between 1982** and **Christmas 1984. Between then and now** we have not written or spoken to each other, but I know he was here in England **between last June and August.**

5 During

'Did you hear the thunderstorm **during the night?'** 'Yes, it went on **for half an hour.** The weather has been so hot and wet **during the whole of this summer!** I'm taking my holidays **during the winter.'**

6 For

My brother has lived abroad **for many years.** He'll be visiting us here **for a few days** soon, **during the Easter holidays.**

7 In

I'm busy **at this moment.** I'll be free to talk to you **in five or ten minutes,** if you can wait **till then.** These reports must leave my office **within the next quarter of an hour** so that the members can read them **by the time** their meeting begins, **at eleven thirty.** I can't finish all my work **within normal working hours.**

8 Over

Harry came to see us **on Friday, in the evening after work,** and stayed **over the weekend until early on Monday morning.**

In: the complement can refer to the name of a month, season, or year. NOTE **on Friday** etc. Often, **on** drops out before the names of days (Am) — **We'll meet again (on) Friday.**

These prepositions can all appear in connection with periods of time. Some of them refer to the whole of the periods, some to points within a period of time and others can give either meaning.

Between can refer to one or more occasions or to a continuous activity during two points in time.

During covers the whole period; one or more occasions, or continuous activities take place **during that time.**

The complement of **for** mentions the length of an unbroken period of time; **for** does not introduce a clause (▶ **9** and **11** below).
NOTE **for** drops out before **all.** He stayed there **all day.**

The complement of **in** mentions the length of a period of time. Notice that in English we generally say, **in** an hour, **in** a few weeks, **in** a minute or two, eg John is out. He'll be here **in an hour** NOT ⟨**after an hour**⟩ (▶ also **12** below).

Over often appears with rather short periods of time eg **over** the weekend, **over** the last few days etc instead of **during.**

9 Since

I have lived here **since I was born, for more than seventy-five years. All through the years, since I was a little boy,** this village has been my home. We visited London five years ago, but haven't gone away again **since then.**

The complement of **since** marks the beginning of a time period already running its course. **Since,** in addition to usual complements, can introduce a time clause.

10 Through

Throughout his life, your grandfather was a careful, honest business man. There were occasional hard times, when he would work **through the night.**

Through can usually replace **during; throughout,** meaning **from beginning to end without interruption,** can also replace **during,** in this meaning only.

11 Until, up to

a We have paid the rent **up to the end** of next June.

b You can have the flat rent-free **up to then.**

c That should help you **until you start** earning a salary.

d We lived in the flat ourselves **up to last Saturday,** as you know. We shan't want it back **until you're quite ready** to leave. **Until then,** good luck!

The complements mention a time at which activities and happenings, already taking place, will stop or come to an end. **Until** (or **till**) can introduce a clause, **up to** cannot do this.

12 Within, in

a This bill must be paid **within seven days.** That is to say, **on** or **before Monday.**

b We allow a discount of five per cent for payment **within the same week,** two per cent for payment **within ten days.**

The complement of **within** mentions a time limit; at or before that time some activity will (or must) take place. **In** an hour, **in** a year, **in** five minutes etc simply mean at the end of an hour etc; when an hour has passed. Sometimes, speakers say **in** when **within** would be more exact.

13 For

a Let's hurry. I want to get there **for the start of the film.**

b John's away on business but he'll be home **for Jenny's birthday** next Sunday.

c Everyone in the family tries to get to our parents' home **for Christmas Day.**

For as a time preposition is often a short way of saying **in time for, in good time for,** with a complement that names a reason or purpose, in terms of time.

30 Prepositional adverbs

A Simple prepositions

> aboard, about, above, across, after, against, along, alongside, around, before, behind, below, beneath, besides (= as well (as), in addition (to)), between, beyond, by, down, in, inside, off, on, opposite, outside, over, past, round, since, through, throughout, under, underneath, up, within, without

Ordinary prepositions have complements that appear with them in the same phrase or clause, as in all the examples in the previous chapter of this book. When the other words in a sentence clearly show what the complement would be, or common sense allows us to understand what the complement would be, the prepositions opposite can stand alone, without complement. We call them prepositional adverbs.

a Jane was coming **up the steps** as Joe was going **down.**

b The **ferry boat** was about to leave. We went **aboard.**

c They gave us **food, good advice,** and money **besides.**

d She unlocked her front door and stepped **inside (the house).**

e **The telephone lines** were cut. I couldn't get **through.**

f If you can't afford **a new car,** you must do **without.**

B Compound prepositions

> in charge (of), in consequence (of), in consideration (of), in danger (of), in front (of), in place (of), in want (of), in common (with), in touch (with) (= in contact (with)), in exchange (for), in payment (for), in return (for)

Many compound prepositions can stand without complement, in the same way as the simple prepositions above. The end preposition in the compound phrase drops out when there is no complement.

a The captain is asleep. I'm **in charge** (of the ship) now.

b Harry and Liz have nothing **in common** (with each other).

c I don't know where Rob lives. We don't keep **in touch.**

d I have dollars and want pounds **in exchange.**

e You'll need an umbrella and, **in addition,** gum-boots.

C Prepositional adverbs in phrasal verbs

1 **a** The meeting will **go on** until six o'clock.
   b A sportsman's pistol **went off** by accident.
   c Father is **coming back** from Brazil tomorrow.
   d The men **stood up** when the colonel **came in.**
   e Cholera has **broken out** in some of the camps.

An ordinary *finite verb + a prepositional adverb* make a phrasal verb; the prepositional adverb usually goes by the name *particle* (of a phrasal verb). The meaning of a phrasal verb can be very different from the usual meanings of each its parts. The phrasal verbs in **1 a-e** opposite are all intransitive.

2

transitive phrasal verb	direct object
Someone was **running down**	our friends.
The driver **turned off**	his engine.
She **ran up**	enormous debts.

verb of movement	prepositional phrase
A boy was running	down the street.
The driver turned	off the main road.
She ran	up the steps.

Some phrasal verbs are transitive; the noun, pronoun or gerund is a direct object, NOT a complement of a preposition. As object of a phrasal verb in the active voice, it can become a passive voice subject.
NOTE *verbs of movement + prepositional phrase of place/direction* are not phrasal verbs; their meanings are exactly the same as the meanings of their parts.

3 **a** People were **taking off their coats and hats.**
      People were **taking their coats and hats off.**
      People were **taking them off.**
   b Someone **turned on the radio.**
      Someone **turned the radio on.**
      Someone **turned it on. I turned it off.**
   c Will you **cut up the meat** please?
      Will you **cut the meat/it up,** please?

The object of a transitive phrasal verb can be a noun or a gerund; these can be after the particle or before it, without change of meaning. Pronoun objects come before the particle of a phrasal verb eg **Put your hat on./Put on your hat./Put it on.**

4 **a** The radio (that) **you turned off** was far too loud.
   b The meat (that) **I cut up** was quite fat.
   c The door (that) you wanted **to break down** wasn't locked.
   d A friend that **I rang up** wasn't at home.
   e The secret, which **she soon found out,** was no secret.

The particles of phrasal verbs are not mobile; that is to say they cannot move about from place to place within a sentence. We do not treat the particles of phrasal verbs as if they were normal prepositions. Particles cannot govern relative pronouns and so cannot stand before them in relative clauses.
For phrasal verbs in passive voice, ▶ **Chapter 25, 7.**

5 A short list of very common transitive phrasal verbs is given below, with some items commonly occurring as objects of the active verbs.

back up (a friend, a proposal)
break down (figures, statistics, complicated reports)

blow up (a bridge, a building, with explosives)
blow up (a balloon, a football; a photograph)
break off (negotiations, an engagement, a discussion)
bring about (a change, an opportunity, a result, consequence)
bring up (a family, a matter for discussion)
call in (the police, a doctor, experts)
call off (a meeting, a party, a search)
draw up (a contract, letter, petition)
draw up (of a car — come to a stop, pull up)
fill out/in (a form, application)
fill up (a glass, a tank, a space)
find out (a secret, information)
get over (an idea, explanation); ▶ also list of prepositional verbs
give away (one's possessions; a secret)
give off (steam, a smell, a vapour)
give up (a problem, a struggle)
give up (smoking, meat)
hold up (of traffic, progress — to delay, hinder)
hold up (a bank, a traveller — commit armed robbery)
let off (the culprit — treat him leniently)
live down (a scandal, a bad reputation)
make out (handwriting, what you say/mean)
make up (a story, an excuse)
put by (money, savings)
put off (a meeting, an appointment, a decision)
rub down (a horse, an athlete)
rub out (a mistake)
set/let off (fireworks, explosives)
set out (ideas, points, arguments)
set up (a firm, a system)
switch on/off (machinery, electrical appliances)
take down (dictation, a letter, notes)
take on (new workers, extra work)
take over (a business, a post, a duty)
take up (a hobby, a new interest)
try on (new shoes, a coat, a hat)
turn on/off (water taps: also ▶ switch)
work out (a solution, method, plan)

Note also the following phrasal verbs:
*let somebody down — fail to meet one's obligations to somebody
*put somebody out — cause inconvenience or disappointment to somebody
*see somebody off (on a journey, at the airport)
*see somebody off (the premises, the property, estate)
show somebody in — conduct him to my room, office etc.
show somebody out — conduct him to the front door
take somebody in — trick, deceive somebody
tell somebody off — scold, reprimand somebody

All of these are transitive. The 'somebody' in the object can become the subject of the passive: The Olympic team **was seen off** by an enormous crowd.

*The particles in these four verbs generally follow the direct object: John **let** the team **down** by failing to turn out. They **put** everyone **out** by the sudden change in arrangements.

31 Prepositional verbs

1 General description

prepositional verbs	objects
Will you **speak for**	the candidate?
Did you **speak to**	the prisoner?
Have you **spoken about**	me?
We have **agreed on**	buying a house.
You must **set about**	getting a job.
I shall **insist on**	doing as you say.
	this/that.

A large number of verbs combine with prepositions that come after them eg **break into, look after, look for,** and so on. We call them prepositional verbs. All prepositional verbs are transitive: an object always follows the prepositional particle (phrasal verbs have adverbial particles; ▶ **C1-2** above).

The object of a prepositional verb is the noun, gerund or pronoun that follows the prepositional particle. *Verb + preposition* has its own meaning which may or may not have a connection with the separate elements of the prepositional verb; eg **take after** someone, **take to** someone, **take up with** someone, all have quite different meanings.

2 Passive voice

The prisoner / The candidate	will be spoken **to** / was spoken **about**	by them.
You	were spoken **for**	
Buying a house / Getting a job / His doing as I say	has been **agreed on.** / must be **set about** now. / will be **insisted on.**	

Passive voice: the direct object of a prepositional verb in active voice can become subject of the same verb in the passive voice; the prepositional particle does not move away from its place after the verb. Some verbs such as **come across, take to,** are seldom passive.

3 Relative clause

a The children (that) we **look after** aren't ours.

b The person we **spoke for** wasn't your candidate.

c The prisoner (that) you **spoke about** is now a free man.

Relative clause: the prepositional particle can stand before **whom** or **which** in a relative clause in the active voice. More often, it comes at the end of the clause after its verbal part; often, the prepositional particle seems unnatural, at the beginning of the clause.

4 Two particles

	objects
I will not **put up with**	your rudeness.
Are you **going in for**	the marathon?
I shall **stand up to**	his bullying.
You can't **get out of**	paying tax.

Some prepositional verbs have two particles; the first is adverbial and the second is prepositional. Generally, the particles remain together at all times, especially when the preposition is **of** or **for.** All these verbs are transitive.

5 The following is a short list of some fairly common prepositional verbs, with examples of objects in brackets. Although all such verbs are considered transitive and therefore can appear in the passive, in practice some of them seldom do so. An asterisk* indicates this.

abide by (the law, the verdict, a decision, promise)
accede to (a plea, request)
account to (somebody for one's actions)
adhere to (opinions, promises, regulations)
admit to (a bad habit, one's weakness)
admit of* (an explanation, interpretation)
agree on (a price, a date, a place)
agree with* (**1** someone, someone's opinions, **2** coffee doesn't agree with me = upsets my stomach)
allow for (future needs, inflation, contingencies)
apply for (a situation, pension, permit, licence)
approve of (behaviour, actions, status, habits, customs)
arrive at (a decision, conclusion, an understanding)
ask for (someone, help, advice)
attend to (someone, his needs, business)
believe in (ghosts, democracy, God)
break into (**1** a house, a shop **2** a conversation = interrupt)
call on (**1** visit briefly, **2** summon somebody)
care for (**1** the sick, the aged, the young, **2** I don't care for ski-ing = I'm not keen on it)
cater for (one's needs, comfort, entertainment)
come across* (an old letter, a lost ring = find or meet by chance)
come by (a sum of money, a rare painting = acquire, obtain, sometimes by devious or dishonest means)
comment on (performance, abilities, the news)
conform to (standards, rules, norms)
consent to (a marriage = give permission for)
decide against/on (a holiday in December, bacon and eggs, the alternative)
depend on (one's father, someone's help = rely on: It depends on* the weather/John/you etc. cannot be passive)
dispose of (rubbish, old newspapers, an argument)
enlarge on (the difficulties, dangers, advantages)
get over (an illness, disappointment, difficulty)
hint at (suspicions, possibilities, undisclosed secrets)
hope for (improvement, success, good news)
insist on (rights, explanation, payment, protocol)
laugh at (a joke = make fun of, be amused at)
look after (the baby, one's interests, one's property)
look at/on (somebody as something: she looked on Louis as a brother)
look into (the circumstances, cause, matter, crime = investigate, examine)
look to somebody for something (we look to the experts for advice)
object to (somebody's actions, presence, arrangements)
persist in (efforts, attempts, denials, refusal)
quarrel with* (a friend, one's wife = fall out with somebody)
rely on (someone = depend on)
resort to (other methods, cheating, threats)
respond to (treatment, kindness, encouragement, stimulation)
see through (a trick, deception, a lie)

set about somebody (a victim = assault somebody, attack somebody)
set about * (the job in hand, the day's work)
set upon somebody (the dog set upon me, he set his dog on me = attack)
speak about/of (the past, one's children)
speak to (the crowd, one's boss)
speak for (one's friend, a cause = speak on somebody's or something's behalf)
speak for (goods or property offered for sale: the interesting items were spoken for before the auction began)
stand by* (a friend, a decision, one's promise)
succeed in (one's intentions, hopes, purposes)
succeed to (the throne, a title)
take to somebody* (= feel a liking for somebody)
take to* (drink, drugs, bad ways)

6 A list of the more common phrasal verbs having two particles follows:

catch up on
check up on
come up to* (expectation, standard)
come up with (ideas, solutions, suggestions)
cut down on (luxuries, holidays)
do away with (responsibility, hardship, suffering = abolish)
fall out with* (=quarrel)
get away with (=avoid or escape punishment)
get down to (work, business, negotiation)
get out of (difficulty, unpleasant work or duty)
go in for (sports, games)
keep up with* (current events, inflation, the neighbours)
lead up to (climax, the main fact)
look down on (=despise somebody)
look up to (=respect, esteem somebody)
make up for (=compensate, replace)
make up to (=flatter, ingratiate)
put up with (=allow and suffer from rudeness, laziness, inconvenience etc)
run out of* (supplies, patience)
stand up for (=support and defend rights, justice, fair play, my little sister)
stand up to (a bully, harsh weather)

The asterisk* indicates verbs that seldom occur in the passive.

32 Adverbs and adverbial clauses

A Adverbs

1 a Richard speaks English **fluently** (*manner*)
   b They sell fresh fish **there** (*place*)
   c We might buy some fish **today** (*time*)
   d Ann plays the guitar **expertly** (*manner*)
   e She often appears **at concerts** (*place*)
   f Let's go **to the cinema tonight** (*place, time*)

Generally speaking, adverbs are words that we add to a sentence in order to say something about the activity of the verb. For example, we mention the time of the activity (**yesterday, tomorrow, last week** etc) with an adverb of time; the place of the activity (**here, there, at home** etc) with an adverb of place, and if we mention the style or manner (**well, badly, beautifully, politely** etc) we use an adverb of manner. We say that an adverb modifies the verb, ie it gives more meaning to it.

2 Adjectives in **-ful** add **-ly** for the adverb: **beautiful(ly), careful(ly), useful(ly)**.
   Adjectives ending in **-le** change **-e** to **-y**: **horrible/horribly, miserable/miserably, possible/possibly**.
   Adjectives ending in diphthongs and in **-y** as a vowel: mostly add **-ly; coyly, newly**. We also have **daily, gaily**.
   When the adjective ends in *consonant* + **-y, -y** usually becomes **-i; prettily, happily** but we also have **shyly**.

Most adverbs of manner are adjective + **-ly: badly, nicely, happily, beautifully, helpfully, willingly, tiredly**.

3 a I'll **get up early** to catch the **early train**.
   b If you **run fast** you might get the **fast train**.
   c We all **work hard**. It's very **hard work**.
   d This is **the right answer**. You've **done it right**.
   e She's a **kindly woman**. She **treats us kindly**.

Some adverbs and adjectives are in the same form; early, kindly, fast, *late, *hard, long, *high, low, *right, *wrong, *dear.
*These can have an adverb form in **-ly** but with a change in meaning.

4 Positions of adverbs in sentences

		objects	adverbs
	copied	a Chinese vase	**expertly** (M).
They	mended	a skeleton	**at the museum** (P).
	restored	a picture	**yesterday** (T).
	painted	a water clock	**last week** (T).

In English, adverbs do NOT come between a transitive verb and its object; adverbs can follow the object, but do not come before it. Generally, when we have two or more adverbs of different kinds, we place them in a certain order: adverbs of manner come before adverbs of place and time; adverbs of place

a Tom waited **patiently** (M) **in the car** (P).

b We all slept **on the balcony** (P) **last night** (T).

c I slept **soundly** (M) **until sunrise** (T).

d Ann went **to Dover** (P) **by train** (M) **yesterday** (T).

e Peter rides **to work** (P) **on his bike** (M) **most days** (T).

5 Position before the verb

a **Ann has kindly offered** to go shopping for me.

b **I willingly agreed** to her doing this.

c **Tom respectfully knocked** on the professor's door.

d **The professor cheerfully called** Tom to come in.

e **He helpfully explained** Tom's mistakes to him.

f She **sings** those old songs **beautifully**.

g You **acted** your part **quite nicely**.

h He **drives too carelessly**, in town.

i She **looks after** the children **perfectly well**.

j I think she should **treat** them **more strictly**.

6 a **She hopefully expects** to do well in the exam.

b **I have carefully read** your latest report.

c **You will be anxiously waiting** to hear my views.

d **Tom might have been kindly trying** to help you.

e **He could have been tactfully meaning** to avoid trouble.

f **I foolishly lost** my temper with the poor fellow.

g **He unintentionally said** the wrong thing at a bad time.

7 a I agree with her **perfectly reasonable** opinion.

b She's **absolutely right**, and you're **quite wrong**.

c I'm **extremely sorry** to tell you this.

come before adverbs of time. So, if we have all three kinds, the order is manner, place, time (MPT) after intransitive verbs and after the objects of transitive verbs. With verbs of movement (**come, go, walk** etc) the order is usually place, manner, time (PMT). Place adverbs are very often in the form of prepositional phrases of location or direction (▶ **Chapter 29, A3, B1-9, C1-13**). For time ▶ **Chapter 29, A2, D1-13**.

Adverbs of manner that refer to the verb can usually take position before the verb, instead of following it; often, they point to some attitude or manner in the subject too, and normally appear before the verb to do this.

Adverbs that express blame, criticism or praise by anyone about anyone's way of doing things do not come before the verb. When the speaker mentions any degree of ability, excellence, cleverness, skill etc and their opposites, as his personal judgement or criticism, the adverb of manner stays in the end position (**4 above**).

When there is no auxiliary, the adverb comes directly before the verb, after the subject; when there is one auxiliary, the adverb comes between that and whatever part of the verb we are using. When there are two or more auxiliaries, the adverb follows them and takes its place immediately before whatever part of the verb we are using. In practice, however, the adverb often comes after any one of the two or three auxiliaries.

We have seen that adverbs modify verbs (**1 above**). Adverbs of manner, when their meanings are suitable, can also modify adjectives and other adverbs. They come before the adjective or other

d I'm sure you are. And I'm **terribly hurt,** too.

e You've behaved **remarkably foolishly.**

f For a grown man, you've been **utterly childish.**

g There's no need to be **so rudely outspoken.**

h Let's have a **truly friendly** talk about things.

adverb, wherever it may be in the sentence. Adjectives often appear in the complements of **be, seem, become** and other state verbs.

8 Outside position

Perhaps
Possibly
Probably
Fortunately
Clearly
Honestly
Naturally
Personally
Definitely
At home
On the train
That day
Last night

This is a position before the subject. The adverb of manner modifies the whole sentence, not just the verb, the speaker offers an opinion or comment about the statement that follows — it seems possible etc to the speaker. The speaker can use an adverb and mention his own feelings or attitudes. He is speaking honestly etc. We place a comma after the adverb.

Adverbs of place and time sometimes take the outside position, to give them more importance, or when the usual end positions are over-full with other adverbs and prepositional phrases. We place a comma after the adverb.

a **Honestly,** I have to work for my daily bread.
I have to **work honestly** for my daily bread.

b **Naturally,** children become adults, with time.
Children **become adults naturally,** with time.

c **I, personally,** have nothing to say to Peter.
I have nothing to say **personally to Peter.**

d **Definitely,** the man on the phone asked for you.
The man on the phone **asked definitely** for you.

e **Regrettably,** our long partnership has ended.
Our long partnership **has ended regrettably.**

Adverbs of manner in outside positions refer to the speaker in some way, as we have seen. So there can be a great difference in meaning when the same adverb, in another position, modifies the verb. The outside position can also be immediately after the subject, and between commas; sometimes it can be the end of a sentence, after a comma. When speaking, there is a short pause for all the commas.

9 Pre-verb adverbs

We
 	
You
 	
They
 	
Ann
and
Tom
	always
	never
	hardly ever
	scarcely ever
	almost never
	often
	usually
	seldom
	sometimes
		visit her on Sundays.
		have coffee at breakfast.
		listen to the radio now.
		go to the theatre
		   nowadays.
		drink beer with a meal.
		disagree with each other.
		mention the cost of living.
		spend the weekend at
		   home.
		discuss political affairs.

Frequency adverbs answer the question:
How often? How many times? They are:
  always, *sometimes, hardly ever,
  scarcely ever, almost never, never,
  *often, *seldom, *frequently,
  *occasionally, *rarely, *usually.

All of these can take positions before the verb.
*These can all take end positions as well as pre-verb positions, and often do so; when another adverb such as **very, so, fairly, rather, more, most, quite** comes before them, they take the end position (▶ **12** below).

10

I can You could	barely hardly seldom scarcely just never	read the headlines see what you write make out his face recognise people	without glasses. in such poor light. at that distance so far away.

Degree adverbs
  barely, hardly, scarcely, just, just about, almost, nearly, very nearly, not quite, quite.
These all take pre-verb positions only when they refer to the activity in the verb.

11a Never do we agree about anything!

  b Hardly ever does he remember my birthday.

  c Seldom have we heard such fine singing.

  d Barely had I fallen asleep when you telephoned.

  e Hardly had he gone out, when he was here again.

  f Never would she tell such a lie!

Negative and near-negative frequency and degree adverbs always appear with an affirmative verb as in the tables at **9** and **10** opposite. These are:
  never, hardly ever, scarcely ever, almost never, seldom (frequency); and
  barely, hardly, scarcely (degree).
When these modify the verb, they sometimes come first in the sentence, for dramatic effect or literary style. The pattern is **Never** etc + *interrogative form of the verb;* there is no question, this is only a matter of style and, exclamations apart, seldom occurs in spoken English.

12 Degree adverbs and other adverbs

An adverb has its own normal meaning eg They lived **happily.** An adverb of degree before **happily** would tell us whether they lived **very** happily or **just** happily or that they lived in **some degree of** happiness or unhappiness.

They wrote	most	interestingly.	10
	quite	clearly.	9
She talked	very	passionately.	8
	so	cleverly.	7
You argued	rather	foolishly.	6
He replied	quite	reasonably	5-6
	—	reasonably.	5
They agreed	fairly	wisely.	4
	not very	politely.	3
She objected	barely	respectfully.	2
	hardly	audibly.	1
He spoke	scarcely	correctly.	1

Note degree adverbs also appear with adjectives (▶ **33 B**).

B Adverbial clauses

1 **a** **As/Since nobody else wants to come out,** I'll take a short walk by myself.

  b I went out by myself **because the others didn't want to take a walk.**

  c **As/Since the man is a complete stranger to me,** I can tell you nothing about him.

  d Tom can't tell them anything about that man **because he's a complete stranger (to Tom.)**

  e **Because of his sleeping on duty** he lost his job as a night security guard.

2 **a** I had received my salary, **so I had some money.**

  b You've eaten a good breakfast, **so you won't be too hungry** before lunch is ready.

  c Old Mrs Green was a very helpful neighbour, **so lots of people became her close friends.**

  d I must clean my glasses **so that I can see better.**

  e He disconnected the telephone **so that it would not disturb his sleep.**

  f Ann wears an apron over her dress, **so that it will keep clean in the kitchen.**

  g I wish I had more capital **so that I could start up a firm of my own.**

  h The salesman talked **so convincingly** about his wonderful washing machine **that I agreed** to let him wash our clothes in it.

In the table opposite, the norms are the **adverbs** themselves as they stand eg **reasonably** and norms = five points on this degree scale. They go above or below the norm when degree adverbs modify them.

hardly and **scarcely** can express near negative (zero) degree, when the speaker, not wishing to be hard, avoids a negative adverb — **unwisely, impolitely** etc. For **too** and **enough** ▶ **Chapter 27, A12.**

Cause, reason and consequence: **as, since, because** can all introduce a clause that states a consequence of the cause in the main clause of the sentence. Generally, the cause clause comes first, but it can also follow the main clause; either way there is a comma between the clauses. **Because** can introduce a clause that states the reason for the situation in the main clause; **as/since** do not do this. Reason clauses follow the main clause without commas. **Because of** can have a noun or gerund complement.

Clause of result: **so, so that, so. . .that.** So introduces a clause of result, after the main clause; the main clause states the cause that produces the result. **So that** introduces a clause of result; the result **may/might, can/could, ought to/should, would be** a consequence of the activity in the main clause. **So that** clauses often express possible or probable results, and purposes, and intentions. In **So. . .that. . .,** so is an adverb of degree (**12** above) followed by a **that** clause of consequence or result.

NOTE **so that. . .** clauses do not say definitely that the results, purposes or intention (of the subjects in the main clause) become actual facts: He gave me a pill so **I slept better** (fact). He gave me a pill so ***that I would sleep better** (and I did/but I didn't sleep better).

*In spoken Am, **that** is often absent.

i The water is **so cold** in early spring **that very few people go in for a swim.**

3 **a** **The harder** you work, **the more** money you earn.

b **The less** you know of my doings, **the less** you can tell.

c **The faster** he talked, **the less** I understood.

d **The older** she grew, **the more patient** she became.

e **The more reasonably** I argued, **the less** she listened.

f **The earlier** we start, **the sooner** we shall finish.

Clauses of proportion: there are two clauses. Each clause makes a comparison with the other, in equal measure and proportion. **The more/The less** + noun or adjective or adverb. When the adjective or adverb ends in **-er** for the comparative degree, we do not need **more/less: the harder, the faster, the earlier** etc. There is a comma between the clauses.

4 **a** **Although Tom and Joe are brothers,** they are quite different in character and looks.

b Alec and I seldom meet nowadays, **though we shall always be good friends.**

c **In spite of the very cold weather,** we must go out and clear away the snow.

d We gave him a job, **in spite of his having a police record against him.**

Clause of concession: **although, though, in spite of.** There are two clauses; the fact in either of the clauses seems surprising or unexpected, when we compare it with the fact in the other clause. **Although, though** introduce concession clauses; **in spite of** has a noun or gerund complement as concessions. Main clauses or concessions can come first. **Nevertheless (formal), still, yet** meaning **in spite of this/that** cannot join clauses together; they appear after semi-colons (;) or full stops. Also **notwithstanding** (very formal) can appear as first word or last word, in a concession.

'The fellow's a rascal.'	'Still	he's my brother.'
'The man's an idiot.'	'Nevertheless	she loves him.'
'He's a lazy lout.'	'Yet	you trusted him.'

5 **a** This coffee is **too strong to drink** (don't drink it).

b Mr Boni speaks Italian **too fast for us to follow him.**

c The battery was **too weak to start the car.**

d Jane speaks **too clearly for anyone to misunderstand** what she says.

e Tom has been **too well trained to make an elementary mistake like that.**

Too... + *infinitive.* **too** is an adverb of degree and combines with adjectives and adverbs to show extreme, excessive degree, so that the activity in a following infinitive should not or does not happen; the infinitive does not take a negative form (▶ **Chapter 27, A12**).

33 Adjectives

A Form/use

a house, **the** house(s), **that/this** house, **my** house, **every** house, **each** house, **no** house, **all** houses

Articles, demonstrative and possessive adjectives (and possessive nouns) and all other items that replace articles move away from their place next to the noun, and adjectives enter:

a **wooden** house, **the wooden** house(s), **these/those wooden** houses, **your/their wooden** houses, **every/each wooden** house, **no wooden** house(s), **all wooden** houses

Adjectives are words that appear with nouns of all kinds and say something about the noun eg **a man** can be a **tall** man, a **tall, dark** man, a **tall, dark, handsome man**, a **tall, dark, handsome, Australian** man, and finally, **This/That** (tall, dark, handsome Australian) man. So adjectives describe nouns and as they do so, they limit the category or group or type in the noun. Not every man is a **tall** man, though each man is a man and nothing less or more. Adjectives usually take their place before nouns or in the complements of **be, become, seem, appear, sound, look** etc. Adjectives have only one base form and it goes with nouns of all genders, singular and plural, without change.

B Order

Group 1	Group 2		Nouns
The first	polite,	pretty	girl(s).
That other	kind,	dark	student(s).
Her second	tough,	long-haired	one.
No	rude,	plain	person(s).
All	serious,	handsome	women.

Group 2	Group 3	Nouns
gentle, long-tailed	big, old	horse.
polite, red-haired	tall, young	woman.
comfortable, well-made	soft, new	divan.
uncomfortable, shiny	hard, narrow	bench.
useful, polished	heavy, oval	table.
awkward, ill-made	bulky, square	parcel.

the other kind, pretty, black girls
that hardworking, big old grey horse
this hard, narrow, short, brown divan

Group 1 is farthest from the noun (▶ A above) and contains articles and any item which stands in place of an article; some of these can be followed by a cardinal or ordinal number.

Group 2 includes personal character and physical appearance in that order; often we reverse the order — a **pretty, polite** girl — a **polite, pretty** girl.

Group 3 pushes Group 2 away from the noun and enters the space. Group 3 mentions physical particulars: height (or length); age; width or bulk; size and shape — all in normal order. Generally, **old** and **young** come next to the noun, when they refer to age. Otherwise, age can come before physical dimensions, **a new, high wall, some fresh, thick cream** etc. Colour adjectives take their place immediately before nouns after adjectives in Group 1, 2 and 3.

Her table.
Her oak table.
Her English oak table.
Her polished, English oak table.
Her large, polished English oak table.
Her large, polished, antique, English oak table.

The only new **red carpet.**
Your first, good-looking new **blue suit.**
The cheapest sweet **white wine.**
That beautiful old **blue china teapot.**

---

bus driver, band leader, petrol pump, front door, washing-machine, frying pan, civil servant, army officer, oil-well, China tea, fire alarm, emergency exit

---

a patient, rather handsome, old-fashioned, London police officer
NOTE A whole sequence of adjectives from Groups 1-5 is very seldom necessary. What we must keep in mind is that items from one group stand nearer to the noun than items from other groups do.

Adjectives in Group 4 are participles eg **polished,** or mention nationality or provenance (where things come from) eg **English,** and materials, eg **oak,** in that order. Group 4 adjectives push Group 3 towards the front of the sentence eg **large,** and move into the space.

Colour adjectives can come before participles: Her large, **dark brown, polished,** English oak table. The colour adjective can have any item in Groups 1, 2 and 3 before it.

Group 5 adjectives always come nearest to the noun because they are actually parts of compound nouns; they express purpose, use, type and so on.
We can, of course, have suitable adjectives from any of the other groups, in proper order, before Group 5 items. Within each group, except 4 and 5, we can change the order — in 2, for example, **a polite, pretty girl** is normal order — **a pretty, polite girl** gives more attention to **pretty.**

C Position

a She was a woman **careful of her good name.**

b He was a man **too proud of his ancestry, to be snobbish.**

c Her father was a doctor **famous for his work with children.**

d They are people (who are) **respected by everyone.**

e I don't know anyone **capable of doing this work.**

f Everybody **willing to help** should telephone 849 630.

g Can you suggest somewhere **suitable for a new hospital?**

h Build it anywhere **less noisy than the airport area is.**

i There's nothing **better than aspirin for her headaches.**

j Something **important** has happened today.

Adjectives can follow a noun when there is a prepositional phrase with it. Often, the *adjective + prepositional phrase* is the remainder of a relative clause. Adjectives can come after the **any-, every-, some-** and **no-** series of pronouns (▶ **Chapter 15, A1-3**); they do not come before them.

34 Comparison of adjectives and adverbs

A Comparison of equals

1   John is **as** tall **as** his father.
     Mary speaks English **as** well **as** I do.
     negative:
     John isn't **as/so** tall **as** his father.
     Mary doesn't speak English **as/so** well **as** I do.

2 **a** Liz doesn't want **as large a house as this** (is).
   b Liz doesn't want **a house as large as this** is.
   c I don't drink coffee **as** often **as** you do.
   d He could always run **as** fast **as** I could.
   e Tom's work seems **as** good **as** his father's.

Adjectives and adverbs of suitable meanings have three levels of comparison: comparison of similarity; comparison of differences (between two) and the superlative degree which shows that among three or more items in a comparison, one is greater in some way than all the others. It is usual to speak of the positive degree (norm), comparative degree and the superlative degree of adjectives and adverbs.
In negative comparisons, **the first as** often becomes **so,** but this is not a rule.

As + *adjective/adverb* + **as** is the normal pattern between the two parties in a comparison of equals. The adjectives and adverbs are in their usual unchanged forms, in their usual places.

B Comparative degree

1 **a** Joe gets up **earlier than I do,** usually.
   b Tom's father is **taller than Tom** is.
   c Tom is **shorter than his father.**
   d Mary speaks English **less well than I do.**
   e I speak English **better than Mary does.**
   f Tom could always run **faster than me.**

2 **a** Ann is **the tallest girl in our class.**
   b She isn't **more intelligent than some of us.**
   c Jane's **the most intelligent woman I know.**
   d **The highest mountain in the world** is Everest.
   e Peter behaves **less foolishly** nowadays.
   f He helps us **more willingly than before.**
   g He talks **the most politely of all my students.**
   h He's **the least hardworking of my four sons.**

Adjectives and adverbs of one or two syllables take the suffix **-er: fast, faster; hard, harder; early, earlier** etc.
Adjectives ending in **-ful** and **-less** do not take **-er.** They take the same patterns as adjectives and adverbs of more than two syllables: **more** + *the positive (norm)* for the comparative and **the most** + *norm* for the superlative degree. We can also have **less** and **the least** in place of **more** and **the most; than** connects the two sides in comparison of unequal values.
NOTE Adjectives ending in **-ing** and past participles as adjectives take **more. . .** and **most. . .** for comparative and superlative degrees.

184

C Different genders

a **A man** much older **than Ann** is wants to marry her.

b **A boy** kinder than **our girl** was didn't exist.

c **A house** as large as **theirs** would cost a lot.

d Liz doesn't want **a house as small as this is.**

The first noun can also be subject or object and take comparative phrases with the second noun following (▶ **A a-b** above).

Comparisons such as **a child/a person as happy as Billy/Jenny is; a happier child/person than Billy/Jenny is** are acceptable; child/person in common gender can go with Billy (male), Jenny (female). We could not say \as tall a man as Ann is; a taller man than Ann is\; The first noun must come before the comparison in order to make sense: **a man as tall as Ann is.**

D Comparisons and pronouns

a John's older **than me (than I am).**

b I'm as tall **as her (as she is).**

c She was the youngest **of them.**

d I know **him** better than **her.**

e She loved **us** as much as **him.**
I know **him** better than I know **her.** She loved **us** as much as she loved **him.**
or:
I know him better than **she knows him.**
She loved us as much as **he loved us.**
= I know him **better than** she does. She loved us **as much as** he did.
We could also say:
I know him better than **she (does).**
She loved us as much as **he (did).**

The personal pronoun at the end of a comparison is usually in the object form in spoken English. This is quite correct when we analyse **as** and **than** as prepositions, and **of** certainly is a preposition. If **than** and **as** are prepositions, the sentences **a-b** and **d-e** are correct as they stand.

In familiar, not careful speech, the intended meaning can be different; **as** and **than** are not prepositions, they are conjunctions between clauses each with its own subject. In quite formal spoken and written English, the subject pronoun can stand without an auxiliary or other verb (see the last two sentences opposite). Generally, we have an auxiliary; without it, a sentence often seems too formal, too careful, especially in spoken English.

E Irregular adjectives and adverbs

good, better, best; bad, worse, worst;
*well, *better; are adjectives.
well, better, best; badly, worse, worst
are adverbs.

A few adjectives and adverbs are irregular in their comparative and superlative degree forms.
***Well, better** refer to someone's health: **I'm very well,** thank you. I hope **your cough is better** today. **Well** is also the adverb that corresponds to the adjective **good.**
These refer to degree in adjectives and adverbs or to quantity and number in nouns. ****Many** appears with plural nouns only.

little, less, least; some, more, most;
some, less, least; much, more, most;
**many, more, most

elder, eldest son/sister/brother

far, farther, farthest; or further, furthest

We use these forms, not **older, oldest,** to place members of a family in order of age. All of these refer to distance; only **further, furthest** can mean **additional,** eg I need **further information.**

F Degree adverbs and adjectives

His letter	seems	**most**	interesting.
Her talk	was	**quite**	clear.
Your	appears	**very**	passionate.
argument	sounds	**so**	clever.
	is	**rather**	foolish.
His reply	will be	**quite**	reasonable.
	was	**fairly**	wise.
Their	should be	**barely**	polite.
objection	might be	**hardly**	respectful.
	sounded	**scarcely**	audible.
His speech			correct.

Degree adverbs can modify adjectives in exactly the same way as they modify adverbs (▶ **Chapter 32, 12**). Usually, adjectives are in the complement of **be** or other state verbs. **Most** is an adverb of very high degree; it does not mean the same as **the most** with the superlative degree of adjectives and adverbs: eg the sentences **John's speech was the most reasonable.** and **John spoke the most reasonably of them.** do not say that John was **most reasonable** — they say only that he was **more reasonable than the others were.**

Index

Numbers in bold type denote chapters